# FLOATING PALACES:
## America's Queens of the Sea
*Maine Island Mariners and the Big Steam Yachts*

*By:*
**William A. Haviland**
*and*
**Barbara L. Britton**

Second Edition, June 2016
Book © Penobscot Bay Press, Inc., 2015
All rights reserved.
No part of this book may be reproduced without written permission,
except for brief quotations for review purposes.

ISBN: 978-0-941238-19-9
Library of Congress Control Number: 2015942168

Editor Caroline Spear
Designer and Paginator George Eaton

Cover photograph: Steam yacht, *Cythera* (ex. *Agawa*), designed by
Cox & King, built by Ramage & Ferguson in Leith, Scotland, 1907.
Collection of Barbara L. Britton

Published by Penobscot Books,
a division of Penobscot Bay Press Community Information Services
P.O. Box 36, 69 Main Street, Stonington ME 04681 USA
Tel: 207-367-2200
Fax: 207-367-6397
Email: books@pbp.me
Web: penbaypress.me
Printed in the USA by 360 Digital Books
Kalamazoo, Michigan USA

*Clayton Gross. Penobscot Bay Press file photo*

*Captain Walter Scott. Courtesy Deer Isle-Stonington Historical Society*

# Dedication

To the memories of Clayton H. Gross and Captain Walter E. Scott, who did so much to keep alive our memory of Deer Isle's maritime tradition.

*Working scale model of Hi-Esmaro on display in the Museum of Science, Boston. Owned by asbestos magnate Hiram Manville, Hi-Esmaro was one of the luxury yachts with a Deer Isle captain and many crew members. Courtesy of Museum of Science, Boston.*

# Table of Contents

**Foreword** — *page 6*

**Preface** — *page 7*

**Acknowledgements** — *page 8*

**Chapter 1:** Introduction — *page 11*

**Chapter 2:** From Farmers to Seafarers:
The Development of Deer Isle's Maritime Culture — *page 15*

**Chapter 3:** Life at Sea Under Sail — *page 27*

**Chapter 4:** The Big Steam Yachts:
*Camargo*, *Hi-Esmaro* and Their Crews — *page 49*

**Chapter 5:** The Greenlaws of Sunset (Part I):
An In-depth Look at a Yachting Family, the Early Years — *page 77*

**Chapter 6:** The Greenlaws of Sunset (Part II):
Captain Edwin B. Greenlaw — *page 95*

**Chapter 7:** The Greenlaws of Sunset (Part III):
Captain Kenneth N. Greenlaw — *page 131*

**Chapter 8:** More Yachts with Deer Isle Men Aboard — *page 160*

**Chapter 9:** The Postwar Period and the End of Yachting — *page 186*

**Appendix I:** S. Appel & Co., by Clayton H. Gross — *page 197*

**Appendix II:** From William to Edwin and Kenneth:
A Greenlaw Genealogy — *page 198*

**Bibliography** — *page 200*

**About the Authors** — *page 203*

# Foreword

Bill Haviland and Barbara Britton have combined to write an absorbing book about Deer Isle mariners and the big luxury steam yachts they commanded, *Floating Palaces: America's Queens of the Sea*. Before a bridge was built in 1939, Deer Isle was as isolated as any island on the Maine coast. The island was first settled in 1761 when William Greenlaw moved his family from the St. George area to Deer Isle. It is significant that Barbara Britton, one of the authors of this intriguing book, is a descendant of the 18th century Greenlaws.

As stated in the Introduction, Deer Isle was unusual for producing many of the men who captained the exotic steam yachts, or "floating palaces," as they were called. The book's first pages summarize Deer Isle's unusual origins. Surprisingly, it began as a farming community in the 18th century. Although agriculture remained important, a robust maritime culture developed as the 19th century progressed.

The authors are both Deer Isle residents and they write about a neglected period in the island's maritime past. Bill is a former anthropology professor from the University of Vermont and the author of twelve books since he retired. As noted, Barbara Britton is a descendant of William Greenlaw. She was born on the island, grew up in a yachting family, and is now a summer resident of Deer Isle. The result of their joint efforts is a fascinating account of the golden era of America's great steam yachts and the many Deer Isle men who captained them.

Haviland and Britton take us aboard these "floating palaces" and transport us around the world. The voyages of the grand yachts began in the late 19th century and continued through the two World Wars of the 20th century. Along the way the authors recount numerous tales of the adventures of elegant craft and their Deer Isle captains. Haviland provides the historical context for the book by placing the luxury steam yachts in the context of their times. Britton concentrates on the lives of selected Greenlaw family members drawn from memoirs, diaries and letters.

By no means was the captain of every yacht a Greenlaw, although they are an important part of the story. We are introduced to other master mariners like Monty Haskell, one of the many Deer Isle men who sailed his ships into often-dangerous waters and weather around the world for half a century. Monty was also remembered as a member of the all-Deer Isle crew of *Columbia*, the America's Cup winner in 1899.

No expense was spared in outfitting the big pleasure boats. Some might have a fireplace, a grand piano or a pipe organ. All the ship's "commanders" outfitted their crews with specially designed uniforms inscribed with the vessel's name. As to cost, it is estimated that some of the larger vessels needed $3,000 a day to operate.

I enjoyed the description of the elegant *Camargo* that was built in 1925 and sailed all over the world until meeting its end off the coast of Malta in 1952. *Camargo's* captain was Charles R. Small. It had a crew of 35 to 40, and carried up to 120 passengers. And *Camargo* is just one of the many ships described in this absorbing book. Each chapter is filled with the adventures of Deer Isle mariners and their yachts as they sailed around the globe.

*Floating Palaces: America's Queens of the Sea* is filled with photographs of the elegant vessels and the men who sailed them. The book is a pleasure to read and serves as a memorial to the age of luxury steam yachts and their intrepid Deer Isle captains.

—Harry Gratwick, 2014

*Harry Gratwick is the author of several books dealing with Maine history, including* Penobscot Bay: People, Ports and Pastimes; Stories from the Maine Coast: Skippers, Ships and Storms; *and* Historic Shipwrecks of Penobscot Bay.

# Preface

The beginnings of this book go back to 1973, when I read an article by anthropologist Ward Goodenough in a professional journal on kinship and residence in the Pacific Islands. I cannot now remember the title, but it was something like "Cognatic Organization in the Gilbert Islands." This resulted in an "aha moment," as I realized that all of my neighbors on Deer Isle exemplified a similar pattern. This inspired me to write an article for another professional journal in which I developed the concept of a distinctive culture of "seafaring farmers." In subsequent years, I documented the kinship and residence patterns in a series of unpublished works now in the archives of the Deer Isle-Stonington Historical Society.

There matters stood until 2010, when renewed interest on the island in the all-Deer Isle crews of the America's Cup defenders of 1895 and 1899—a story ably told by Mark Gabrielson—led to an interest in the island's involvement in yachting in general. At the historical society, the decision was made to mount an exhibit on yachting, and I set about organizing a series of guest columns in the local paper on Deer Isle in the yachting era. Some of the articles I wrote myself, but several were written by members of families that had contributed officers for several of the large private steam yachts. Among them was Barbara L. Britton, whose father, grandfather and uncle all "went yachting." The series ran periodically through 2012.

There matters might have ended, had it not been for attendance at a party for volunteers at the historical society in the fall of 2013. In a casual conversation, Barbara Britton asked me what project I was currently working on. At the time, I had begun nothing new, and in an off-hand manner, said I was toying with the idea of a book about the great steam yachts and the Deer Isle men who went on them. She replied that she, too, had been thinking of doing something about her family's involvement in yachting, and perhaps she could provide some assistance. This galvanized me to action, and what had been a vague idea suddenly became a good idea: we could join forces to produce a book, at once scholarly and readable, on Deer Isle and the men who served as officers and crews on so many of the yachts of the rich and powerful families of the United States. For the title, I was captivated by Captain Walter Scott's characterization of them as "floating palaces," but it was Barbara who came up with the full title.

Here, then, is an account of the big steam yachts and the Deer Isle men who were aboard them. We haven't touched on them all, as the intensity of the island's engagement with yachting would require more than one volume. Moreover, information on some of the yachts is sketchy at best, nor are all who served on them clearly remembered today. Still, we have touched on enough of the men and boats, including those best remembered, to be able to place them in the context of the culture that made it possible for island men to go down to the sea in yachts.

—William A. Haviland, 2014

# Acknowledgements

This book could never have been written without the help of several people. Those who provided specific information are: Neva Beck (wife of George Lane Beck), Arthur J. Billings, Hubert Billings, Tinker Crouch (granddaughter of Merle Greene), Rena Day (granddaughter of Ralph Haskell), Hans-Jochem Droste in Germany, Nancy Gross, Almont Haskell ( grandson of Monty Haskell and Alton Torrey), Carroll Haskell, Lucy Hopkins (daughter of Grover Small), Cynthia (niece of Franklin Hardy) and John Melnikas, and Eric Ziner (friend and one-time neighbor of Dud Haskell). In addition, Carroll, Lucy, Neva and Rena read sections of the manuscript, and Tinker read it all. Their comments and reactions have been absolutely vital.

During interviews conducted with Col. Kenneth N. Greenlaw Jr. and Roger L. Greenlaw, men with whom the junior author shares a common memory, details relevant to Greenlaw family history were gathered, remembrances shared, and experiences validated. Gratitude is extended to both men for their individual interviews, their willingness to share photographs and copies of memorabilia, and their warm encouragement.

Also vital have been the resources in the archives of the Deer Isle-Stonington Historical Society. These include photos, genealogies, obituaries and interviews. Truly, we could not have done without these. We cannot state strongly enough how fortunate the island is to have this treasure.

Another treasure is Connie Wiberg (great-granddaughter of Charles Scott), archivist at the historical society. Her assistance in locating photos and documents was invaluable; moreover, she went beyond the call of duty in scanning into the computer most of the photographs in this book. We cannot thank her enough!

Others who have been helpful include Maynard Bray and Aaron Porter of Woodenboat Publications, Louisa Watrous, Intellectual Property Manager at Mystic Seaport, Brittany Dunn of the Directorate of History and Heritage, National Defense, Canada, Violetta Wolf of the Museum of Science, Boston, and Sofia Yalouris of the Maine Historical Society. Of vital importance for the Greenlaw narrative has been the search for and retrieval of images pertaining to early sailing vessels, their detailed descriptions and owner names. At Mystic Seaport, Carol Mowery, Reference Librarian, G. W. Blunt White Library, responded to the challenge with enthusiasm, support and professional expertise, as did Jeanne Gamble, Library and Archivist Specialist at Historic New England. As a result, definitive descriptive material and early photographs of each vessel were recovered.

An email to the Boston Yacht Club requesting information regarding Commodore John A. Stetson brought an immediate and affirmative response from Michael Mentuck, a member and acting historian of the club, followed by a photo of the Commodore (1892-1898) and his yacht, *Rusalka*. A copy of the book, *The Boston*, a history of the Boston Yacht Club, was sent to Barbara Britton with the compliments of Commodore Peter Barnet and Michael Mentuck, which was much appreciated.

Valuable and little-known information related to the steam yacht *Cythera* during her service to the U.S. Navy as a patrol boat in World Wars I and II, and, sadly, her sinking by a German submarine in the latter conflict, was provided in the article, "Overdue Atlantic" USS *Cythera* (PY 26) by Robert P. Sables, LTC, MSC.AUS, Ret., courtesy of the NavSource Naval History Website.

Especially helpful was Earl Taylor, president of the Dorchester Historical Society, who secured colorful images of the George Lawley Shipyards on early postcards; Astrid Drew, at the Steamship Historical Society, who provided several photographs of the luxurious passenger liner SS *Washington* from which to choose; and Tom Moore, Senior Curator of Photos at Mariners Museum, Newport News, Virginia, who was able to produce specifications and an "elusive" photograph of the motor yacht *Dolphin*, so difficult to find.

Welcome additions from T. Horodysky's marine photo collection included a Liberty Ship photograph and the naming procedure for these ships during World War II. Hard-to-find images of the vessels *Steel Seafarer* and *Haparangi*, accompanied by detailed background information, were sent by marine photographer Victor Young from New Zealand, and greatly appreciated.

Immensely helpful was the well-documented and formatted piece, "The History of the Isthmian Steamship Company," by researcher Skip Lewis, in which he presented Isthmian's vital role in shipping during wartime and the new frontier called "containerization" that confronted the company in peacetime.

Of special note is a unique photo of Robert Manry and his tiny boat *Tinkerbelle*, on their way to the "finish line" in Falmouth, England, courtesy of Steve Aystrach and the Robert Manry Project. Noteworthy too is the work of Lynn Smith, Librarian and Archivist at the Episcopal Diocese of Massachusetts, who "never gave up" and finally succeeded in finding an obscure photo of the Church of the Redeemer in South Boston, now long gone.

Noteworthy as well is the work of Anita Haviland, who responded on numerous occasions to cries for help from the senior author as he encountered computer problems. In addition, she scanned several photographs, and took on the daunting task of organizing all of the images on the computer. Her skills go way beyond those of either author, and we could not have done without them!

Welcome financial support came from the University of Vermont through a Retired Faculty Award to defray costs of permissions and research assistance.

Finally, we are grateful for the encouragement received from Caroline Spear, editor for Penobscot Books, and the crew at Penobscot Bay Press for their skill at producing the book.

To all who have shared text and photographs for this project, willingly contributed their time and expertise, or given support and encouragement, we extend our thanks and appreciation.

*The Penobscot, leaving Rockland, Me.*

# Chapter 1: Introduction

To most people today, when they hear talk of yachting, they think of men and women in sailing vessels, cruising or racing for fun and sport. To be sure, this is how it all began, and, to a large degree, continues today. Almost forgotten, however, is the era of the great "floating palaces," luxurious steam- or diesel-powered ships owned by wealthy industrialists and financiers such as the Vanderbilts, Morgans, Fleischmanns and Manvilles, to name just a few. These began to come into prominence in the latter part of the 19th century, but were at their height in the 20th century, up until World War II.

Less widely known is that many of the officers and crews for these large vessels came from the small island community of Deer Isle, Maine. As described by Captain Walter Scott:

> During the early part of the 1900s the Steamer *Penobscot* ran from Boston to Bangor. Capt. Frank Brown was first Pilot, George Sawyer second Pilot, Sam Cole and myself were Quartermasters, all from Deer Isle. *[See photo 1.1.]*

After the *Penobscot* had left Rockland for Boston, each of us took turns to go down to meet those from Deer Isle on their way to Boston or New York, or Bristol, RI to join yachts. There would be at times 100 sailors or officers from Deer Isle. The forward end of the freight deck was piled high with sail bags that had been transferred from the Bar Harbor Steamer *Mt. Desert* that ran through Stonington at that time.

These men were the cream of the crop of Deer Isle's finest. Their sail bags would soon be on board those great floating palaces, such as the *Constellation*, *Sea Fox*, *Camargo*, *White Heather*, *Corsair*, *Hi-Esmaro*, and others. In the social hall you would meet the pioneer officers of those yachts, such as Capt. Grover Small, Capt. Charles Small, Capt. Edwin Greenlaw, Capt. E.L. Haskell, Capt. E.Y. Haskell, Capt. Montaford Haskell, and others. *[See photo 1.2]*

1.1 Steamer Penobscot, on which Deer Isle captains and sailors traveled on their way to Boston, Bristol or New York to join their yachts. Courtesy of Deer Isle-Stonington Historical Society

As recently as 1952, the island newspaper commented:

> We wonder how many communities have the number of men around with unlimited licenses as we have from this little island. Many of them got their licenses when they were in their early twenties and were masters of ships going around the globe, while several have unlimited licenses for sail and steam. Here are a few of them: Sherman Hutchinson, Willie Green, Phil Haskell, Grover Small, Franklin Hardy, Avery Marshall, Merle Greene, Lyle Cleveland, Randall Haskell, Edward Hutchinson, Wildred Conary, George Torrey, Walter Scott, Ernest Foster, Cecil Hardy, Alton Torrey, Henry Morey, George Knowlton, John Duke, James Coombs, Frank Hardy and Albert Coombs. These men have sailed the Atlantic and Pacific; they are familiar with the West Indies and South America; they can tell you about rounding the Horn or sailing through the Strait of Magellan. The world has been their dooryard.

Worth noting is that most, if not all these men at some point in their careers served on yachts. As for "the world as their dooryard," the captain of the first merchant ship through the Panama Canal was Ernest Torrey of Deer Isle, whose brothers we shall meet in Chapter 3. The pilot aboard that vessel was another Deer Isle man, Captain George Dow.

Such was the reputation of Deer Isle mariners that, as Ralph Eaton observed: "Anybody from Deer Isle… who applied for a yachting job at City Island, New York, a place where all the yachts fitted out, could get a job. If you'd go there looking for a job and you told them you came from Deer Isle, that's all there was. You'd get a job." Nor was Eaton exaggerating, as confirmed by others. Who were these mariners, and how did they, coming from a small community, gain such large reputations? Deer Isle is Maine's second largest island, while the town itself includes several nearby islands. Originally, it included Isle au Haut and the islands south of Merchant's Row, but these all separated and became their own town in 1868. In 1897, the southern third of the town of Deer Isle separated to become Stonington. The total area encompassed by the town of Deer Isle today is 123.67 square miles, of which 29.72 are land and 93.95 water. For Stonington the figures are 37.84 square miles, 9.81 being land and 28.03

# Introduction

*1.2 Captain Grover Small, photographed around 1952. He was one of the Deer Isle men with unlimited master's licenses mentioned in the newspaper of that date. Photo by William A. Haviland*

*1.3 The farm of Joseph Smith Greenlaw, which he settled in 1836. Although a cooper by trade, his farm is representative of those operated by Deer Isle mariners, including some Greenlaw relatives. Photo by William A. Haviland*

water. The 2010 census gives an island-wide figure of 3,018 year-round residents, 1,975 for Deer Isle and 1,043 for Stonington. The island-wide figure does not differ greatly from that of 1860, which was about 3,600 (and which included Isle au Haut). **[See map on page 14]**

Over the decades since 1860, the population of what today is the town of Deer Isle has remained more or less constant. That of what today is Stonington, however, has not. Initially, there was no settlement south of Webb's Cove and Crockett's Cove, and not until quarrying began around 1868 was there more than a handful of people where the downtown is today. With the quarrying, however, Stonington became a boom town and its population exploded into the 20th century. Then, with the decline of the granite industry, it too declined to its most recent level.

In 1899, an article in *The New York Sun* reported: "Deer Isle, Maine produces two commodities in profusion. One is a sailorman, and the other is granite." Indeed, so many islanders followed the sea that Captain Oscar Eaton, in 1914, went so far as to claim that there were "…400 able seamen to every square acre of ground." Of course, this was a gross exaggeration, but it reflected the reality that a great many islanders were mariners. In Chatto and Turner's *1910 Register*, out of 474 male heads of households in the town of Deer Isle, 169 (36%) had their occupations listed as "yachting" (81) "mariners" or "sea captains" (the other 88). For the other 305 heads of households, the most commonly listed occupations are "farmer" and "fisherman," often together. This is somewhat misleading, however, for several of these had been or were to be mariners. To cite two examples, Elmer Hardy of North Deer Isle spent about 20 years at sea, including service on the America's Cup yacht *Defender*, before he came ashore to take over the family farm. William I. Conary of Sunshine (a village within Deer Isle), listed in the *Register* as "fisherman," had been a member of the all-Deer Isle crew of the America's Cup defender *Columbia*, and would later skipper newspaper magnate Joseph Pulitzer's sailing yacht. We shall meet both men later in this book. **[See photo 1.3]**

In the following chapters of this book, we shall see how Deer Isle's distinctive maritime culture developed, and how it led to the prominence of Deer Isle men in the era of the big steam yachts. We shall go on to look at some of the big yachts themselves, and profile some of the Deer Isle men who ran them.

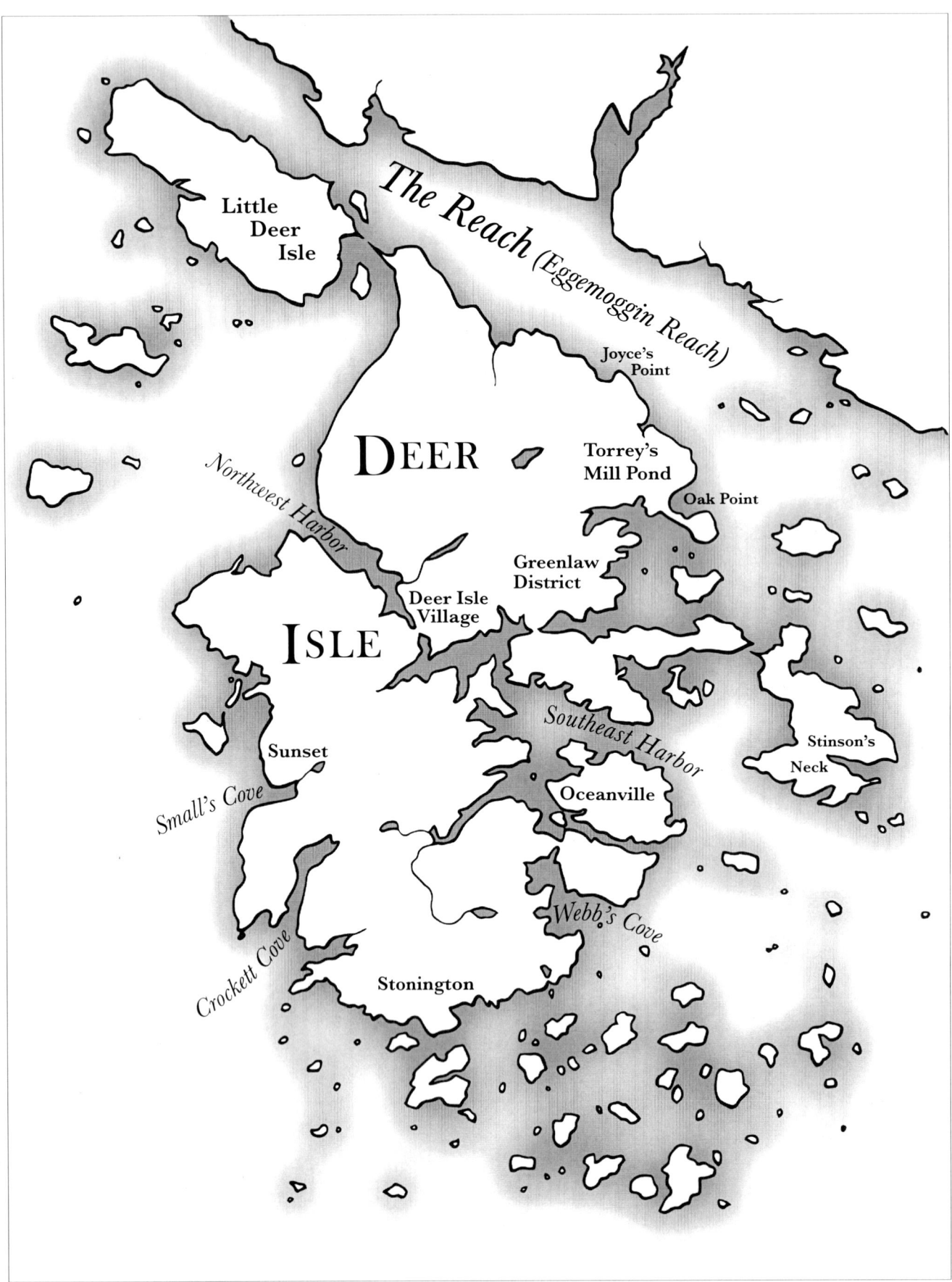

*1.3 Map of Deer Isle, showing localities mentioned in the book. Map courtesy of Jane Crosen*

# Chapter 2: From Farmers to Seafarers: The Development of Deer Isle's Maritime Culture

*"A unique feature of…coasting was the proportion of skippers, mates and even men, who owned farms on or near the seacoast."*

George S. Wasson, *Sailing Days on the Penobscot*, page 53.

## Historical Background

Given the reputation that men from Deer Isle earned for themselves as skilled seamen, it may come as a surprise that their ancestors came to the island to farm, not to follow the sea. They came late to Maine, long after the first fishermen arrived, as part of a wave of immigrants from Massachusetts and elsewhere looking for land from which they could provide for their families. Prior to their arrival, the coast from Pemaquid east was a war zone, as Indians, who had lived here for millennia, sought to prevent the takeover of their homeland by English speaking invaders. Supported by the French, a few of whom settled among them, they were successful, though at great cost, until the French were defeated in 1760 and forced out of North America.

The first of the new immigrants to settle on Deer Isle were William Greenlaw and his five sons, who established farms along Eggemoggin Reach from Oak Point to Torrey's Millpond. They came from Greenock, Scotland in 1761, having stopped first in Warren, Maine. They were followed a year later by William Eaton and his family, who settled on the Reach at the north end of Deer Isle. Other families followed soon after, filling in along the Reach between the Eatons and Greenlaws, and spreading as well along the island's western shore.

These earliest settlements were made on that part of the island most suited for farming. As Deer Isle's early historian, George Hosmer noted: "The Town of Deer Isle contains a large proportion of land that can never be cultivated; especially in the southern part…The northern part of the island is better adapted to agriculture than the southern, as the proportion of land incapable of being cultivated is smaller." In particular, south of a line running from Small's Cove on the west to Joyce's Point on the east, the island is underlain by granite, and the further south one goes, the closer this is to the surface. North of this line soils are deeper and are underlain by softer rocks of sedimentary origin that have been altered by volcanic action. The earliest settlements tended to be north of this line, but were limited south of it. Up until 1812, there was no settlement on the west side of the island south of Crockett's Cove, where soils become especially thin. For similar reasons, on the east side, there was no settlement south of Webb's Cove until 1800. Green's Landing, now downtown Stonington, was not settled until 1810, 41 years after North Deer Isle, and then only by a handful of people. Eventually, the residents of much of the granitic portion of the island developed quarrying and fishing as the basis for their economy, following which they separated from the Town of Deer Isle to become Stonington. *[See photo 2.1]*

Consistent with their focus on farming, the early Anglo settlers were granted by the General Court of Massachusetts 100 acres each to those present as of January 1, 1784, although there were some larger holdings. By modern standards, 100 acres may not seem large, but it is considerably larger than required, for instance, by people concerned primarily with fishing. In fact, it was what authorities at the time considered necessary for successful farming. Statements from the settlers themselves also testify to their preoccupation with farming. For example, Captain Edmund Sylvester, who came in 1788, did so at the behest of his wife in order to leave seafaring. She expressed herself willing to live anywhere if he would but remain at home. For another example, Thomas Stinson, who established the first settlement on Stinson's Neck in 1765, regretted that he had not settled on what he referred to as more "valuable" land; instead, he chose a place convenient for the procurement of waterfowl and fish to tide him over until his farm was in production. The clear implication here is that "valuable land" was good farmland. Stinson's Neck is part of granitic Deer Isle.

A general description of the eighteenth century settlements, based on verbal accounts given him by descendants of the pioneers, was provided by Hosmer. Apparently, they were as close to self-sufficiency as settlers came in those days. Slash-and-burn was the method of agriculture, with corn the most important crop. Hay and potatoes came next in importance, along with some other grains. Plow agriculture was not to come until later, after the tree stumps had sufficient time to rot out of the fields. Even then, the first plows were homemade affairs, as were virtually all tools. As time passed,

2.1 Pastureland on the farm established by Peter Hardy, ca. 1795. The rocky pastureland shows what the fields looked like before they were cleared of rocks. Photo by William A. Haviland

farming increased, both in size of fields and numbers of crops grown. At the same time, cattle and sheep, kept initially in small numbers, became more numerous. As they did so, oxen became available for use as draft animals. This, coupled with the rotting of the tree stumps, permitted the switch to plow agriculture. *[See photo 2.2]*

There was minimal dependence on the outside world for tools or other equipment. Although the iron came from outside, axes were forged at home; boats were dugout canoes, houses were built with logs, and grain was ground with log mortars and pestles. The need for ammunition seems to have been slight; hunting techniques were notable for minimal use of guns. A great deal of hunting concentrated on waterfowl, which were taken in nets or by communal bird drives during the molting season, when birds couldn't fly. The expressed rationale was the idea that birds rapidly became "gun shy", so hunting was better without firearms. Be that as it may, the net result was that ammunition, which had to be brought in from outside, was not used in great quantity.

Because domestic livestock were too few at first to provide much meat, other sources of protein were important. Besides sea fowl, these included clams and fish. Therefore, many of the earliest settlements were not far from good clam flats. At the north end of the island, where Indians dug clams, speared flounders and built fish weirs, the early Anglo settlers did exactly the same things (and their descendants continued to do so thereafter; they still

# From Farmers to Seafarers

2.2 A team of oxen at work. Photo by Thomas P. Haviland

2.3 Fish weirs, for herring and mackerel, were tended by islanders to supplement other economic pursuits. This one was tended by Elmer Hardy, a former mariner turned farmer. Photo by Thomas P. Haviland

dig clams today, built fish weirs through the first half of the twentieth century, but abandoned flounder spearing earlier in that century). Over on Stinson's Neck, however, Thomas Stinson, as already noted, regretted having paid too much attention to the sea and not enough to the farming potential of his land. To preserve from spoilage the produce from the sea, salt was a necessity. Rather than trading for it, as was the practice among professional fishermen, islanders produced it locally by boiling down sea water. This was a time consuming process, but the wood for fuel was abundant locally. Salt was made in this way up to 1786 at least. By contrast, elsewhere along the Maine coast, salt was the main item of import, as all salt for the fisheries was imported. This difference again reflects the emphasis on farming, rather than fishing, on the part of Deer Islanders. *[See photo 2.3]*

More equivocal as indicative of self-sufficiency, but suggestive nevertheless, is information on Deer Isle during the revolution. Out of 69 men, a mere three served in the colonial army, although some others served in the ill-fated Penobscot Expedition to expel the British from Castine. Following this, however, most islanders returned to their farms, trying to get by as best they could. Writing in 1886, George Hosmer noted: "I do not remember hearing of any person in this place being arrested…"by the British on suspicion of sympathy with the rebels. Moreover: "Although there were acts of violence between Whigs and Tories in other places, I never heard of any here…" Perhaps too much should not be made of this; certainly, Deer Isle was not totally immune to the turmoil of the time. One sign of this was the expulsion of the Greenlaw families for their loyalist sympathies. It does convey a picture, though, of people pretty much minding their own business, consistent with other indications of a great deal of self-sufficiency. As for the Greenlaws, although the original settlers joined other loyalist refugees at St. Andrews, New Brunswick, two sons of one of the brothers returned to Deer Isle, one within a year of his parents' evacuation to New Brunswick.

Farming seems to have gone well on Deer Isle at first, but with time, problems developed. A

*2.4 Grist mills powered by tidal currents, established at various places around the island, were easily accessible by boat. This one, on Torrey's Mill Pond, was built in 1837 and dismantled in 1883. Courtesy of Deer Isle-Stonington Historical Society*

statement by Hosmer on this is revealing:

> "The soil originally produced large crops, and had the early settlers been more judicious in the use of fire in clearing their lands, the soil would have retained its fertility much longer. It was by them an object to have the ground as dry as possible when fire was used, so as to clear it up more effectually; but the consequence was that with the wood the vegetable matter upon the top of the soil was destroyed which was necessary to the durability of its fertility. After the benefit of the ashes was gone, the soil soon became less fertile and required much manuring".

At the same time that the settlers were intent on the business of establishing their farms, they did not turn their attention from the sea to the land alone. They had, after all, come by sea in the first place, and their homesteads were initially close by the shores, as was characteristic of most seacoast towns. And, as already noted, the sea afforded an important source of protein foods to supplement the produce of the farm, as well as salt to preserve it. The sea also continued to serve as the main transportation artery. On the land, one had only the slow cumbersome ox drag, or else one carried things on one's own back. Indeed, it was a full 26 years (a whole generation) before there were any roads. Grist mills, once established, were located at tidal rapids, which were the source of power. As a consequence, they were easily accessible by boat. Similarly, when saw mills were established, they were powered by tidal currents as well. Thus, one hauled the logs to the water with a team of oxen and then towed them to the mill by boat. Nevertheless, no matter how self-sufficient islanders aspired to be, some items, however few, still had to be obtained from the outside world. Money for this came from cordwood, which went by sea to the Boston area. *[See photo 2.4]*

Given this kind of pattern, it is not surprising that, as the productivity from farming slacked off, the maritime component of the economy became increasingly important. As luck would have it, Deer Islanders were able to profit from a boom in the maritime industry. For some time, transportation by sloop, shallop, schooner or brig had been the order of the day along the coast. Although times were hard during the revolution, with a great depression in shipping especially around 1783, things got better toward the end of the century. By 1794, just over a generation after Anglo settlement of Deer Isle, things were looking up. Between 1794 and 1812 on the coast of Maine, there was a 300% increase in shipping tonnage, and the gain was particularly noticeable in the Penobscot region. Here there was

# From Farmers to Seafarers

*2.5 The fishing fleet at Southeast Harbor, about the time of the Civil War. The vessels voyaged far afield, to the Bay of Chaleur and Grand Banks. Courtesy of Deer Isle-Stonington Historical Society*

a fivefold increase from 3,685 to 20,480 tons, an increase in which Deer Isle participated.

So seafaring, in both coasting and deep water voyages, increasingly became the primary pursuit of the men from the part of the island that today is the Town of Deer Isle. It wasn't that they planned it this way, but rather seizing an opportunity to make up for deficiencies of farming, using skills already available. Although some went into fishing as a means of livelihood, among the first generation of the early pioneers were a number of master mariners. Fishing was mostly secondary to other pursuits, with the major exception of South Deer Isle and Oceanville, on the shores of Southeast Harbor. Here, a substantial fishing fleet regularly traveled under sail to the Bay of Chaleur and the Grand Banks. Thus, this pursuit had much in common with other maritime ventures, as opposed to inshore fishing. *[See photo 2.5]*

One indication that Deer Isle was actively involved in deep water voyaging, important to coastal Maine generally until the 1890s, is indicated by the establishment of a custom house in the town. The town was also heavily involved in the coastwise trade in which Maine shipping was supreme until 1905. Important in the latter was lumber, with Bangor (up the Penobscot River) a leading lumber port; lime, with Rockland (across the bay) a leading producer; and granite, with Stonington (the southern portion of Deer Isle) and Vinalhaven (out in the bay) and Mount Waldo (up the Penobscot River) being leading producers for Boston and New York. Ice and sawdust, carried from up-river and Walker's Pond, were also important, as was cordwood for the lime kilns in Rockland, and coal to power the granite quarries. In addition to coal, rum, cloth goods, spices, molasses, coffee, some food and citrus fruit, as well as salt (after 1786) were among items imported.

Especially hazardous were lime and granite. In the case of lime, if it became wet, it would start a fire among the casks in the hold. The only way to extinguish such blazes, short of sinking the vessel, was to seal it up, cutting off all oxygen. Even then, the fire might burn for months. As for granite, any shifting of the great weight would upset the stability of the vessel. Should any of the cargo break loose in heavy seas, the pounding would cause the ship to split open.

Ownership of Deer Isle's shipping did not differ significantly from usual practices on the coast of Maine. Despite some large owners, Maine's shipping was for the most part widely distributed in the several small, independent villages. Ships were generally officered and manned by townspeople, many of whom owned shares in the vessels along with merchants, schoolteachers, and hundreds of others. Shares were usually sixteenths, thirty-seconds or sixty-fourths although sometimes they were as small as one two hundred and fifty sixth. Commonly, the captain and his family owned the controlling interest. This seems to have been the practice on Deer Isle. For example, there is the case of Captains Horatio and Abijah Hardy. The latter served as mate for the former on a schooner owned wholly by the family. In the case of the much larger brig *Cinima*, with all Deer Isle crew and officers, Boston interests owned some shares, but three Deer Isle merchants owned shares of one thirty second each. Presumably, smaller vessels were more likely to be wholly owned by families than larger ones. In any event, even though Deer Islanders were participating in a money economy, normal ownership of controlling interests in vessels by captain, family and crew harmonized well with the old idea of self-sufficiency.

Important though seafaring became for Deer Isle, the family farm continued to be important as well. Deer Isle must not have been unique in this. George Wasson, describing lumber coasting, commented on the large number of officers and men who owned seacoast farms. It was, apparently, a common thing for a captain to "hang up" his vessel in a sheltered harbor while he got in the hay, or performed some other important farm chore. And on lumber schooners tied up at Bangor talk commonly concerned such non-maritime topics as the merits of a newly invented mowing machine drawn by horses, a new sort of churn, the milk-producing capabilities of certain breeds of cows, and such. So common was this sort of talk that the term "cow yard tar" was coined.

The reason that farming continued to be important was quite similar to what caused men to go to sea in the first place. Just as seafaring offered a substitute to a drop-off in farm productivity, so farming offered a substitute when seafaring fell on hard times. Indeed, shipping did undergo declines from time to time. The first, after the revolution, was Jefferson's embargo of December 1807, which prohibited United States ships from departing for foreign ports. This led to an unemployment rate in Maine seacoast towns of at least 60%. That the effects of the embargo, which lasted 14 months, was seriously felt on Deer Isle is indicated by an appeal, voted in town meeting, January 1809, to the General Court of Massachusetts for relief from distress caused by the embargo. In such circumstances, the family farms were once again of primary importance, as at least people were able to put food on the table.

The next blow to shipping was, of course, the War of 1812. This was to lead to a blockade by the British of the New England coast which began in April 1914. That the war was not popular on Deer Isle is vividly indicated by an incident related by Hosmer. Late in 1814 or early 1815, an English brig loaded with beef, pork, salmon and lumber was forced into Small's Cove by a United States privateer. In response, a mob of islanders gathered that threatened not the British vessel, but rather the United States privateer.

Following the end of the War of 1812, a shipping boom developed that lasted until about 1860. These were the great days of the lumber trade centered on the Penobscot River, as well as the Rockland lime trade, notable as much for the immense amounts of wood that had to be shipped in for lime burning as well as for the amount of lime shipped out. Granite shipping was also getting under way. These were the great days of the square rigged vessels, in which Maine men shipped to all ports of the world. They were a part of a global economy, before anyone realized there was such a thing. So it was that, once again seafaring became preeminent for Deer Islanders, for it was at the end of this era that Hosmer made his observation as to the importance of seafaring for the inhabitants of the northern part of the island. Between 1886 and 1889, Deer Isle held first place in marine commerce over all ports east of Portland, with the exception of Bangor. According to Captain Walter Scott, raised on the island in the last two decades of the nineteenth century: "During the 1880s, it was the dream of every Deer Isle boy to follow in the footsteps of his father or older brothers. He played 'going before the mast' with his chums in the schoolyard, and with his brothers at home... It was not uncommon to see him a hardened sailor before he was 18." Indeed, qualifying as a captain by that age or soon after was about as common on Deer Isle as earning a high school diploma is today. *[See photo 2.6]*

As before, the shipping boom did not last. Captain Scott's statement above to the contrary notwithstanding, by 1855 along the coast generally cargoes were hard to secure, freights were low, and there was a decline in the demand for ships. By 1857, the worst economic depression for shipping interests since the embargo was in full swing, and ships along the coast were rotting at their piers. Deep water voyaging for State of Mainers never did recover, but coasting did, only to slack off again before a final, brief resurgence during World War I. Still, a few coasters continued to haul cargo up

# From Farmers to Seafarers

*2.6 A three-masted schooner at the John L. Goss quarry wharf on Crotch Island, off Stonington, ready to take on a load of granite. Courtesy of Deer Isle-Stonington Historical Society*

into the early 1940s, the last being the *Annie and Reuben*, commanded by John Duke of Stonington. She continued to haul granite from the quarries until sold in 1943. For the most part, though, vessels under sail were yachts or old coasting schooners refitted for the summer "windjammer" trade. *[See photo 2.7]*

Deer Isle men were engaged on both windjammers and yachts, but no longer were they manning vessels in which they and their families owned controlling interests, or even shares. Instead, they were in the employ of others, working for wages. This change correlates with the last days of significant farming on the island. There was still farming going on into the 1940s, though not a great deal. By 1950, it was for all intents and purposes dead.

*2.7 The* Annie and Reuben, *last of the schooners to carry granite. Courtesy Deer Isle-Stonington Historical Society*

In summary, it is evident that seafaring has waxed and waned a number of times as a means of making a living since the time Deer Islanders began going to sea. In the first place, they began to do so after the productivity of their farms (their first interest) had fallen off. Perhaps, had seafaring waxed and held steady, farming would have lost its importance long ago. Instead, periodic depression presented a situation where farms continued to be important. The family farm would carry one through an economic depression; similarly, the good times of shipping compensated for mediocre results from farming. Both this and the custom of hometown ownership of vessels on shares fit well with the ideal of self-sufficiency established in the later part of the 18th century.

## Deer Isle's Distinctive Maritime Culture

Their dependence on the mixture of farming and seafaring just described had profound consequences for the way people lived on the island. If one is going to tend the farm and at the same time furnish officers, crew, or both for a vessel, there have to be available a sufficient number of able bodied men. It is ordinarily beyond the means of a single married couple with their unmarried offspring to provide these. By contrast, some form of extended family is well adapted to handle the problem. Under these circumstances, where the cooperation of men was so essential, what anthropologists call the patrilocal extended family might be expected to be common. In such a situation, men upon marriage would remain in or near their natal households, their wives coming to live with them. This would provide several adult males, all "blood" relatives of one another, to cooperate in farm tasks and manning a vessel.

2.8 The homestead built in 1795 by Peter Hardy, as it looks today. Photo by William A. Haviland

There is no question but what there was a patrilocal bias in the case of Deer Isle extended families. There was, however, flexibility in the system that would have been impossible had patrilocal residence been strictly adhered to. With ambilocal residence –the option of living with either the husband's or wife's family – a couple had a choice. They could go live with which ever family could offer the best opportunities, in shipping and/or farming, or who had the greatest need for their labor (or who they got along with the best). From a different perspective, a particular group could theoretically be "swamped" by more members than their resources could support under rigid patrilocal residence; under ambilocal residence there was a means whereby surplus manpower could leave to go elsewhere.

So it was that a common pattern on the island was for a man, but sometimes a woman, upon marriage, to take up residence with his or her spouse in a house on a small plot of land carved out of the family farm. To illustrate this pattern, we may look at the example of Peter Hardy and his descendants.

He and his wife came to the island in 1784 from Bradford, Massachusetts and acquired just under 100 acres at North Deer Isle from William Eaton. In 1795 he built his homestead on Hardy's Hill. Typically it was not close to the shore, as settlers, once sawn lumber was available, abandoned their original log cabins in favor of wood frame houses on higher ground, away from the salt water. This was no doubt prompted by the usual presence of "wet ground" near the shore. On the island, a deposit of marine clay deposited at the end of the last Ice Age lies beneath the surface, but is exposed by erosion near the shore. Rainwater, upon soaking into the ground, hits this clay and travels above it, to seep out wherever the clay is exposed or the soil above is thin. The resultant "wet ground" was regarded as of no use either for growing crops or grazing livestock. *[See photo 2.8]*

Peter Hardy was joined by two sons who acquired farms of their own; when Peter died (in 1831) his farm was inherited by his grandson, George Campbell Hardy. Married three times, George had a son and five daughters by his first wife, who died at the time of her last daughter's birth. By his second wife he had three more daughters and two more sons. All three sons followed the sea. As time passed, pieces of the farm were acquired by his oldest son and three of his daughters along with their families. Meanwhile, he kept the most productive part of the farm for himself, eventually passing it on to his youngest son. The other son

# From Farmers to Seafarers

2.9 George Campbell Hardy, grandson of Peter Hardy, from whom he inerited the farm. He conveyed pieces to three daughters and his oldest son; his youngest son inherited what remained of the farm. Collection of William A. Haviland

moved into a house next to that of his wife's family. By 1950, the farm had been carved up into 17 parcels divided among descendants, with the best farmland still being worked. Thereafter, piece by piece the farm was sold off to outsiders, so that today, there are no longer any Hardy descendants living on Hardy's Hill. *[See photo 2.9]*

Living close to one another fostered the habit of reliance on each other for all sorts of tasks. In fact, so closely connected were such families that they were constantly in and out of each other's houses, without the bother of having to even knock.

The case of the Hardy farm is illustrative of a pattern of inheritance frequently seen on the island. This was the practice of the family farm passing either to a man's youngest son, or to a grandson. In the case just seen, Peter Hardy passed the farm to his grandson. It did not go to any of his own sons, as they were well settled on their own farms. Capt. Peter Hardy Junior, for example, had been given 100 acres of his wife's father's farm on the Reach. George Campbell Hardy, the grandson who inherited Peter senior's farm, in turn passed it on to his youngest son, Elmer. His oldest son, Captain Amos Hardy, had already acquired a piece of the old farm and built a house on it. The other son, George Leslie, was well settled in a house next to his wife's parents. Elmer, who had gone to sea until 1899, when he signed on the crew of the Americas cup defender *Columbia* (aborted by a trip to the hospital), came ashore to help his father, who by then was 85 years old. Although Elmer was already the father of three sons, with the fourth born in 1899, he was less settled than his brothers.

The labor pool was further enlarged by marriage to members of other families living close by, creating a web of kinship that could be called upon for assistance. Often, marriages were to cousins and sometimes involved sister exchange. A man would marry a woman, whose brother would marry the first man's sister. So it was, for example, that Samuel Jordan Greenlaw married the sister of Deacon George Barbour, who married Samuel's sister Nancy. *[See photo 2.10]*

The importance of close cooperation among kin for the success of Deer Isle men as mariners cannot be overstated. Consider this comment by Richard Phillips, a twenty first century merchant marine captain:

> It's a tricky thing to be in charge of a ship with several other guys, most of whom you hardly know. The merchant marine is different from the navy or the army or the marines in that you don't have a crew or a battalion that's grown to know you over several months or even years. You walk on a ship and you have to earn instant respect, instant faith in your leadership, or the whole thing falls apart. You need to do on-the-spot appraisals of what every man is capable of and bring them up to their potential in a matter of hours or days.

Obviously, if you have an intimate knowledge of your crew, and a history of cooperation before you

*2.10 Captain Amos Torrey (seated in chair) with his family. His daughter Comfort (far left) married Solomon Barbour Greenlaw, whose sister married Comfort's brother. Courtesy Deer Isle-Stonington Historical Society*

even set foot on the deck of a vessel, you are at an enormous advantage.

Besides promoting cooperation, family structure and the web of kinship also served to keep the community relatively classless. Freely sharing equipment and labor worked against significant differences in status. Egalitarianism was further promoted by men serving together on schooners, the most common vessels on which islanders sailed. Even large schooners required relatively small crews, compared with square rigged ships. As a consequence, regardless of rank, men on schooners had to pitch in and handle just about every task that came along. And of course, they were usually all relatives to begin with.

The essentially egalitarian nature of Deer Isle society was reflected in its housing. Unlike Searsport (on the North Shore of the Bay), where sea captains lived in large and imposing mansions, Deer Isle captains dwelt in modest farmhouses. Attached to each was a big barn where horses and cows and oxen

*2.11-2.13 Three houses represntative of those in which Deer Isle captains lived with their families. These belonged to Grover Small, Albert Coombs and Arthur Haskell. Captains Small and Haskell lived in the houses in which they were born. Photos by William A. Haviland*

*2.12 The Albert Coombs house.*

# From Farmers to Seafarers

*2.13 The Arthur Haskell house.*

*2.14 The Shakespeare school as it appears today. Typical of the island's one room schools, it was named not for "the Bard of Avon," but for a schooner, built on the island in 1816, but lost with all hands two years later. The school was built in 1858, and closed in 1921. It now serves as the home of the community band. Photo by William A. Haviland.*

were kept. With few exceptions, they did not stand out in comparison with other peoples' houses. *[See photos 2.11 through 2.13]*

Growing up on the island, children were schooled in the one room school houses scattered around town. In 1847, there were 19 of these schools on Deer Isle, with another nine on smaller islands. Besides reading and writing, navigation was an essential part of the curriculum. And as already mentioned, in recess boys commonly played "going before the mast." By 1800, there was scarcely a family on the island without a son, father, brother or husband at sea. It was not uncommon for a boy to put to sea by the age of six. Youngsters would often go off for a stretch, returning to take up their studies where they left off. At graduation, those receiving diplomas might be of almost any age. *[See photo 2.14.]*

A product of Deer Isle's maritime culture was Capt. Walter Scott, who grew up on Deer Isle in the last two decades of the 19th century. Part of this time was spent on a farm with his family on Pickering Island. A fitting conclusion to this chapter is his recollection of one vessel and its crew from this era. *[See photo 2.15]*

One of the most beautiful in the fleet was the brig *Cinima*, in command of Capt. Frank Marshall; Capt. Ezekiel Marshall was mate, with Cook and sailors all from Deer Isle and Stonington. The name, Marshall, has been prominent in Deer Isle's Marine history since long before the Civil War. Capt. E. A. Marshall, grandfather of our present living Capt. Avery Marshall, guided the famous schooner, *Alpine*, through most of her career. His son, Capt. Ed Marshall, sailed her on her last voyages and was on board when she was beached on John Haskell's beach, condemned from old age after paying their owners the highest dividends of any of the two masters of that era.

The brig, *Cinima*, was undoubtedly the most beautifully kept ship of her era. Capt. Marshall, being a perfectionist, lived up to every tradition that was typical of the clipper ship era. His ship could've been called a Sea Goddess in review...

Her masts painted buff, "Horses" painted black against white Fiddlehead and cross trees, neatly served standing rigging painted black which made her glistening white swifters stand out prominently. Her buff – colored

*2.15 Captain Walter Scott, born in 1887, was the youngest of 21 children. He went to sea at age 14, had his master's license by 21, and eventually became marine superintendent of the Eastern Steamship Co. After his retirement, he wrote several accounts of Deer Isle men at sea. Courtesy Deer Isle-Stonington Historical Society.*

bowsprit entered a shiny black thrust band from her breasthooks, with the inboard end buff against her white railed Poop extending in an unbroken line along her entire waist.

Her "dolphin striker" was black with white shackles that secured her martingale. On deck, varnished belaying pins decorated dark stained life– rails, a wide gallous frame supported a long boat to the starboard of her mizzen hatch. Decks were holystoned and were protected by canvas covers when coal cargoes were carried. In spite of the cost of upkeep she paid dividends to three Deer Isle merchants who owned a one thirty– second share each, other shares being owned by Boston ship brokers.

It is an almost unbelievable fact, that the Deer Isle boys who braced their feet on the deck of the *Cinima* to "let go and haul" left school at recess, to join the ship. At the end of the voyage many would again take up their studies. Capt. Ezekiel Marshall made three trips to the West Indies as mate, and was able to finish two terms of school at the same time.

Most crews, of the clipper ship era, were made up of sea hardened sailors, many of the cutthroat type. This was not the case in Deer Isle's early maritime history. Our sailors were sea hardened but there was a generous amount of culture and refinement among the rank-and-file which accounted for the great demand of our island's ship officers in the Marine commerce of the world.

A sailor on the brig *Cinima* in 1875, could look forward with hope of being master of the schooner, *Princeton,* in 1880.

# Chapter 3: Life at Sea Under Sail

*"...on the sea, nothing goes like you expect it to. You have to be prepared for a staggering amount of possibilities..."*

Captain Richard Phillips, *United States Merchant Marine: A Captain's Duty*, page 60.

## Men at Sea

Before turning our attention to the big steam yachts, it is worth taking a look at what life at sea was like in the era of commercial sail. It was, after all, in this setting that the men of Deer Isle honed the skills that led to the island's fame, as *The New York Sun* put it in 1899, as "the producing place of sailors of superlative quality." It was that reputation that led to their selection by yacht owners everywhere, including their selection as the first all-American crews to man the yachts that successfully defended the America's Cup in 1895 and 1899. These were the only races for the cup where the officers and crew, with the exception of the captain, came from a single community. Deer Isle men sailed on other Cup defenders as well, but with sailors from other places.

We are fortunate that, for the period in question, we have a number of newspaper accounts of life at sea, several of which we reproduce below. We also have accounts from people who themselves went to sea, or who remembered men who did. We begin with an account of Montaford Haskell, one of the last of the old time schooner captains. Although merchant sail was in decline by the time he came along, his early career is fairly representative of Deer Isle mariners.

Born in 1874, Monty was one of three children of Captain Charles E. and Emma F. (Thompson) Haskell. The family lived in North Deer Isle at what is now 436 North Deer Isle Road, in a house that later burned in the mid-20th century. The house that stands there now was converted from a barn behind the original dwelling.

At the age of six, Monty went to sea for a short trip with his father. In his teens, he was going as mate on the schooner *Susan N. Pickering* under his father's command. Often, the cargo was granite from the Stonington quarries. In 1910, for example, they made twenty-one trips in the summer alone, carrying paving blocks to Brooklyn. Crews could be pretty rough in those days, so on trips when his vessel was laid up in Boston, Monty went to Professor George Godfrey's Gym, where he learned the fine points of what then was called "The Manly Art of Self Defense." This stood him in good stead, as illustrated by an incident when he was mate. As he told it to Lew Dietz of *Down East* magazine in 1956 (p. 34):

> There was a bluenose aboard, a big, loud-mouthed fella from St. Stephens. He licked every man forward but that wasn't enough for him. This day he comes swaggerin' aft in nail-shod boots right across a fresh varnished deck. I was there awaitin'. 'Git forward and git yourself a hammer, and take every blasted nail out of them boots.' And he says to me, 'Matey, I won't take no nails out of no boots for any s...o...b'. Well, he *did* take them nails out. It was two months before I could get my hands in my pockets they were that swole up.

At the age of twenty-five, Monty signed on to the all-Deer Isle crew of *Columbia* for the 1899 defense of the America's Cup. He was one of the fifteen-man bowsprit crew. In his interview with Lew Dietz (pp. 34-35), he recalled that the crew spent the summer training

> under the exacting supervision of the skipper [Charlie Barr] and designer [Nat Herreshoff]. A stopwatch was used on the handling of every one of the forty-five sails the *Columbia* carried. "And they weighed everything aboard", Captain Monty recalls, "even the mate's pipe".
>
> The *Columbia* won by eight minutes on that 30-mile course off Sandy Hook. She would have won by considerably more, according to Monty, if the skipper had not mistaken a passing freighter for the lightship that marked the finish line and stood in too soon.

Monty's first command was the three-masted schooner *George H. Ames*, which he skippered for ten years. Owned by several Deer Isle investors, the majority of shares were held by various Haskells. Much of the time she hauled coal from New York to Rockland. According to Monty:

> Ye had to know a thing or two to be a shoal-water sailor, I can tell ye. There was no part of the bay that wasn't foul ground in a snow storm or fog mull. Many's the time I've come through this Reach a'goin' by ear. You make your course and let her come with one ear for the bell buoys and the other for the sound of seas on reefs. In a dungeon o' fog it's mighty thick pokin'. (Dietz, p. 34)

On another occasion, he reminisced:

> Why, I mind the time when I was mate of father's vessel we was four days out of Norfolk with a fair wind when we made Isle au Haut. Just as we head in by the Western Ear it come in thick-a-dungeon fog. Well, sir, we strikes up the bay by dead reckonin'. We can hear the whistle on Saddleback Ledge to port, gives the Brown Cow a good berth and picks up the bell off the Porcupines. When we figures we're off Hardhead we luffs her over and sets our course for Northwest Harbor. I tell you, we didn't see nothin' till we raised Heart Island dead ahead.

Since Heart Island lies at the mouth of Northwest Harbor, that might not be considered too bad a job for, say, close to three hours in a fog mull.

Going in the other direction in fog, according to Nancy Gross (p. 4), a schooner would sail three hours out into the bay from Northwest Harbor. At that point the skipper would put a bucket over the side and draw up some sea water. If it didn't taste of clam flats, he knew he was seaward of Saddleback Ledge.

Shoal water and fogs weren't the only hazards Monty dealt with. He also sailed through ten or so hurricanes, like one he experienced aboard the *Ames*. As he told it to Lew Dietz (p. 32):

> There was one real howler, I recall. I was with the *George H. Ames*. We'd unloaded 630 tons of coal at Bermuda and were heading in light for Jacksonville to take on a load of lumber. The gale hit us off St. Augustine,

# Life at Sea Under Sail

*3.1 Captain Montaford Haskell, in his days as a yacht captain. Collection of William A. Haviland*

"In five minutes we were bagging out coal," the captain said. "That's the way we had to do things in those days to make a dollar."

Although a few coasters did continue to carry cargo—often stone from the quarries—into the 1930s and even the early '40s, by then most vessels under sail were either yachts or old coasting schooners refitted to carry vacationers on summer windjammer cruises. For a time after World War I, Monty, out of necessity, went on yachts cruising waters he had once sailed carrying coal and stone. But when Captain Frank Swift of Camden began in 1936 to offer summer cruises in converted coasting schooners, Monty could not resist the temptation to return to his roots. By around 1940, he signed on with Captain Swift to command one of his windjammers. *[See photo 3.1]*

Monty's last command was the *Mercantile*, a schooner built by the Billings family on Little Deer Isle in 1916. He skippered her for fourteen years before he retired at age eighty-two in 1956. It was aboard her that he rode out his last hurricane in 1954. With Hurricane Carol on the way, as reported by Lew Dietz (p. 33),

> [h]e had taken her into Buck's Harbor and dropped both anchors close to the lee shore of that tight little cove. The big wind hit. He sent all passengers below and stood by on deck to watch how his anchors would hold. They didn't. The anchors started crawling. At the height of the storm a passenger's head appeared in the companionway. It seemed to this uneasy passenger that the *Mercantile* was moving. "Aren't we dragging anchor, captain?" he wanted to know. Captain Monty shook his

Florida. I ran her west a spell and head into it, but she wouldn't right at all in that wind. So we made 830 miles in three days, the rail ten feet under. Ended up off Charleston. If that wind had lasted a few more hours we'd a ended up ten miles into the woods.

With the end of World War I, a few coasters continued to haul cargo. Monty liked to recall the last load of coal he brought into Camden Harbor. As Lew Dietz (p. 34) tells it:

> It took seamanship to bring a vessel into a narrow harbor under full sail and that was the way Monty liked to do it. The deck hands stood by at the sheets and halyards waiting for orders to take off canvas. Not until the skipper was fifty yards from the coal wharf did he give the order—and then only to drop the tops'il halyard. The schooner still had a bone in her teeth as she came alongside the wharf. A small boy was standing idly by on the dock. "Take a line, lad!" the skipper bellowed, "and if you make it fast you've earned ten dollars." The boy caught the flying line. He laid a couple of hitches over the bitt. Sparks flew from the bitt as the line snubbed up and held. Only then did the skipper give the order to drop the fore and mains'il.

*3.2 Captain Montaford Haskell's house, as it looks today. Photo by William A. Haviland*

head and said calmly: "Not a mite of danger, Mister. She's not draggin', just stretchin' her chain." It was a close call, however. The schooner found holding ground a hundred feet from the weather shore and rode out the storm.

In 1900, Monty married Grace A. Hatch, whose mother was one of the daughters of George Campbell Hardy by his first wife. As noted in the previous chapter, the latter had parceled out bits of his grandfather Peter's farm to four of his children, one of them Grace's mother. Grace, in turn, acquired some of this land on which she and Monty built their house, in 1905, next to her mother's. The house is still there, at 705 North Deer Isle Road, and looks much the same as when Grace and Monty lived there. Like most Deer Isle families, they did some farming, though in their case this was minimal. Behind the house was a hen house and yard, and in back of that a pasture and woods. Over time, Monty cut back most of the woods, expanding the pasture into productive blueberry land (one harvest in 1964 was six tons). *[See photo 3.2]*

Grace and Monty had two daughters and a son, who brought both joy and tears. One daughter died young, and their son, having earned chief engineer's papers and started a family, drowned in 1947. Still, his son and daughter brought joy, as did Grace and Monty's surviving daughter's daughter and granddaughters.

After Monty came ashore, he devoted himself to farm and family. Soon, however, health problems took their toll, and his wife of over fifty years died. He himself succumbed in 1964 at the age of ninety.

An earlier Deer Isle mariner of some note is the subject of the following piece written by Captain Walter Scott, who we met in the last chapter.

This article I would like to call "From Schoolroom to Forecastle"—as it concerns one of Deer Isle's ablest old time shipmasters, Capt. E. A. Richardson. At the age of 16 he was considered a model scholar at the old "Shakespeare Schoolhouse" [pictured in the previous chapter]. Deacon Closson was the teacher and a great friend of the boy's father who himself was a master mariner who had died at the age of 26 years.

It was then the last year of the Civil War. Men were in great demand for all purposes—soldiers, sailors or landsmen—and anyone else of small ability could easily obtain a better position and more pay than he was worthy of. This boy had been told many times how his father had straddled the sky-sail yard before he was old enough to shave. He decided to do something about it. He loved Deacon Closson. He had many favorites among his schoolmates, but if he was to follow in his father's footsteps, no time should be lost, as the fuzz was beginning to show up on his chin.

The Brig *Meteor* was due in Boston from the coast of Africa. She was commanded by a relative of his mother, and from pressure, Mrs. Richardson consented that he might apply to the captain for a chance to sail on the next voyage. His application was promptly mailed, and within 10 days a favorable answer came and was handed him while at recess on that January Saturday afternoon. (In those days school was six days a week.)

The very next day he borrowed his grandfather's horse and sleigh, and with his sister in charge he drove to North Deer Isle. Eggemoggin Reach was neither open nor closed, but the ferryman and his passengers punched a way across through drifting ice, and a farmer drove him to the Doritys' house at Sargentville for the night. In the morning the Doritys drove him to the Castine ferry before sunrise where he took the Stage for Bucksport.

He arrived in Bucksport in time to have dinner at the house later made famous by the Jed Prouty Play. Then he took a stage to the Bangor House where the night was passed.

The next morning he began his long journey to Boston. He picked up an acquaintance with a man named Judson Freethy who was enroute to New York to go mate on a ship from that port. He gave the boy much fatherly advice and asked him how it was he was traveling without a nurse.

In Boston he found his ship, *Meteor*, loading a general cargo. Only the Mate was on board. He was an able sailorly man, but not over-scholarly, and he lisped. He wore ear-rings containing loose, cockbilled anchors, and blond whiskers parted in the center of the chin colored to the tone of iron rust from unpainted Chain-plates, where the tobacco juice had formed a natural scupper from his lower lip, finally dripping to form uneven patterns of rusty brown on his blue waistcoat.

This was only the beginning for this Deer Isle boy. They sailed the very next day on the dying end of a northwest gale. The very next day they were caught in a January blizzard. Sail was reduced to meet an ordinary blow, and he overheard the skipper say: "No more sail off tonight unless the Lord takes it off." Before the night was over, "He did", leaving only the boltropes holding whipping rags and twisted threads. Before this voyage was ended, the happenings would make another long chapter: provisions soaked and spoiled, water barrels briny from salt spray, insubordination crushed, chased by a confederate cruiser until welcome darkness and a sudden storm came to their relief.

He made two voyages on the *Meteor*. Then he joined the clipper ship *Charles Luling*, bound for Calcutta, at $18 in gold per month. After this one voyage he was induced to return to his first ship the *Meteor* as second mate, pinked-cheeked and beardless, wishing for whiskers and a Bo's'n complexion, as being more in harmony with such exalted office.

He sailed on this ship a year, and following that was on the beach in New Orleans at that time the vilest seaport on earth—and was there during that historical riot—hence by that time he had become familiar with the common life of a sailor of that day, both afloat and ashore.

This is the simple and unvarnished tale how a Deer Isle school boy became a sailor. During the years following Captain Ed Richardson's name was heard on the docks of Singapore, Calcutta, and Rangoon, and many other ports of countries that he had learned about in his Geography at the old Shakespeare schoolhouse with

Deacon Closson on the quarterdeck.

Our maternal grandfathers of that era had the whimsical theory that one should be qualified to mold the frame, build the ship, rig her and go in command of the finished product, before aspiring to the title of "Able Seaman". Captain Ed Richardson was one of the ablest skippers that ever stood on the quarter-deck.

Another of Captain Scott's articles describes a voyage by the *Jane Palmer*, a five-masted schooner built in East Boston in 1904. Her commander was Captain Delmont Torrey, one of four brothers who were master mariners. The complications of this particular voyage illustrate the problems skippers faced, ashore as well as at sea, and the resourcefulness needed to deal with them.

In 1919 I resigned after serving 8 years as Marine Supt. of the Eastern SS Co, and the Metropolitan Lines, and accepted a position as purchasing agent of the France and Canada Steamship Corpn, and its subsidiary line United States Mail SS Co, that operated several trans-Atlantic steamships with offices at 120 Broadway, N.Y.

These steamships included the reconditioned ex-German Liners that had been interned in Boston during World War One. In addition to the steamships, my company owned and operated the 6 masted schooner *Wyoming*, and *Edward J Lawrence* and the five masted schooners, *Jane Palmer* and *Dorothy Palmer*. On July 16, 1919, I was appointed as marine consultant to the Vice President Stewart H. McIntosh in connection with the operation of these vessels.

The *Jane Palmer* was commanded by Capt. Delmont Torrey of Deer Isle. Captain Torrey in my book was an "educator of the sea lanes". The Southern Cross or the Magellan Clouds held no secrets from his vast knowledge of celestial navigation. To him they were just another guide post to the heavenly corn field. *[See photo 3.3]*

He was noted for quick decisions, and his unlimited courage could never be questioned by the close brushes he had experienced through his long career on the quarter-deck. In August of that year Capt. Torrey sailed the *Jane Palmer* from St. John, NB enroute to Garnston, England, with a full load of lumber. All went well until he had passed the Virgin Rocks which lies to the east of Cape Race, Newfoundland. Here under all sail with a freshening breeze the mate reported to Capt. Torrey that water was visible in the pump wells but the pump strainers were plugged. *[See photo 3.4]*

Investigating, Capt. Torrey discovered that his vessel was leaking badly with all pumps disabled and the water was rising at a rapid rate. He swung his ship for St. Johns, Newfoundland and shortened sail to prevent his ship from going on her beam ends in case she became water-logged before they could get the pumps in working order.

The entire crew, including Capt. Torrey, took turns at the pumps. After working to a point of exhaustion for 6 hours the pumps cleared only to become plugged again in less than half an hour. With his crew in a state of complete exhaustion he ordered them all to abandon the pumps and rest to recuperate in case they should be needed if the ship became water-logged. In this case, with a load of lumber with a fifteen foot deck load and her towering masts, she would undoubtedly turn turtle. Capt. Torrey kept on as much sail as he dared, feeling confident he could reach port before this could happen.

In the meantime the fishing steamer *Thetis* owned by the Job Brothers

# Life at Sea Under Sail

*3.3 The Jane Palmer, commanded by Captain Delmont Torrey, was the largest five-master ever built. She is shown here at dockside in England. Courtesy of Deer Isle-Stonington Historical Society*

fisheries of St. Johns, was returning from the Banks. They saw the *Jane Palmer* with her distress signal in the rigging. She drew alongside and her captain was invited on board by Capt. Torrey.

Capt. Torrey said he was sure he could make St. Johns, but he would agree to pay him $5,000 to tow him to St. Johns. The agreement was accepted by the captain of the *Thetis*. The vessel was towed to St. Johns and on the arrival at a berth near the Job Brothers Fisheries a Custom House officer boarded the *Jane Palmer* and nailed an arrest to her mast demanding $50,000 salvage.

This was a very valuable cargo, as lumber was badly needed in Europe having been depleted by World War One. So badly was it needed that the freight charges on the vessel's cargo was over half the value of the cargo.

*3.4 Captain Delmont Torrey, seated right, with his brother, Captain Winsor Torrey. Courtesy of Deer Isle-Stonington Historical Society*

Capt. Torrey wired our New York office. I was ordered to proceed to St. Johns at once to put the case into court. The highlights of this trip for me was the beautiful ride the full length of Newfoundland by train from Port Au Basque to St. Johns on the Reid-Newfoundland railroad.

This was the first cargo of long lumber ever carried on the *Jane Palmer* as she had always carried Coal or Linseed in bulk. She had become somewhat hogged over the years and the solid weight of the long lumber had straightened her out to open her seams, and the pump strainers had become plugged with the Linseed that had gradually shifted to her bilges from previous cargos.

The case was brought to court and the first day was spent with details of the case. On the second day however, Capt. Torrey was put on the stand and cross questioned by the Barrister for the fish company.

This attorney was face to face with a great "Educator of the Sea Lanes". The repercussions of Capt. Torrey's answers held his learned opponent at bay and proved himself to be the expert he was on all the laws governing that great field of sky and water where he had spent his entire life.

The text books of that little white school house at the Reach taught him the fundamentals that enriched his mind to a degree that made him worthy of distinction as a scholar on land. *[See photo 3.5]*

*3.5 The one-room schoolhouse at North Deer Isle (not in the Reach District) where Captain Delmont Torrey received his formal education. Courtesy of Deer Isle-Stonington Historical Society*

His entire life spent on the sea lanes of the World fitted him for this task as he faced the able Barrister at St. Johns, Newfoundland. Capt. Torrey won his case, with much applause from Newfoundlanders.

The deckload of lumber was removed from the deck of the *Jane Palmer*, new pump lines with strainers were installed, the ship was reloaded and sailed for England, still leaking, but with good pump lines, Capt. Torrey was confident he could make it.

Capt. James E. Creighton, that great Thomaston shipmaster, said: "None but a crazy Deer Islander would sail for England with half of the Atlantic Ocean inside his ship's hull".

Before reaching England, Capt. Torrey had two brushes with the elements. The Tramp steamer, *William O'Brian*, was slowed down on the northern track in a gale. The *Jane Palmer* passed him with five lowers set, racing before the gale, her jib torn to ribbons with rags fluttering from the bolt ropes and every sea broaching her deck load from stem to stern. Five men were on

*3.6 The house in which Captain Delmont Torrey grew up, and later lived with his wife, the daughter of Captain Charles Scott. Its modest size is typical of the houses of Deer Isle captains. Photo by William A. Haviland*

the *Jane*'s quarter deck waving their so-westers. Their shouts could be heard, "We Are Bound For England".

Capt. Torrey arrived in England. The faces of every member of his crew gave the evidence of their hard struggle to keep their ship afloat by constant hours at the pumps. Their whiskered faces were drawn, with blistered lips from the salty spindrift that drenched them every hour of the voyage.

Lloyds of London surveyed the *Jane Palmer* and condemned her as unseaworthy and she never returned to her home ports. Capt. Torrey and his crew returned by steamer.

So ends the career of the *Jane Palmer*, the last of that great fleet of 5 masters, her last voyage made successful under the command of that great Deer Isle shipmaster, the late Captain Delmont Torrey.

Delmont Torrey went on to command other schooners, his last being the four-master *Virginia Dare*. In 1926, the vessel had to be abandoned in a hurricane near Puerto Rico and although other crew members were able to swim ashore, Captain Torrey was drowned. *[See photo 3.6]*

The next glimpse of seafaring under sail by islanders comes from the *Deer Isle Messenger* of August 12, 1904. The author is simply listed as "Richardson," probably the same E.A. Richardson who was the subject of Captain Walter Scott's article reproduced earlier. "Edw A. Richardson" is the only one of this surname in Deer Isle listed in the *1910 Register*, his occupation being given as "Sea Captain."

The Schooner H. Curtis.

In accord with many others, I regret to learn that the *Curtis,* after weathering the storms of more than half a century, has at last surrendered to the hand of the vandal, who has "veiled her topsails in the sand/And bowed her noble mast."

The *Messenger* would like to know her history, from her youth up. I cannot attempt the task, but can tell some patches of her most faithful career.

She was built in Harrington, by Harmon Curtis in 1850, and rigged as a brig. Early in her history she was partly dismasted and then became a schooner. She was purchased at Deer Isle in about 1856. She carried 225 tons and was considered a monstrous schooner and hard to manage; none but tried and trusty commanders, with a picked crew of six to seven lusty men, were allowed to go in her and in that way she was managed very successfully through times of maritime evolution— while she was growing smaller and men were growing larger. Prescott Johnson, H.T. Carman and Haskell Reed were among her first Deer Isle masters. The first new master she made was George Courtney. He engaged a Harbor boy for Mate (Ben Haskell) but the owners decided that she must have an older and more experienced chief officer, and so Capt. Henry Weed was engaged for that very responsible position. Her general field of operations in those days was that through which all paths lead to the West Indies.

After George Courtney, she was commanded by Eben Brown and carried army stores for the Government to ports in Virginia, during the war.

In 1866 she was almost entirely rebuilt at Deer Isle and was at that time commanded by William Haskell, of the Dow Road, followed by William Richardson. When the latter took charge she was quite as good as new and then had a master who never showed mercy to any vessel, old or young. He was very successful in her—making much money, both for himself and the owners. At one time, when homeward bound from Cuba, the mainmast was carried away and he bore up for Wilmington, N. C. for repairs. This captain had a rather free command of language and was even something of a pleasing speaker; but when running in for the Wilmington bar, on a hazy day, with tackles and hawsers doubtfully supporting a tottering mast, he met a vessel working off and surprised her master by asking "How does the boo bar boo?" twice repeated. The stranger told him how the bar-buoy bore. So long as Captain Richardson lived, to tell many other amusing stories, he never liked to be asked how the boo bar boo.

He once brought a cargo of molasses from Cuba to Belfast in the *Curtis* and stopped in the Harbor on the way; that was possibly the most valuable cargo that ever stopped in the Norwest Harbor. The same vessel, when in charge of Capt. Johnson, bound from Cuba to Portland with molasses, brought up in Sou-west Harbor, through stress of weather and under very trying conditions. *[See photo 3.7]*

After Richardson's administration, the *Curtis* next made a brand new captain of G. Dudley Haskell, and he was perhaps followed by John S. Greenlaw; but coming down from her ancient history to what may be termed her medieval age, I cannot tell much of the latter as I myself was in those days following false lights and visiting the tents of the stranger, while the faithful *Curtis* held

*3.7 Taken about 1892, this photo shows schooners in Northwest Harbor. Courtesy of Deer Isle-Stonington Historical Society*

quietly on in her paths of peace and year by year gained in the affections and admiration of those who knew her best. I believe that at various times she was commanded by such men as Edwin L. Haskell, Herbert Spofford and many other well-known masters of today—always without mishap.

Of her ancient commanders, all are dead excepting Reed, while those of her medieval and modern ages are probably living and rather prosperous.

After Capt. A.O. Gross became the owner, he once elected himself master of the *Curtis* on a voyage from Deer Isle to Belfast, for repairs to the vessel. It was said that he allowed both chronometers to run down on the passage, and meeting heavy weather was out nearly all night, reaching port only by expert dead reckoning and observations of the North Star. Soon after that he discharged himself and appointed a new "navigator-in-command"—a man of broad experience and possibly nearly seventeen years of age.

So far as I know and believe, this faithful old craft never lost a life in her whole career.

When her remains have followed in the ways of others—when the timbers have been sawed, barreled and shipped to other States, there to throw out changeable blue flames from the open gates of wealth, there will be no ghostly eye wickedly leering from the colored lights, nor will any avenging spirit or demons of hate dance around the hearth. The spirit of some dead commander may hover near and silently offer the broad benediction, "Peace to these ashes of all the dead who have lived thus righteously!"

One of the men mentioned by Richardson who served at one time as master of the *Curtis* was Herbert Spofford. Another of his commands was the schooner *Hattie*. His cook, Joshua Dow, described a trip in which "Capt. Spofford beat her up through the Musselridge Channel when the fog was so thick it bent the stovepipe." He figures in another incident related by Captain Scott, in which his brother was lost at sea, from the *Hattie*; here it is, retold in 2009 by Nancy Gross:

> The *Hattie*'s greatest battle of her career with the elements was on the night of May 29, 1893, on a voyage from Providence. She passed over Nantucket Shoals during a northeaster of moderate intensity. Darkness overtook them off Chatham (Massachusetts) where the wind increased to gale force. Capt. Walter Scott's brother and his cousin Charles Scott were ordered out on the jib boom to cut away the slatting jib. "These were two Deer Isle sailors with a job to do." They worked their way inch by inch, unable to see the mountains of water coming at them. They were submerged in the onrushing sea. Cousin Charles inched his way back and was washed into the scuppers by breaking combers. He did gain his feet and worked his way aft to report to Capt. Spofford that John Scott had been washed off the jib boom. "John was somewhere out there in the darkness with no help at hand." Capt. Spofford was able to bring the *Hattie* safely into port, proving to all who knew him "that a more capable navigator never walked the quarter deck of a sailing ship."

Captain Scott's cousin, Charles Scott, who survived the incident, was typical of island men at the time. Born in 1860, Charles was the son of William Pitt Scott, the third generation of the family to run a ferry across the Reach to Sargentville. His mother was the daughter of Asa Richardson, a master mariner. As a young man, Charles had his own coasting schooner, and from this, went on to become a yacht captain. When the New York Yacht Club recruited all-Deer Isle crews for the America's Cup defenders in 1895 and 1899, Charles signed onto the first as seaman, the second as quartermaster.

His older brother, William Dayton Scott, was second mate. *[See photo 3.8]*

If 1899 was the high point in Charles' yachting career, it was also the end of it. In that year, his mother died, and his father was having health problems. So Charles, the youngest son, inherited the family home, and took over operation of the ferry. On the side, he tended a fish weir in partnership with a neighbor, Captain Meredith Ellis. It was the ferry, though, that was to occupy him for the rest of his life up to his death in 1939, one week after the new Deer Isle-Sedgwick Bridge opened.

Tragedies at sea, such as the one just described, were simply the risk one took on a sailing vessel. Here is another account of an even greater disaster, as told by Clayton Gross:

> The *Brave* was built at Hancock in 1872 and was 85 feet long, of 25.2 foot beam, 7.9 feet of depth of hold, and 113 gross tons. At the time of her loss she had just been thoroughly overhauled and refitted at a St. George shipyard.
>
> Up to 1890 her owners were S.G. Haskell (5/8) of Deer Isle; Elvin J. Torrey (1/8) of Bar Harbor; Seth Perkins (1/8) and H.H. Carter (1/8) of Boston. In 1891 one of the previous owners had sold his share, leaving the division as follows: S.G. Haskell (39/64) and H. P. Greenlaw (9/64) of Deer Isle; Seth Perkins and H.H. Carter of Boston (8/64 each). W. L. Greenlaw was listed as master in 1890. In June of 1892 he was succeeded by Joseph W. Lane of Oceanville, who was destined to be the final master of the *Brave*.
>
> The *Brave* carried a load of stone on her final voyage from Green's Landing [Stonington] bound for New York. On board in addition to Captain Lane were Sumner Stinson, Ed Norton and Fred Thompson, all of Deer Isle.
>
> With a favorable northeast wind, midnight of May 3rd found the heavily

*3.8 This flyer shows Captain Charles Scott and his brother "Billie" Scott, who served as quartermaster and mate on the America's Cup defender Columbia. Some of the other crew members shown have their names wrong. "Manter" Haskell is Monty (see photo 3.1). The correct surname of Wm. I and Alva (discussed in Chapter 8) is Conary. Courtesy of Deer Isle-Stonington Historical Society*

> laden vessel in the area of Plum Island in Ipswich Bay. It was at this moment that a sudden storm struck the entire coast from Block Island, R.I., to Eastport. At sundown on May 3rd the light station at Portland Head had reported a moderate sea with a five mile visibility and no storm reports received up to that time.
>
> The northeast gale began as sudden squalls accompanied by sleet and hale. The cargo of granite made the *Brave* wash badly, and it would be safe to assume that her crew quickly became aware of her dangerous situation. To those on board the *Brave*, three possible courses of action were open.
>
> The first was to head offshore to try to ride out the storm under reefed main and jib. Due to the nature of the cargo this was ruled out. Even if the wallowing vessel could be

turned to sea, a shift in the cargo could capsize or disembowel her.

A second course would have been to try to pass Thatcher's Island and make Gloucester. There were no breakwaters at the Sandy Bay Harbor of refuge at that time, and the ship would never have weathered it. There was also the possibility that they were too far into Ipswich Bay to even make Thatcher's Island.

The third choice was to run before the gale and make the shelter of Newburyport. It was a slim chance, but the only one that gave any hope at all.

The cross tides of Ipswich Bay near Plum Island are dangerous even in good weather. In pitch darkness, even if she still had her sails, there was little the crew of the *Brave* could do in regard to those cross tides. It is a safe guess that by that time most, if not all, of the *Brave*'s sail had been carried away. About all her crew could do was to keep her afloat and take the short end of the odds on making Newburyport.

At 9:15 a.m., on May 4, 1893, the *Brave* struck hard and fast amid the breakers of the outer shoals of Plum Island. The officer in charge of the lifesaving station was Capt. Frank Stevens. As was the custom in those days, the crew of the station was furloughed from May 1 to October 1. Thus it took him some time to get help enough together to attempt a rescue.

In the meantime the crew of the *Brave* had secured themselves in the rigging. A line was shot off and one man came out onto the main gaff and caught it. Before he could haul in the heavier line attached to it, a massive sea snatched him away to his death. Before another attempt could be made, the masts and rigging were carried away, taking the rest of the crew with them.

The remains of the crew were recovered and returned home for burial. The Deer Isle *Gazette* carried the long and drawn out text of the funeral of each victim.

W.L. Greenlaw, acting as agent for the owners, took over what personal effects had been salvaged and sold the wreck where she lay to Nathan Dole of Newbury for five dollars.

One more account of a marine disaster involves two men from Little Deer Isle who we mentioned in passing in the previous chapter. According to Captain Walter Scott:

> No greater courage was ever displayed than that of Captain Horatio G. Hardy, 36 years of age, and his mate and brother Captain Abijah W. Hardy, 42 years of age, when their schooner the *Charles K Burkley* met disaster off the New Jersey coast on April 15, 1914. Both these men were typical of all others from Little Deer Isle who like Capt. Sherman Hutchinson was the veteran master of that famous schooner, *Brina Pendelton*. Their names will always be forefront on the pages of the log book of time.

The fate of the schooner *Charles K Burkley* can best be described by the actual report of Seaman George Martinson, who was rescued. He told the following story from his hospital cot:

> "I saw every one of the 9 die and I believed my turn was next. I was lashed to one mast that didn't break off flush with the deck. When all the rest including the Captain's wife had been lost, I grabbed a line shot out by the life savers; tied it about my body and leaped overboard. They pulled me ashore through the breakers and here I am. Soon after the schooner had grounded on the bar late Wednesday night, after dragging her anchors from Atlantic Highlands in the Northeast gale, Capt. H.G. Hardy ordered his

brother, who was mate, and his wife into a yawl, with a seaman, and they were lowered into the lashing seas. This was a terrible sight for me to witness. The yawl had hardly touched the water when she was swallowed up by the mountainous seas, the Captain's wife, brother and the seaman were swept to oblivion. The rest of us climbed into the rigging and lashed ourselves, while the onrushing mountains of water was carrying away our deckload of lumber. The first line that was shot out by the life savers hit the side of the schooner. I saw the Captain leap for it. He missed it and the sea washed him back on deck. The next instant another sea swept the deck washing Captain Hardy overboard where he perished. I happened to be lashed to the only mast that wasn't broken off at the deck. When I looked around everybody had been washed overboard. The life savers shot another line across the schooner's deck and I grabbed it. I couldn't make it fast, so I lashed it about my body and leaped into the sea. While I guess they pulled me ashore. I was unconscious, and remember little about what followed."

Martinson was on the danger list for days but recovered fully, the only survivor of the ill-fated schooner *Charles K Burkley*.

Three things about this account are worth noting. The first is the presence of the skipper's wife on board. Although most Deer Isle women stayed ashore to look after the farm and raise the children, not all did. We shall return to an example at the end of this chapter. The other two things are the relative ages of the captain and his brother, as well as the latter's service as mate despite his rating as a captain. This is not the only case of an older brother with the rank of captain serving under a younger brother on board a vessel. To cite one other, the cook on Joseph Pulitzer's yacht was Captain Alvah Conary, older brother of the skipper, William I. Conary. It illustrates the point previously made about the egalitarian nature of Deer Isle society.

Before taking up the topic of Deer Isle women at sea, we look at three more examples of the challenges confronting Deer Isle mariners at sea. The first is again from the *Deer Isle Messenger*, with the author as before identified simply as "Richardson."

Though perhaps such a blizzard and heavy snow as we have lately had, in nearly mid-April, has not often occurred, yet it is not impossible or unknown.

Twenty-three years ago [in 1884] we had come up rather quickly from the very mild climate of the southern coast of Cuba, had seen no winter-weather and were looking for none, as the first week of April had passed before we approached the northern coast.

We came into the Vineyard Sound and drifted through with mild spring-weather and baffling winds—without any promise of any good or bad weather. Were in no way suspicious or much interested—only hoping to see our way safely off the shoals before there should be any sort of thick weather.

I have always believed that the time to come off the shoals, when bound to northern ports, is when one can safely see the way clear and almost entirely regardless of what the chance may turn out to be after one has reached where one side at least is free from dangers. It was the eighth of April, at the edge of darkness when we came out of the "Eastern Way," in close company with the fine collier *Augustus Hunt*, and were so reported. We were bound for Boston, the *Hunt* for Portland. We were not entirely clear of the shoals and intricate channels before it began to snow, with the wind at southeast, which was fair. It held moderate through the night but the snow was so thick that we saw no lights or other guides. By dead reckoning and soundings we sailed up past the Cape and well into Boston Bay, believing the wind would veer to the westward and

# Life at Sea Under Sail

clear up. But it went the other way—to the east and to no'theast and soon became a strong, stormy gale and we in a "tight place". So long since we had seen anything that our position was too entirely uncertain to permit running for Boston or any other harbor.

The vessel was nearly new and none were better or more able. The cargo of sugar was worth 80-odd thousand dollars and ten lives were at stake. I never more keenly felt responsibility of action! The greatest danger was ahead and to leeward—safety lay to windward only, and why not try for it! Sails were reefed and the craft hauled by the wind and put to as hard a test as any vessel has ever been asked to try! Several turns were made, back and forth across the bay, deeper soundings were gained and appreciated. The seas that she could not get over we went through. It was a wild night!

Just before daylight the wind backed further to the north, the driving snow became more thin, showing a light close under the lee. We were further out of the bay and more to the south-east than our long reckoning seemed to call for—it was Cape Cod light. Capt. B. George Johnson (now a late bridegroom) was the mate and Ned Haskell (now of the village variety store) was the engineer. On making the light so close under the lee, Mr. Johnson called Ned: "Get on deck and be ready to eat sand."

*3.9 Ned Haskell in front of his Deer Isle village store. Earlier, he had served as engineer on sailing vessels. Perhaps his brush with disaster off Cape Cod caused him to abandon seafaring as a career. The senior author of this book remembers getting his hair cut by "Neddie." Courtesy of Deer Isle-Stonington Historical Society*

Ned was then quite youthful—had no previous strenuous experience—and he wondered how much better it might be to "eat sand" than to die comfortably in the engine room. *[See photo 3.9]*

Slowly the vessel forged ahead without striking bottom until so far past the light that we were safe and it became only a clear and easy drift down channel. How we cleared Race Point and Peaked Hill Bars will ever be a mystery and it were none too soon, as our sails were fast giving way from the long and fierce strain upon them.

When clear of the Cape and danger, there was relaxation indeed! For my part, I poured the ice water out of my boots, where it had been swashing about for thirty-odd hours, turned in and dreamed of home. One should never regret that he has sometimes been called upon to meet with such trials and stress, but rather be grateful and proud that he once had the needed strength to meet his full share of abuse and to have been of some use in the world and in the battle of life.

Some time later we learned that Emery's bark *Belmont* went on Peaked Hill Bar at the very hour we had passed them so closely. Of all her crew, one man alone drifted ashore alive. The commander, Capt. Hagan, had been a longtime friend of mine.

As our sails gave way more and more, we drifted down channel and far out to sea. Then after two dull and threatening days another gale came from the east with torrents of rain, and again backed no'th-east and to the north, in which we drifted away to the south-west, far outside of Nantucket. As before mentioned, we had been reported as passing off the Shoals, and then as time passed, and nothing more was heard, Boston shipping men and friends became interested. The insurers of cargo gave up hoping for the safety of the "risk", while others declared that we would yet come in all right.

When our former company-keeper, the *Augustus Hunt*, limped into New York (so far from, and so opposite to her objective point)—sails gone, spars broken, hull damaged and leaking badly, there was more and more speculation on shore regarding our fate.

When hearing of it afterward, it was pleasing to learn that the optimistic side of the arguments came from those who best knew the combination.

We ourselves knew that we were still afloat, and after long waiting a wind came from the southward, and with such repairs to sails as it had been possible to make we again came in by Gay Head and this time anchored safely in Vineyard Haven—fourteen days after we passed there before.

The able tug *Wrestler* came from Boston to tow us around, and we arrived there safely—no one hurt, none drowned and the cargo dry!

Another challenge successfully dealt with by Captain Richardson was reported in the *Deer Isle Gazette* for March 6, 1897:

> The schooner *S.G. Haskell* recently arrived from Cienfuegos was thrice fired upon off the Cuban coast.
>
> The *Haskell* left Cienfuegos, Feb. 7 and as she was bearing out to sea that night off the mouth of the San Juan river, those aboard observed two flashes and the reports of guns from somewhere toward shore.
>
> The *Haskell*'s people paid no particular attention to the guns. A third report was then heard and a solid shot passed close by and plumped into the sea beyond the schooner.
>
> With his night glass the captain made out a steamer following close after them and showing no lights. The steamer approached quite closely and without hailing them steamed shore-wards again.
>
> It is thought she was a Spanish gunboat and mistook the *Haskell* for a filibusterer.
>
> The *S.G. Haskell* is a Deer Isle vessel command by Capt. Ed A. Richardson. She is a three-masted schooner of about 800 tons. She was built in 1891 at Milbridge, Me.

Captain Richardson's success at dealing with the elements and Cubans was not matched, unfortunately, by the captain if the *Ida L Ray* early in 1901. On board were Belcher Howard and two others from Deer Isle. Built in Harrington in 1864 as a brig, the *Ida L Ray* was later rerigged as a two-masted schooner used to carry granite from Stonington to New York, returning with coal. As of 1891 her owners were as follows: Sylvanus G. Haskell, 48/64ths; A. Richards, 4/64ths; Joseph Otis 4/64ths; Henry L. Ray, 4/64ths; and John Walters, 2/64ths. Although the controlling interest remained the same until her loss, smaller shares were exchanged among others.

# Life at Sea Under Sail

*Captain Belcher Howard*

3.10 Captain Belcher Howard. Courtesy of Deer Isle-Stonington Historical Society

What turned out to be the *Ida Ray's* last trip began after unloading a third of her cargo in New York and taking aboard a twelve-foot-high statue of General Logan and his horse. After unloading this in Washington, she proceeded to Norfolk, where she took on a load of lumber, consigned to Portland.

Besides Belcher, another crew member was Allen Barter, a quarry boss and shareholder, who had signed on as cook because heavy snows had closed the quarry. This was his first time at sea. The other crewman was "Billy the deckhand" (Billy Graze) who was regarded as "not quite bright." The captain, not from the island, was Anders Anderson, a Swede, said to be in love with "the lighthouse keeper's daughter." Which lighthouse we are not told. *[See photo 3.10]*

All was well, apparently, until they were hit by an Atlantic storm off the coast of Delaware. What happened next is pieced together from accounts by Clayton Gross and an anonymous writer in a newsletter of the Deer Isle-Stonington Historical Society.

> It was midnight on February 10 when the storm hit. In the succeeding days two port holes (used in earlier years for loading lumber into the hull) were broken open and flooded the hold, despite the efforts of two men on the pumps. At some point the topmast and sails were torn away, the anchor chain broke, chains on the deck load came loose and the dried lumber in the hold started to swell, splitting the ship's seams. The captain set the American flag upside down in a universal signal of distress, and stood on the mainmast crosstrees to watch for a sail. He saw several steamers, one so close that he could make out the figures on the bridge, but none responded to the distress signal. Seas washing over the deck took the yawl boat, and washed the oars out of the dory. The axe was already gone, so Belcher pried a plank free from the cargo and, using makeshift tools, set out to make oars. Water rising inside the cabin had destroyed all food and fresh water, and the ship sank lower as time went on. While Belcher worked on the oars, the others unladed lumber from the decks, to lighten the vessel and to keep from freezing to death. After three days and two nights the oars were finished, and the crew decided to "face death head on" in the dory. The *Ray* was so low that all they had to do was step from the deck into the small boat, which soon began to leak.

> Belcher and Billy manned the oars, exchanging port and starboard oars every two hours. Barter and Anderson took turns bailing and keeping watch for ships. Gradually, they were blown out of the shipping lanes. At one point, a freak wave blew Howard and Allen out of the dory; they were hauled back in by their shipmates. To keep the captain from falling asleep and freezing to death, his companions beat him with the end of a rope. The story includes an account of a period of time when two whales appeared, one on each side of the dory and so close that the men had to ship their oars. For a long time, the two whales kept the dory between them, watchful. At last they seemed to lose interest, and together they sank beneath the surface so quietly that it seemed

as if they were trying not to rock the boat.

On February 22, after twelve days, the men were rescued by the *Alleghany*, a steamship of the Atlas Line. When they were rescued, Belcher Howard had to climb the Jacob's ladder onto the steamship on his knees, because his feet were frozen and black. As for the captain, he had held the steering oar for so long that his clothing had frozen to it. It had to be cut off before he could be taken from the dory.

As for the steamer that passed close by, another source has it that the *Bellenden* reported passing "…close to a derelict schooner having two masts standing with the head of the mainsail set. The schooner was waterlogged, with the decks awash, and abandoned…." And what of the crew of the *Ida L Ray*? Captain Anderson is said to have married the lighthouse keeper's daughter, Billy never went to sea again, and Barter went back to the quarry, where he was killed in an accident. Belcher Howard did go back to sea, soon became a captain, and had at least one other close encounter in 1903. This was aboard the *Carrie E Pickering*. Owned by the "Deer Isle Pickerings," this two-master also carried stone and coal from and to the quarries. Off Cape May on Thanksgiving Day, she was struck by a gale, grounded, and broke up. Of the crew, all from Deer Isle, Captain Frank Haskell, Arno Weed, Frank Knight and George Knight perished; only Belcher Howard and Edward Rogers survived. [See photo 3.11]

*3.11 The schooner Carrie E. Pickering, on which Belcher Howard sailed. She was wrecked off Cape May, with the loss of all but two crew members. The boat was named for the daughter of Timothy and Susan N. (Haskell) Pickering, and married Captain Edwin L. Haskell (noticed in Chapter 8). Their house, built by her father, is the first on the right after the telephone exchange building going north from Deer Isle village on Route 15. Courtesy of Deer Isle-Stonington Historical Society*

## Women at Home and at Sea

Our consideration thus far of life (and death) at sea has focused on men, but we need to ask: what of the women? Men on ships obviously had to be strong, not only physically, but in character as well. The same was true of women, who for the most part stayed ashore. There, they were the ones who managed the household, took care of the children, and organized activities on the farm. Usually, a family had at least one cow that had to be fed and milked. Chickens had to be fed and eggs collected, horses and oxen had to be fed and pastured, their stalls had to be cleaned, and so on. Gardens had to be planted, harvested, and crops "put up" for the winter. A familiar sight in the late summer or fall was a woman in her kitchen, working over a wood-fired cook stove, canning vegetables. Sheep had to be sheared, wool spun, hay gotten in, fences mended, animals slaughtered, wood cut, split, and brought in as fuel for cooking and heat; the list goes on and on. Many of these jobs could be and were done by women and some by children. For the heavy jobs, however, if a woman's menfolk were off at sea, other men had to be recruited to help out.

The following account by Captain Edwin Greenlaw illustrates the point:

# Life at Sea Under Sail

*3.12 The house in which Captain Edwin Greenlaw grew up, as it looks today. Photo by William A. Haviland*

Our father was a sailing master, and over the years was in command of several fine schooner yachts for wealthy owners. He was away from home from April to October. During his absence mother planted a large garden, which always produced a variety of vegetables for the table, and preservation for winter. Poultry was raised for the egg production, and the eggs were shipped to the wealthy families in Boston. Wild berries were plentiful and could be had for the picking, which were preserved for the winter. During the months that the hens were prolific layers, any surplus was pickled, and later utilized for cooking purposes only. The small cucumbers from the garden were pickled, and green tomatoes made into picallili. A pig, and sometimes two, were raised and butchered in late fall, and each and every part except the squeal and tail were processed: the hams and bacon were cured with sugar and smoked. Lard from the fat was rendered and stored in earthenware crocks. The head of the animal was made into hog'shead cheese, and the feet pickled. The lean meat was kept frozen and eaten during the winter months. Any remaining fat was placed in a special container and made into soap for washing purposes, and had a strong lye content. [See photo 3.12]

As we did not keep a cow, milk and butter was purchased from a neighbor.... Father returning home in the fall, always purchased sufficient groceries to last through the winter: A couple of barrels of flour, a barrel of sugar, fifty pounds of coffee beans, which had to be pulverized in a coffee grinder. He owned a boat, and would catch fish at the turn of freezing weather. Some he split, salted, and dried, and others he buried in the deep snow to be consumed later in the winter.

As we will see in Chapter 6, Greenlaw goes on to discuss the sixteen cords of wood that had to be cut and split for fuel; the job of keeping the wood box full was his. And much of his mother's time was devoted to making and mending clothing for the family. Truly, women's work was never done, and all the while was the constant worry about the safety of their men at sea. One could, at the drop of a hat, become a widow. When this happened to the wife of Captain Henry Lufkin's brother, it was left to Henry to look after the widow. The task was daunting, as the woman went quite mad, to the extent that he had to make her a strait jacket! This he did, sewing the canvas with the same skills used to make and mend sails. As this demonstrates, sea captains had to rise to the occasion of all sorts of unexpected emergencies, even when not at sea. In his diary, Captain Henry wrote about the incident as just one more event in the course of a day.

Not all widows, of course, lost their minds. Most

coped as best they could, often under trying circumstances. The widow of Captain Nathan Lowe, who died young from complications associated with measles, was left with a two-year-old daughter. She survived by taking in boarders, sewing, and as a milliner. One thing in her favor was that the property was held in her name, not her husband's. Eventually, she remarried, as many widows did. The widow of Captain Delmont Torrey, for example, went to live with her father, Captain Charles Scott, running the household after his wife's death, and staying on in the old homestead after his death. Eventually she, too, remarried, to Captain Merle Greene, who we will meet in the next chapter. Another example is afforded by the widow of Ambrose Haskell who, like the women just noted, lived in North Deer Isle. He was a yachtsman, who died in a nursing home on Staten Island, New York. His widow then married Ambrose's male nurse, and the two returned to Deer Isle to run her farm.

If life was difficult for a woman without a husband, so it was for a man without a wife. Thus, George Campbell Hardy, who we met in Chapter 2, when his first wife died in childbirth, remarried a second, who was herself a widow. By her, he had five more children and adopted a sixth. Following his second wife's death he married once more, again a widow. After George's death, she stayed on in the family of her late husband's youngest son, Elmer, who had taken over the farm.

This is not to say that Deer Isle women never ventured out on the water. In an 1899 article in *The New York Sun*, the following was reported from a conversation with one Captain J. W. Green:

> "...by ginger, there's some of the gals that's better sailormen than the boys, though they don't work at it steady," he said, and the little "gal" who was as pretty as a picture with rosy cheeks and snappy eyes, and who made the *Sun* man's dinner pleasant, wore Eastern Yacht club buttons and reckoned she could sail a boat with the best of 'em, and she looked it.

*3.13 The* Hesper *and* Luther Little *are two schooners that were skippered by Capt. George Torrey's brother Winsor (pictured in photo 3.2). They ended their days, as shown here, rotting at a dock in Wiscasset. Photo by William A. Haviland*

As we saw in the case of Captain Horatio Hardy aboard the schooner *Burkley*, women sometimes accompanied their husbands on voyages when they were able to do so. Another example is this, from the June 1, 1939, issue of the *Island Ad-Vantages*: "Mrs. Grace Haskell has returned from Daytona Beach. She reports a fine trip on the yacht with Capt. [Montaford] Haskell."

Sometimes, women spent considerable time on board vessels with their husbands. One who did so was Essie Gray, who honeymooned with her husband, Captain George Washington Torrey (a brother of Delmont), on a voyage to South America in 1916. Nor was this the last time she sailed with her husband. She later accompanied him to Lisbon, Portugal, and other European ports. Essie's father Leslie was a captain, and at the age of ten she sailed with him from New York to St. Simons, Georgia. Her name came from a fishing schooner named *Essie* that Leslie saw when, at the age of nine, he sailed with his father to the Grand Banks. He liked the name so much that he gave it to his daughter.

Like Essie's father, her husband's, Jacob Torrey,

was also a captain. He died of yellow fever when George was fifteen years old. As the oldest of four brothers, George took it upon himself to teach the others the skills of seamanship. All three also became captains. *[See photo 3.13]*

George Torrey's first command was the schooner *H. Curtis*, noted earlier in this chapter. On board with him was Herbert Gray as mate and Charlie Morey as cook. As Essie told it: "He and a friend dug her up out of the sand, patched her up, and sailed her to New York and back," leaking all the way. He went on to command first three-masters, then four-, and eventually a five-master. Later, despite his dislike of them, he was in command of a steamship when, in 1942, he was torpedoed on a run from Saint John, New Brunswick, to Newfoundland.

Before her marriage to George, Essie had been to sea a second time with her father. The second was when, at the age of sixteen, she talked her father into taking her on a trip carrying paving blocks to New York, and from there went on to Richmond. After her marriage, she went with her husband on every trip for a year, to Hampton Roads to load coal, which was carried to Pernambuco, Brazil. They returned with sugar for Boston, or went to Jacksonville to load lumber. Eventually, Essie went with her husband off and on for eight years. At first, she was officially signed on as stewardess, and later as assistant navigator.

Essie and George Torrey had two children, George Jr. and Jane. George Jr. went to sea with his parents at the age of nine months, Jane as soon as she could walk (George found it easier to crawl). At fifteen months their son went with them to Lisbon, and as he grew up, sailed with them until after the primary grades in school. They would take him out of school in the spring, but Essie schooled him every day through each summer on board the vessel. By the time he returned to school in the fall, he found himself ahead of his classmates.

In a 1970 interview, Essie recounted some of her experiences at sea. On long voyages,

> [w]e had an icebox, so that we could have fresh meat for about 10 days, as long as the ice would last. After that we had salt food—salt corned beef,

*3.14 Essie (Gray) Torrey. Courtesy Penobscot Bay Press.*

> ham. We had canned fruit, peaches and pears and things like that.
>
> We always had the tanks full when we left port and when it rained there was a tank on deck to catch water, but we were always saving of water.
>
> We always had plenty of scraps. You see, there was a crew of 10 or 11 and so I don't remember that we ever bought any special feed for the hens. We had about a dozen hens, so we always had fresh eggs, along with what we took with us. And when we got down south we always had plenty of fresh fruit. When we were in Jamaica we got a stalk of bananas which we hung up and everybody could help themselves. Where there were orange groves we had plenty of oranges. When there were watermelons we had those, and in Puerto Rico we had oranges and grapefruit. In Jamaica there were pineapples, and I remember six miles of banana groves on both sides of the road. So we had plenty of fresh fruit when we were in port and as long as it lasted out to sea. *[See photo 3.14]*

One time I brought back a coconut and they told me what to do to make it grow. I put it in the skylight of the after cabin and sure enough, soon a little coconut tree began to grow from it. When we got back to New York we left the ship for a few days and when we got back the little plant had frozen. Then I had a tub on deck that somebody was good enough to fill with soil and I had some plants in it. I planted some watermelon seeds and they grew and blossomed. When the men washed down the deck they were very careful not to get any salt water or hot water on it. I guess it was an awful nuisance but I never heard anybody complain.

*3.15 The* Ella Pierce Thurlow. *Like several other schooners, she ended her days in use as a barge, her masts having been removed. In March of 1932, she sank off the coast of North Carolina. Photo by Thomas P. Haviland.*

She also recalled a hurricane, which lasted through two days and two nights.

> Well, I'm not the kind to get panicky, but I realized every bit of danger and I wouldn't have bet one cent whether we'd come out of it alive or whether we might not get out of it. I had been at sea long enough so that I didn't get seasick. We took on a lot of water and it kept me busy drying things out so that I didn't have time to get frightened.
>
> I used to go up the gangway and look out the windows at the seas once in a while and they were terrific seas. She'd pitch way up and dip down in and put her jibboom out of sight. One time when I was looking out, the hen-coop was washed overboard. We had had good Sunday dinners from them and they used to lay eggs pretty good. I think we had four left then.

Essie recalled that her favorite ship was the four-master *Ella Pierce Thurlow*.

> Some people didn't like her at first, they said she was so cranky. She'd roll way over on one side whichever way the wind was putting her. They were afraid she'd roll over. They were talking about putting more ballast in her to hold her up straight. But we weren't afraid of her. She'd made a trip to Africa and didn't roll over. She'd had a load of wool and that was pretty light. I guess the reason I liked her was after we had the two children: whatever side she was down on was the side we'd put them on because they couldn't fall out of the bunk. *[See photo 3.15]*

Essie's husband lost his life in 1942 when torpedoed on the way to Newfoundland. Left a widow, she did what so many other women did in similar circumstances: she remarried, to Harry Beck, himself a widower, who ran a meat market and grocery store in Deer Isle village. Her son, George Jr., carried on the family tradition, becoming a captain himself.

# Chapter 4: The Big Steam Yachts: Camargo, Hi-Esmaro and Their Crews

*Fact is, what many landlubbers call "yachts" nowadays would have served as admirals' barges for the truly large pleasure vessels parading through the decades from the mid-1800s into the 1930s.*

Bill Wisner, "The Golden Age of Yachts," 1975.

## Introduction

Although island mariners continued to go to sea in sailing vessels well into the 20th century, by the late 19th century, the days of such vessels were already numbered. The decline of merchant sail began with the appearance of steamships and railroads, which increasingly took over the transport of freight. First to succumb were deep-water voyages, while coastal trade under sail was kept alive by periodic resurgences until the end of World War I.

Responding to the downturn in maritime shipping under sail, island men began to take advantage of a new opportunity afforded by an increase of interest among people of wealth in owning private yachts. As early as the 1840s, yachting began to come to prominence in Europe, although it lagged somewhat in the United States. Here, it began in 1854 with the launching of Commodore Cornelius Vanderbilt's yacht *North Star*.

Besides opening up new opportunities for employment, there were additional benefits to yachting. For one, the work was less dangerous. Even today:

> When you enter the merchant marine, you're walking into a different world. Danger is your frequent companion. There are any number of things that can kill you: there are people who want to steal what you're hauling, or the ship itself. It's not rare to lose a man. Containers drop, wires part, a heavy piece of cargo shifts and turns into a man-killer. A fire onboard can be a death sentence, because there's nowhere to run and no one to come to your aid. And the loneliness is a fatal part of our lives, too. Men simply lose the desire to return to their lives on land and just disappear in the middle of the night. (Richard Phillips, *A Captain's Duty*, page 91)

For another, the pay was better. Moreover, most yachts were laid up over the winter, allowing the men to return to their families for the winter months. As explained by James Aldrich in his book *Centennial* (p. 16):

> In late winter or early spring each year the exodus began. Scores of men, young and old, experienced and novice, went yachting. Although the majority were from the town of Deer Isle, every island community was represented. The employment period varied depending upon the size and type of the yacht, but with a few exceptions the yachters would be back home for the Thanksgiving holidays.

Finally, on the big steamships that were displacing sail as cargo carriers, as Captain Edwin Greenlaw (in Chapter 6) noted, "Many members of the crew…were alcoholics, convicts and degenerates." That was not the case on private yachts. As Captain Greenlaw observed when he left merchant steamships for yachting, "I did not have drunken crews to contend with." It must have been quite a contrast, dealing instead with wealthy socialites.

The comings and goings of yachtsmen were duly noted in the island newspapers. Below is a representative sample, all from the *Deer Isle Messenger*.

November 25, 1898:

> Capt. Jasper W. Haskell is in New York this week on business in connection with his vessel, the *Hugh Kelley*.

> Capt. Chas. Greenlaw, who was master of the steam yacht *Penelope* when she was sold to the government last spring at the breaking out of the [Spanish American] war, has been appointed to the command of the steam yacht *Eicedo* of Phila. and will leave for that city Monday. Capt. Greenlaw will take from this place a mate, boatswain, two quartermasters, and five of the crew, who will go Monday Dec. 5th.

October 27, 1899:

> Moody P. Eaton arrived home on Saturday. He has been on the yacht *Volunteer* this summer.

> Grover Small came from New York Wednesday, where he has been yachting this summer.

> Roland Torrey came home from New York Saturday, where he has been on a yacht.

> Alvah Emerson, Herbert Conary, and Alfred Dunham, who have been yachting this past summer, arrived home Saturday.

> A part of the *Columbia*'s crew is expected home Saturday. [The *Columbia* was the current Cup defender, with an all-Deer Isle crew.]

October 5, 1900:

> Capt. E. C. Haskell of the yacht *Norseman* returned home last week. His yacht having gone out of commission.

> The yacht *Gundridge*, Capt. C. E. Dow, came into the harbor Friday, for a day or two. The owners are on board on a gunning expedition.

> F. Lermont [sic] Green returned home Tuesday from his first yachting season.

> Kimball B. Barbour, who has been on the yacht *Malay* this summer, arrived home Tuesday.

> Amos Scott, who has been steward of yacht *Akela*, was reported to have been in the Salem hospital last week of abscess of the throat.

> Yacht *Hazel*, owned by Frank Hodgkins of Ellsworth, was at this port Friday. She had as a guest on board Mr. B. T. Soule, agent for the Union Mutual Life Ins. Co.

# The Big Steam Yachts

Warren Powers, who has been yachting this summer, arrived home Saturday.

September 13, 1901:

The yacht *Lucile*, commanded by Capt. John Lowe, has been in the harbor this week.

Mrs. Charles Ames went to Bar Harbor Saturday, returning Sunday on the yacht *Lucile*, of which her husband is steward.

Capt. George Eaton, who has been employed on a New York yacht the past season, is at home, his yacht having gone out of commission.

Mrs. W. S. Green left Friday for New York to visit her husband, who is in command of the steam yacht *Akela*.

H. C. Holden spent Friday night at home, while the yacht on which he is employed was at North Deer Isle bound to Bar Harbor from Bangor.

Roland Torrey made a short call at home last Friday while the yacht *Athene* on which he is employed was in the harbor.

January 15, 1904:

Mr. and Mrs. E. A. Greene left Wednesday for New London, Conn., where Mr. Greene will have the care of the steam yacht *Coranto*, of which he is the chief engineer, relieving Capt. F. M. Holden, who has had the care of the yacht since she went out of commission. Mr. Greene's son, Merle, will stop with his grandparents until school is done, when he will join his parents. Past experience leads Mr. Greene to believe that the boy makes better progress here than in a strange school in the city, which speaks well for the public schools of Deer Isle.

Grover Small has gone to New York, where he will study navigation for a few weeks.

July 22, 1904:

Capt. Charles H. Greenlaw, of the yacht *Seminole*, came up from Bar Harbor Monday on a visit to his family.

The yacht *Coranto* came up from Bar Harbor Wednesday and went to Camden to coal up, returning to Deer Isle yesterday for the night.

Mrs. Charles A. Small and Mrs. Judson T. Haskell have been spending the past week at Islesboro, where their husbands have been for a while in the yacht which Capt. Small commands.

Capt. Judson Torrey left for New York Monday to bring on a yacht which William Hitz has had built out there. Mr. Hitz will accompany him on the homeward trip. The yacht is larger than the *Georgie* and will be used by Mr. Hitz for bay cruising.

W. J. Waymouth has gone assistant cook on the yacht *Seminole* commanded by Capt. C. H. Greenlaw.

April 22, 1910:

Capt. John Marshall left for Philadelphia Monday to take command of his yacht for the season.

Ernest H. Pickering, who will go mate on the yacht commanded by Capt. W. S. Greene, left for New London, Conn., Tuesday to assume his duties.

Harry Annis left for Philadelphia Thursday to join the yacht *Iroista*.

Capt. F. M. Holden arrived from New York Friday, where he has been looking after his yacht. He will return in about two weeks.

Lester Gray left Monday to go with Capt. Charles Gray in the yacht *Athene*.

From a March 1917 issue:

Some of our yachtsmen have left to join their respective yachts but many others are awaiting orders from their captains, who, owing to war conditions [World War I] and the fact that so many of the yachts are being taken over by the government, are uncertain as to whether their boats are coming out or not. This unsettled condition of the yachting business will, however, probably clear itself after congress assembles next week, when those who have offered their boats will learn whether or not they are to be used for war purposes.

March 25, 1921:

Charles Greenlaw, Arthur Eaton, Courtney Bray, Lewis Sylvester, Gordon Scott, and Ernest Pressey leave Saturday morning for New York to join J. P. Morgan's yacht the *Nevette*.

July 8, 1921:

The steam yacht *Shada*, owned by Mr. Darling of Boston and commanded by Capt. Whitney B. Lowe, was in the harbor over the Fourth. The yacht is on a cruise east with the owner and party aboard and Mr. Darling kindly stopped over that the crew might enjoy the Fourth at home.

May 11, 1923:

Winfield L. Greenlaw went to Camden Monday to go steward on the yacht *Robin*.

S. T. Lowe went to Boston Tuesday to put his yacht in commission. Mrs. Lowe accompanied him as far as Rockland, where she is visiting relatives.

Arthur Annis, who is fitting out his yacht at North Haven, spent Sunday with his parents, Freeland H. Annis and wife.

January 22, 1926:

Maurice Powers left home a week ago to go to New York to join yacht *Ventura*, Capt. Merle Greene, and from there they go to Florida. [This is the same Merle Greene who was reported in a 1904 item reproduced above, as then in school. We shall hear more of him in this chapter.]

In April 1928, the *Deer Isle and Stonington Press* reported that "of 100 captains in command of commuter's yachts, sailing in and out of New York harbor, 70 were Deer Isle men." *[See photo 4.1]*

And so it went, even through the depression of the 1930s. Most of the wealthy yacht owners had sufficient reserves to insulate them from the economic hard times. Consider the number of yachts with Deer Isle men aboard that were caught in the hurricane of 1938, one of the worst to ever hit southern New England. According to Clayton Gross:

At Glen Cove, L.I. the *Sybarita,* an 85 foot power boat commanded by Capt. Burton Haskell, broke her moorings but was able to make Port Washington where she anchored without suffering any major damage.

Capt. Avery Marshall was in the 75 foot power boat *Katherine II* at Hadley's Harbor near Woods Hole when the storm struck. By stretching a 100 fathom [600 foot] hawser to a tree on the shore and maneuvering with the engine, Capt. Marshall was able to keep the yacht from joining those piled up on the beach. Also with him at the time were Arnold Morey and Waldo Taylor. Even though he saved the boat, Capt. Marshall lost his car when the garage it was in blew down.

The 270 foot yacht *Vanda* was anchored off City Point, Boston. She dragged her

*4.1 The Mystic, shown here, was a typical commuter yacht, transporting wealthy owners from their estates in the country to their offices in the city. Eighty feet long, she was owned by Gordon Dexter of Boston. In her crew was Alton Gross of Deer Isle. Seventy percent of commuter yachts in the New York area had Deer Isle captains, among them Cleveland and Eugene Eaton of Little Deer Isle, Albert Coombs and Percy Joyce of Stonington (later Deer Isle) and Harry Annis and Alton Torrey of North Deer Isle. Courtesy of Deer Isle-Stonington Historical Society*

anchor for a considerable distance but was large enough to keep off shore. Crewmen lay prone on deck hanging onto anything they could get hold of to keep from being blown off while watching smaller boats pile up on the beach. In her crew were George Lane Beck, Ralph Thompson, Kenneth Pickering, Gilbert and Herbert Marshall, George Barbour and Pearl Eaton.

The yacht *Hi-Esmaro* had left Greenwich, Connecticut and was on the way to New London when the storm struck. She rode out the storm on Long Island Sound until she could return safely to Greenwich. On board at the time were her master Capt. Grover Small, Gilbert Gross, an uncle of the writer, Martin Snowden, Melvin Pickering, Goodwin Eaton and Charles Fifield.

Norman Woolworth's yacht *Naparo* (ex *Viking*) rode out the storm safely at New London. In her crew were Randall Haskell, Beckwith Hardy, Leroy Eaton, Perly Kent and Ernest Smith.

Capt. Eugene Eaton was at Marblehead with the power yacht *Gitana*. He moved her to Manchester where the harbor was thought to be safer. Together with two other yachts the *Gitana* was one of only three vessels in that harbor to survive the storm. Capt. Eaton's son Earl was with him. Six days later the *Gitana* arrived in Stonington at the yacht basin to be laid up for the winter.

Capt. Vern Haskell was at City Island (N.Y.) on the 65 foot yacht *Maritor*. She held her position with two anchors and a mooring. His son Henry Haskell was also at City Island in the yacht *Tara*.

Capt. Walter Scott in the schooner yacht *Stella* was at Darien, Connecticut, but rode out the storm with no damage. Robert Billings of Stonington was at

*4.2 The New London, Connecticut, waterfront after the 1938 hurricane. Collection of Barbara L. Britton*

Fairhaven, Massachusetts on the yacht *Gypsy* at the boatyard of Pierce and Kimball. When a storm surge struck, it snapped her lines and threw her onto her side. By pumping and throwing ballast overboard the crew was able to keep her afloat. *[See photo 4.2]*

Continued employment on yachts, with the family farm, coupled with time off in winter to tend to cutting, splitting and stacking firewood and myriad other tasks, provided islanders with a cushion against the worse effects of the depression. In July 1932, the *Deer Isle and Stonington Press* reported that "the island will be richer by approximately $200,000 when the men return to their homes with the wages paid by their affluent employers." It went on to claim that the yachts of both Julius Fleischmann and George F. Baker were manned "from Capt. to cabin boy, by Deer Isle sailors, and one third of the men sailing on J.P. Morgan's three yachts signed on from this island."

As recently as April and May of 1941, as many as a dozen men were reported as "going yachting." At that point, World War II intervened, in effect sounding the death knell for the big yachts. With this, those islanders still active in yachting went into the Merchant Marine. Others who had retired by then found other occupations, such as Captain Harry Annis, previously in charge of a commuter yacht, who became a produce wholesaler. During the war, the Haviland family enjoyed a regular supply of chickens raised by Captain Annis.

Employment on yachts began soon after the Civil War, and yachting rapidly surpassed both the fisheries and the Merchant Marine in importance. Although some of the early yachts were steam powered *[see Table 4.1]*, many were still wind driven vessels. There seems to have been some prejudice against engines at first. Clearly, in his last years, Captain George Washington Torrey went on steam ships only because cargo carriers under sail were no longer an option. And we have this, from *The New York Sun* in 1899:

> If you continue talking to the average Deer Isle man he'll say: "They ain't many o' our boys that goes wrong; they ain't many. Once in a while they's one that goes into the engineering department; but they ain't many."

Nevertheless, steam yachts became increasingly popular among the moneyed classes. As the ultimate status symbols, there was a certain amount of "one-

# The Big Steam Yachts

**Correct Yachting Uniforms**

Crews Uniformed at shortest notice

*Our representative will call on request*

Send for Illustrated Catalog of Correct Yachting Uniforms

**S. APPEL & COMPANY**
14-16-18 Fulton Street          New York
Telephones John 5382 to 5389

*4.3 S. Appel and Co. in New York supplied uniforms for yacht owners, officers and crews since 1856 (see Appendix I). Their ads appeared regularly in the Deer Isle newspapers; this one is from the Deer Isle and Stonington Press for March 7, 1930. Courtesy of Penobscot Bay Press Note the name on the life ring in the background: Ara was a yacht commanded by Merle Green, who served as First Mate on Camargo. From Centennial—A Century of Island Newspapers, p. 109*

upmanship" as some owners sought larger, faster, and more luxurious yachts than those of their peers. Many of the yachts were over one hundred feet in length, several were over two hundred feet, and some were even larger. Hulls were like those of the old clipper ships, with ornate bows, and interiors that could be truly palatial. They might have wood-paneled walls of mahogany or carved walnut, rich carpets throughout, with silk drapes and curtains. Marble bathtubs and gold fixtures were not unknown, as was Chippendale furniture. There might be a fireplace, a grand piano, and, in at least one case (the *Delphine*, owned by the widow of auto tycoon Horace E. Dodge), a $60,000 pipe organ. On some yachts, food was served on fine china, and valuable art decorated inside walls.

To build such "floating palaces" cost in the millions, nor were they inexpensive to run. Payrolls varied with the size of the vessel. Smaller yachts had smaller crews, but in many cases, they numbered over twenty, and sometimes more than fifty. By the late 1800s, a crew of forty to fifty could cost the owner $2,000 to $2,500 per month, to which would be added $1,500 or so per month to feed them. All told, costs probably added up to some $50,000 per year. Back then, of course, $50,000 was worth a good deal more than today.

Crews, and even owners, had to be properly outfitted. Yacht enthusiast Bill Wisner describes this as follows:

An owner required at least two types of uniforms. One was for general daytime wear and strolling about the deck. This combination dictated a dark, smartly tailored, lapel type jacket, white trousers and white shoes, surmounted by a white-topped yachting cap adorned with the owner's club insignia in gold and enamel. Jacket sleeves carried a three-loop stripe, in gold, identifying him as Mr. Big. Owners' and officers' jacket buttons were gold color, decorated with an anchor. Stewards' uniforms sported silver anchor buttons.

Formal wear at dinner and social functions aboard demanded another outfit for the owner. Its components were a snug mess jacket, dark and trimmed with a kind of black braid, white shirt and a bow tie, dark pants, black shoes. In black braid on the jacket's sleeves was that looping stripe showing who was boss.

Nor could her captain look like a slouch. He had to be as sartorially resplendent as his employer. In those days you could buy a good civilian suit for $50. A yacht skipper's dress uniform—only one of his ensembles—cost about $65, of which $20 was for his gold sleeve stripes. Certain uniforms for all officers carried gold braid. Appel imported the gold, and even then it came high. *[See photo 4.3; Appel ad]*

These are yachts whose crews numbered one or more Deer Isle men, as reported in the Deer Isle Messenger, 1898-1909. Only very rarely are these vessels described other than as noted below.

| | | | | | |
|---|---|---|---|---|---|
| *Ada* | Yacht | *Hindra* | Yacht | *Ranger* | Schooner yacht |
| *Admiral* | Steam yacht | *Iantha* | Yacht | *Rascal* | Racing sloop yacht |
| *Akela* | Steam yacht | *Inia* | Steam yacht | *Razmatang* | Yacht |
| *Alert* | Yacht | *Jessie* | Steam yacht | *Riveria* | Steam yacht |
| *Athene* | Yacht | *Joker* | Yacht | *Rodenia* | Yacht |
| *Augusta* | Yacht | *Jolly Tar* | Fast sloop yacht | *Rosalie* | Yacht |
| *Aztec* | Palatial steam yacht | *Josephine* | Steam yacht; crew of 57 | *Roxana* | Yacht |
| *Centa* | Yacht | | | *Sapphire* | Steam yacht |
| *Cigarette* | Fast steam yacht | *Laurita* | Yacht | *Scud* | Yacht |
| *Clermont* | Steam yacht | *Lillias* | Yacht | *Seminole* | Yacht |
| *Clytie* | Yacht | *Lyndonia* | Yacht | *Spendthrift* | Yacht |
| *Commanche* | Yacht | *Malay* | Steam yacht | *Surf* | Yacht |
| *Consuelo* | Yacht | *Maria* | Yacht | *Swifan* | Steam yacht |
| *Coranto* | Steam yacht | *Merle* | Yacht | *Tramp* | Steam launch |
| *Coronilla* | Yacht | *Navitte* | Yacht | *Uncas* | Launch |
| *Diana* | Steam yacht | *Nectan* | Yacht | *Viking* | Steam yacht |
| *Duquesne* | Steam yacht | *Nirvana* | Yacht | *Weetamos* | Yacht |
| *Elreba* | Steam yacht | *Nourmahal* | Palatial steam yacht of J.J. Astor | *White Heather* | Yacht |
| *Fawn* | Launch | | | *Windward* | Schooner yacht |
| *Georgie* | Yacht | *Onawa* | Yacht | *Wissihickon* | Yacht |
| *Glendoveer* | Schooner yacht | *Onward* | Sloop yacht | *Zara* | Yacht |
| *Gundridge* | Yacht | *Rambler* | Yacht | | |

The inventory of officers' uniforms was impressive. The list called for regulation dress, service dress and a sharp-looking white outfit with standing-collar jacket. Shipboard apparel for the chief engineer included "semi-dress" for engine room wear so he'd look like an officer even in the black gang's domain. Officers also had service and dress caps in blue and white, plus a warm, full-length bridge coat for the cold weather.

Appel could get out a tape measure for the chief steward's set of uniforms. His job was important. Its broad scope included food, drink, accommodations and passengers' comfort in general. Therefore, his underlings also had to be properly attired. Mess jacket ensembles for them. For the chef and his aides were ordered the traditional white galley-service clothing.

Now bring in the seamen. Their outfitting started off with a regulation sailor's blue uniform, its blouse carrying the vessel's name in white across the front. To this were added such items as working suits of blue denim or unbleached duck, jerseys, white dress blouses with the yacht's name embroidered in front, sneakers, assorted hats and sweaters, also with the vessel's name inscribed. For cold climate the inventory provided watch caps, pea jackets ("reefers") and such foul-weather gear as oiled suits lined with warming corduroy, long oilskin coats, sou'westers and boots in short, three-quarter and hip lengths.

We're not finished yet. Since the great yachts cruised far and wide in a variety of climes, it was necessary that everyone, owner to lowliest crewman, be outfitted with clothing of both summer and winter weights.

If all of this isn't expensive enough, there were the added costs of fuel, other equipment, maintenance,

**The Big Steam Yachts**

and so on. In the case of some really big yachts, it cost in the neighborhood of $3,000 a day to run them. As John Pierpont Morgan is said to have commented: "If you have to ask how much a yacht costs, you can't afford one." In the rest of this chapter, we will take a close look at two of the large, luxurious yachts, and the Deer Isle men who ran them.

*4.4 Camargo at anchor in Amoa Bay in the Marquesan Islands. Courtesy of Tinker (Gross) Crouch*

## *Camargo, Hi-Esmaro* and Their Crews

### *Camargo*

One of the yachts best remembered on Deer Isle was *Camargo*, built by George Lawley and Sons at Neponset, Massachusetts, for Julius Fleischmann of Cincinnati. Fleischmann, whose wealth came from the gin, yeast and margarine that still carry his name, had a summer home at Eastern Point in Groton, Connecticut, on the Thames River. His yacht was launched in 1925, and her captain from the start was Charles E. Small of Deer Isle. Many of her crew members, too, were from the island. *[See photo 4.4]*

The yacht was a grand one, with her clipper bow and sleek hull. Originally painted black, it soon showed streaks of white from sea salt, and so was repainted white. Length overall was just over 225 feet, her beam was 32 feet 4 inches, with a draft of 17 feet 4 inches. Although called a "steam yacht," she was powered by a pair of Krupp diesels, innovative at the time, and was capable of cruising at 12 knots. An indication of her fuel consumption is provided by a stopover in the Fiji Islands, where she took on 40,000 gallons, having "steamed" all the way from New York. She sported a one-pound cannon, used for signaling and in celebrations.

Including a crew of thirty-five to forty, *Camargo* could carry up to one hundred twenty people. Her interior boasted most of the comforts of home. Her "living room" was complete with a fireplace, and her dining room had a table on tracks that could be pushed onto the fantail for outside dining. There was a well-equipped gymnasium on board, and even the crews' quarters in the forecastle were described by one crewman as "quite nice." She was truly a "Queen of the Sea." *[See photo 4.5]*

We know little of *Camargo's* travels before 1931. In 1928, she cruised from Eastport to Trinidad. In 1930, she went through the Panama Canal to the Cocos Islands, the Galapagos (bringing back two tortoises for the Bronx Zoo), and Peru. In 1931, however, she embarked on a far more ambitious journey from New York via Bermuda, Jamaica, the canal, the Cocos and several other islands in the South Pacific to the East Indies, Philippines, Southeast Asia and Singapore, westward to the Suez Canal, Mediterranean and Black Sea, and home across the Atlantic. *[See photo 4.6]*

Aboard were Fleischmann, his wife and two very young children, three friends and a photographer (Amos Burg) from *National Geographic*. His color pictures appeared in a 1934 issue of the magazine, to accompany an article by Ian Hogbin, a noted British anthropologist. Several of his black and white photographs appeared in Julius Fleischmann's account of the voyage. At several ports along the way, a number of dignitaries were entertained, among them opera star Lawrence Tibbett at Cannes, the Prince Consort to the Queen of Tonga, and the King, Queen and Crown Prince of Romania on the Danube.

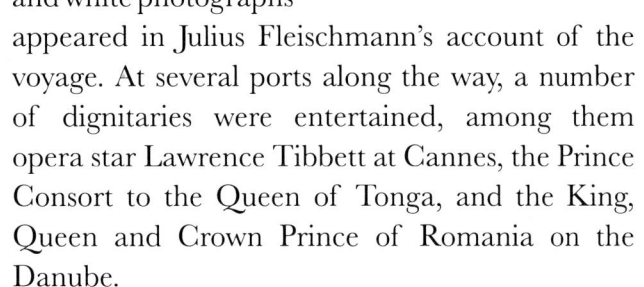

Mixing business with pleasure, Julius Fleischmann acted at several island ports in the Pacific as special representative of the U.S. Department of Commerce, drumming up trade, but had some other projects as well. One was to release six hens, two roosters, three pairs of pigeons and some ducks on the Cocos Islands, to see if they would naturalize there. These islands, some 500 miles southwest of Panama, were uninhabited at the time, but once were the site of a small settlement of treasure hunters. Fleischmann worried about competition to his introduced fowl from resident seabirds, but seems to have been oblivious to the threat posed by the wild hogs and rats that overran the islands.

At the Cocos Islands, besides releasing the poultry, passengers and crew from *Camargo* went ashore to replenish their fresh water and do some fishing. They landed at the abandoned settlement where they found three shipwrecked sailors had been camping. At the time, these castaways had gone to the other end of the island in search of coconuts,

4.5 Roughing it on the high seas: Camargo's "living room." Courtesy of Tinker (Gross) Crouch

4.6 Mrs. Fleischmann (on right) at Chatham Bay, Galapagos Islands. Courtesy of Tinker (Gross) Crouch

the local supply having been depleted. There ensued a search, eventually resulting in a rescue of the men who had spent six months on the island. They arrived on *Camargo* stark naked, having swum out from shore. From the yacht they were taken aboard a naval gunboat, dispatched from Balboa in response to a message radioed to the naval base there.

The voyage was not smooth sailing all the way. In Fleischmann's account of the voyage, there are several references to heavy weather: On the way out from Bermuda, passengers had difficulty staying in their beds; there was seemingly endless rain in the Cocos; many on board were seasick on the run from New Britain to New Guinea. At one

# The Big Steam Yachts

*4.7 Julius Fleischmann, boarding Camargo. Courtesy of Tinker (Gross) Crouch*

point crewman Gilbert Gross wrote in his diary, "Quite a job to stay in our bunks" and a day later, "Sure is rough down this way when it wants to be." Leaving Manila for Hong Kong, they ran into a Pacific cyclone that forced them to divert to Saigon. Gilbert Gross wrote in his diary: "I fed the fish last night for the first time on the trip." They couldn't serve breakfast and things were thrown all over the fo'castle. On the way to Thailand, according to Gross, "A sea struck the port side midships and split the rail and cracked the steel bulwarks about fifteen or twenty feet." A sea also struck him on the upper deck, almost knocking him over. More seasickness was caused by the pitch and roll of a heavy storm on the way to Ceylon (now Sri Lanka). At one point, the sea broke two windows in the Fleischmanns' bedroom, soaking the occupants in their beds. *[See photo 4.7]*

On the way from Saigon to Bangkok, sickness struck several of the crew. At the time, the Fleischmanns were traveling overland between the two cities, their vessel sailing to meet them in Thailand. On March 4, Gilbert Gross' diary reports "four men on sick list" and on March 7, "The skipper is very sick, with fever. His temperature is 104." So worried were the crew that men were assigned to stand watch over him, one hour apiece. On March 10, he was reported weaker. By March 12, he was reported better, but meanwhile, other crewmen were reported sick through late March. By the time they reached Singapore, however, the sickness seems to have passed. *[See photo 4.8]*

*4.8 Gilbert Gross, a seaman on Camargo, later went into the Merchant Marine. While on Camargo, he kept a diary. This photograph dates from 1943. Courtesy of Tinker (Gross) Crouch*

At Singapore, *Camargo* spent one day in dry dock, having her bottom scraped and painted. After five and a half months at sea, marine growth had reduced her speed by about one and a half knots. Supplies of water and fuel were also taken on. A month later she was refueled again at Colombo, Ceylon. This was not without mishap, as reported by Gilbert Gross: "The oil boat came along side today [April 14] and stove in one of our life boats in doing it. The skipper was fit to be tied."

Fleischmann's account of the trip has little to say about life aboard ship, devoting most of his attention to descriptions of places, people and activities ashore. His account stops with their arrival at Aden, and a continuation of the trip to northern Europe and Scandinavia was postponed on account of a family matter at home.

The trip to northern Europe took place in 1934. After layup at Tebo Yacht Basin in Brooklyn, New York, in June, a full crew of forty (including officers) came aboard, supplies were loaded, and the ship set sail for Naples. There, the Fleischmann family boarded, having crossed the Atlantic on the Italian

4.9 Officers and Deer Isle members of Camargo's crew. Seated are, from left, Second Mate Norman Gray, Captain Small, First Mate Merle Greene, and Chief Engineer Maynard Killen from Islesboro. Deer Isle men served above deck, Islesboro men below deck. Courtesy of Tinker (Gross) Crouch

liner *Conte de Savoia*. From Naples, they visited several ports around the Mediterranean, before heading south through the Suez Canal. There were then several stops along the east coast of Africa before stopping at Cape Town, where they spent several days in dry dock for bottom cleaning and painting. Next, *Camargo* steamed up the west coast of Africa, again with several stops along the way. One was at Lagos, Nigeria, where they docked, but had to keep watch fore and aft to keep monkeys that lived under the docks from boarding via the mooring lines.

From Africa, the trip continued north to the Scandinavian and Baltic countries, with stops at various places, for activities including trout fishing in Ireland, and visits to Lapp reindeer herders in Norway. They then returned across the Atlantic to Halifax, steaming from there to New London, Connecticut, and then to Tebo Yacht Basin to lay up.

## The Crew of *Camargo*

As long as the Fleischmanns owned her, *Camargo's* captain was Charles Elwood Small of North Deer Isle. Many islanders served aboard as well, as both officers and crew: Merle Greene (son of Charles Small's sister Kate) as First Mate, and Norman Gray as Second Mate, and crew members George Barbour, Gene Billings, John Eaton, Maurice Eaton, Martin Greene (grandnephew of Merle), Gilbert Gross (husband of the oldest daughter of Charles Small's youngest brother), Gene Hutchinson, Howard Hutchinson, Gardner Joyce, George Lufkin, Eugene Robbins, Myron Shepard (husband of the daughter of the captain's sister), and Weston Small (son of Charles's youngest brother and brother-in-law of Gilbert Gross). No doubt there were other kinship ties besides those just noted. To cite one more example, one of George Lufkin's sisters was the wife of a grandson of Captain Small's mother's older brother. *[See photo 4.9]*

Charles Small, born in 1864, was the oldest son of Lucy Augusta ("Gustie") Tower Hardy and George Washington Small, who married in 1863. George was a fisherman and quarryman, Lucy the daughter of George Campbell Hardy, a farmer who also ran a food and marine supply store on

# The Big Steam Yachts

*4.10 Yacht Calypso, commanded by Charles Small. Picture by Tom Willis of New York, courtesy of Deer Isle-Stonington Historical Society*

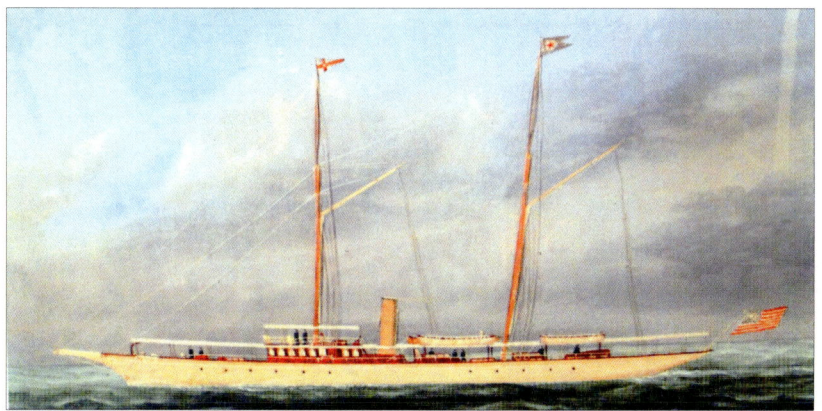

*4.11 Yacht Sapphire, commanded by Charles Small. Picture by Tom Willis of New York, courtesy of Deer Isle-Stonington Historical Society*

*4.12 Crew members from Deer Isle aboard Sapphire in 1899. Front row, left and right: Herbert Bray and Judson Haskell, Quartermasters; Launchman George Torrey between them. Back row, from left: sailors Parker Eaton, Clarence Dow, Frank Holden. Courtesy of Deer Isle-Stonington Historical Society*

Torrey's Millpond. As discussed in Chapter 2, George Campbell Hardy inherited the farm established by his grandfather, Peter Hardy, Sr. Lucy was the fourth daughter of George Hardy and his first wife, and when she married, she and her husband built a house *[see photo 2-11 on page 24]* on a piece carved out of her father's farm. In it, they raised six children (a seventh died young) and, for a time, ran a post office. Of the six children, three sons became captains, and one of three daughters married a captain.

Charles Small went to sea as a young man, in the days of the square riggers. By the time he took command of *Camargo* in 1925, he had been a deep water sailor for some fifty years. Before *Camargo*, he was Master of the yachts *Calypso* and *Sapphire*. *[See photos 4.10 and 4.11]* We have no information on the former; the latter was a wooden single screw steam yacht built in 1900 in the Herreshoff yard in Bristol, Rhode Island. Of 53 gross tons, she was 98 feet long overall, with a 14-foot beam and draft of 5 feet 9 inches. *Sapphire's* owner was Jeremiah Milbank of New York City, whose grandfather amassed a fortune speculating in Texas territorial bonds and as founder of the Borden Company. For a year in 1917-18 the vessel was taken over by the Navy and, as SP-710, used for patrol service in the New York harbor area. She was then returned to her owner; her ultimate fate is unknown. *[See photo 4.12]*

When the *Camargo* arrived back in New York from its around-the-world cruise, coverage in the *Nassau Daily News* on September 23, 1932, spotlighted Captain Small with pictures of the *Camargo* in dry dock at the Tebo Yacht Basin in Brooklyn,

Captain Small with fishing spears from the South Seas, and Captain Small with Prince Michael of Romania on board *Camargo*. Charles R. Becker, author of the *Nassau Daily News* article, referred to Captain Small as a "man of action and not of words… disclosed details of the tour only after being virtually goaded by this interviewer" and that he "…referred to the rescue [of the Cocos Island castaways] in a matter-of-fact way as though it was part of the day's work of commanding one of the world's most commodious yachts." *[See photo 4.13]*

Charles Small was a member of the Marine Lodge, No. 122, Deer Isle, Maine, and was a 32nd degree Mason. He had lived in the Bay Ridge section of Brooklyn, New York, and for seventeen years prior to 1932 lived in Lynbrook, New York. He married Lillian Burton Jordan of Deer Isle. Their two sons died, Frank as a child and Arthur at age 23. Charles had a son and daughter in later years from a second marriage. Charles Jr. joined the Navy in the 1930s, served on the battleships USS *Mississippi* and USS *Detroit* and in World War II served on PT boats in the South Pacific.

Gustie Small's boys, besides Charles, included two other sons and, like their older brother, both went yachting. Forrest Clayton Small, born in 1870, as a young man served on various coastal schooners and was mate on the yacht *Jathneil* owned by Josiah B. Thomas of Peabody, Massachusetts. He later became sailing master of various steam yachts owned by George R. Sheldon, W.K. Vanderbilt Jr., R.A.C. Smith, Peter W. Rouse of New York and Arthur Masker of Chicago. With the outbreak of World War I, he left yachting to take command of various merchant ships. By the time of World War II he had retired, but then served as a coastal pilot until the end of the war. He died in 1949.

Gustie's third son (and youngest child), Grover Cleveland Small, began his yachting career with his brother Charles, and we will look at his career below.

Another descendant of Lucy and George Small was Merle Greene, First Mate on *Camargo* and a captain in his own right. Born in Deer Isle in 1895,

*4.13 Captain Charles Small with Prince Michael of Romania on the bridge of Camargo. The Romanian royal family were entertained aboard on the Danube River. Courtesy of Lucy (Small) Hopkins*

he was the son of Kate Small, one of Charles Small's sisters, who married Captain Eugene Allen ("Allie") Greene. When his son was in school, Allie served as first engineer on the yacht *Coronto*. Upon graduation from high school, Merle was accepted to the U.S. Naval Academy, but decided he didn't want to "take orders" so opted not to go. Instead he served on the U.S. Coast Guard Cutter *Bear* during World War I, as a sailor.

After the war, he became a merchant mariner, working his way up to officer rank. In 1920, he was Third Mate aboard a molasses tanker when, during a storm off the coast of Florida, the captain with his family and the crew were forced to abandon ship in two lifeboats. A brief account of the incident appeared in a local newspaper:

> Merle V. Greene, who was third officer on the tank steamer *Mierlero*, which foundered Jan. 26th, one hundred and fifty miles east of Savannah, Ga., arrived home Monday and gives a graphic account of the catastrophe. The second day after leaving the ship his boat fell in with the captain's, in which among the others was the second officer, Carroll Conary of Sunshine,

# The Big Steam Yachts

*4.14 First Mate Merle Greene ashore at Raugiroa in the Tuomotus. Courtesy of Tinker (Gross) Crouch*

but in the tempestuous weather of that night they again became separated. It was feared that this boat was swamped in getting away from the ship. She has not been reported as picked up as yet but there is still hope that the men have been rescued.

After five days Merle's lifeboat was picked up, but the one with the captain and his family was never found. Merle returned to Deer Isle vowing not to go to sea again. But after pacing the shore for six months he couldn't resist the call. This was the beginning of his yachting career. He was captain of W.K. Vanderbilt's yachts *Ara*, the *Moana* and the *Ventura* (see Chapter 6). In 1928, with a second daughter added to the family (he married Ruth Powers in 1917) he joined the yacht *Camargo* as First Mate under his uncle, Captain Charles Small, with Second Mate Deer Islander Norman Gray, and several other Deer Isle men in the crew. His granddaughter remembers Merle saying, "Any man from Deer Isle who wanted a job on a yacht had only to present himself to the agent in New York and he had a job—no questions asked." *[See photo 4.14]*

Merle Greene seems to have been less self-effacing than his uncle. Still, we have only occasional glimpses of his activities on *Camargo's* around-the-world cruise. Among them is Julius Fleischmann's account of King Neptune's Court, upon crossing the equator.

On the last day of October, *Camargo* crossed the Equator for the first of the many times which she was destined to do so during the cruise. At half-past two the Captain called us up to the bridge to be present when Neptune came on board. Among both passengers and crew there were many who had never crossed the Equator before. We were to "go over the bump" at about three-thirty, it was his duty to hold court. Neptune, in the guise of Mike McCarthy, the third mate, appeared out of the fo'castle head demanding the captain. He said that he understood there were some people on the ship who had never before been in his realm and asked permission to hold his court. This having been granted, he called for his retinue; "Castoria," Neptune's wife, was impersonated by the bo'sun, Silas Clarke; the Court Crier was the second assistant engineer, Harry McDonald; and "Frothmore," the Policeman, was Mr. Greene, the first mate. Frothmore had several assistants from the engine-room who were called the "Mud Guard."

The costuming was very cleverly done. Neptune wore a short tunic made from a potato sack, a beard of shredded rope, and on his head a golden cardboard crown. He carried a cardboard scepter and a pair of binoculars made by tying together two Poland-water bottles. His face was made up with Dorette's [Mrs. Fleischmann's] indelible lipstick. His queen wore a hula skirt of the same material as his beard; however, with lady-like modesty, it was longer. Her blouse, made of sacking, was so filled out as to make her bosom a billowy affair of more than ample proportions. On her head, topping off a flaxen rope wig, was a gold crown. The Crier's tunic, also of sacking, had a wide red band painted around the bottom. About his waist was tied a wide red sash; on his head he wore a dilapidated brimless straw hat decorated with a large feather. The red color note was further emphasized by smears of lipstick on his face. The Policeman wore a high cardboard stovepipe hat painted black, a black tail coat over a bathing suit, and an unattached stiff collar. The Mud Guard were appropriately dressed in hip-boots and slickers.

Neptune and Castoria being duly enthroned on two chairs with a background of flags, the Crier called for the first prisoner, Miss Rohan. She was delivered to the prisoner's box by the Policeman and the charges against her read from a scroll by the Crier. They were "that Miss Rohan has a gross and confirmed habit of beer consumption; that it has been sworn to, vouched for and proved that on or about October nineteenth, nineteen hundred thirty-one, in the city of Panama, she is known to have consumed great quantities of beer—sixteen bottles, more or less; to have behaved riotously; and to have stayed out all night, coming home at six o'clock in the morning, and how!"

*Crier*: "What sayest thou to these charges?"

*Prisoner*: "Guilty, I guess."

*Crier*: "Miss Rohan, the charges brought against you grieve me terribly. I had hoped that when you went out into the world you would adhere to the straight and narrow way. Such does not seem to have been the case. How well do I remember old Smith College! You were a good girl then, and I hope you are a good girl now. You were then a bashful co-ed, Queen of the Campus, as it were. Look at you now! Nevertheless, Miss Rohan, I alone am convinced of your innocence and will plead for mercy in your behalf before His Majesty the King. Almighty King, I recommend for her a Lux Bath!"

The King and Queen, after a conference, agreed to the Crier's recommendations. The prisoner's back was turned to Their Majesties, who quickly produced a bucket of soapsuds mixed with flour and water which had been hidden behind the throne. Then the prisoner was lathered with a large paint brush and shaved with a tremendous wooden razor. After this, the Mud Guard turned the hose on her, washing off what remained of the lather and thoroughly drenching her. Neptune was satisfied, the crime was expiated and the prisoner was dismissed.

One by one eighteen additional prisoners were haled into court. Tom Keck, who seldom misses a good opportunity to take a daytime nap, was charged with having sleeping sickness; Miss Dean was ironically charged with being too noisy about the decks; Mademoiselle and Fred Meng, the cabin steward, were jointly accused of "reckless love-making on the high seas, thereby obstructing the sailors in their work." Various members of the crew had to explain why they had done a variety of things ranging from photographing local girls at Coconut Grove in Panama, fraternizing with brown-skinned ones in Port Antonio, and making whoopee in Bermuda all the way down to being so slow that, in one case, his washing dried before it could be hung on the line. All were meted out the same punishment as Katie Rohan, the degree thereof varying with the charge.

Those who passed through court received a certificate addressed to "All Sailors Around the World," stating that the holder belongs to the "Order of the Bath." This entitles the erstwhile prisoners to become a part of the gallery at the next crossing of the Equator. Skipper and Dielle [the Fleischmann children] were given honorary certificates. The former shouted vehement protests while watching the proceedings and the latter looked on placidly from the vantage point of Deanie's or her mother's arms.

Also mentioned in Fleischmann's account is Merle Greene being hoisted in a bo'sun's chair to the foremast peak to watch for reefs upon entering the lagoon at the South Sea island of Rangiroa in the Tuamotus. At the time of the cruise, the waters around many islands were poorly charted, and Captain Small did not take any chances with sometimes tricky maneuvering. In fact, the crew produced improved charts of the waters. Later on, though not created for that purpose, these charts proved useful to the Navy in World War II as allied forces advanced through the islands against the Japanese.

Another anecdote, from Merle Greene's granddaughter, has to do with a set of Champagne glasses, each one etched with Fleischmann's personal house flag. Because he didn't like the way they looked, he was all set to have them thrown overboard. The mate intervened, however, taking possession of them himself. Today, the glasses are split between his two granddaughters.

From Gilbert Gross' diary comes an entry for February 10: "We had a battle in the forecastle with wet rags. We had a lot of fun until Greene came down and stopped us." Finally, it is clear that those on *Camargo* were not immune to the cultural stereotypes of the time. Thus, there was a tendency to think of the islanders, especially those of the western Pacific, as savages, or even cannibals, who were potentially dangerous. So it was Mr. Greene who carried a pistol when men went ashore. And as their launch was being pushed off from one island, he leaned down and pulled a wooden comb from a native's hair saying later, "The next white man that went ashore was probably eaten."

*Camargo*'s second mate, Norman Gray, was the son of Walter P. Gray, a master mariner who commanded several sailing vessels. Sailing between New York or New Haven and southern ports, he had a reputation as one of Deer Isle's most successful captains. His only son, Norman, one of seven children, was born in 1892. Nine years later, his mother died in childbirth, after which the grandparents and later the oldest daughter and her husband took over the running of the household.

On summer vacations, Norman sailed with his father, signing on as deckhand at age fourteen. Three years later he quit school and signed on first as engineer, then mate on various vessels. When the U.S. entered World War I, he sailed with Captain George Torrey carrying war supplies to Europe. Luckily, they survived several near misses from mines and bombs.

After the war, Norman made several trips as engineer on a boat commanded by his uncle, Captain Arthur Gray, and then one trip to France, again as mate, with George Torrey. In 1920, he married Georgia Haskell, and got his license as master of all oceans. Again he sailed as mate with George Torrey, suffering a bout with typhoid fever on the way to Norfolk. Upon recovery, he assumed command of his first ship, a three-masted schooner, the first of several three- and four-masters, on which his wife sailed with him.

It was in 1931, when he had a shore job, that Merle Greene contacted him about the job on *Camargo*. Neither Fleischmann's book nor Gross' diary, however, has anything to say about Gray's activities on the voyage.

One other member of *Camargo*'s crew about whom we have information is Weston Cleveland Small,

4.15 The full crew of Camargo in 1932. Captain Small is behind the binnacle. Courtesy of Tinker (Gross) Crouch

4.16 Though not from Camargo, this is the sort of starboard launch she would have had to transport the owner, his or her family and guests to and from the yacht. The cockpit aft of the main one was for the launchman, who had to scramble out of this severely confined space to handle the lines when the launch docked. Photo by William A. Haviland

the only son of Charles Small's brother, Captain Grover Small. Born in 1915 and raised on Deer Isle, he was educated at the one-room school house at North Deer Isle (the same one attended earlier by Delmont Torrey), before going on to high school. When the family moved to New London in 1931, as Weston wrote:

I convinced Dad I should get a job on a yacht. A body was needed on *Camargo* where Uncle Charlie was captain and Uncle [actually cousin] Merle Greene was chief mate. No doubt the opening was ideal for my situation. I signed on board as a seaman. *[See photo 4.15]*

I wasn't the teacher's pet, however, things that I did do or didn't do I was reprimanded [for] whereas other crewmembers got by scot-free. Soon the other crew members found I was not to receive any special treatment because of relationships—probably a part of my training—also I was pretty green as a sailor and became the butt of jokes of the others, so decided [to study] some books [to] brighten up.

# The Big Steam Yachts

*4.17 Deer Isle seamen on Camargo in 1936. Front row, from left: Howard Hutchinson, Myron Shepard, George Barbour, last two unidentified. Second row, from left: unidentified, Maurice Eaton, John Eaton, unidentified, Weston Small, unidentified. Courtesy of Tinker (Gross) Crouch*

> At the time of my joining [the *Camargo*] was in lay up at Tebo's Yacht Basin in Brooklyn, N.Y. We had a skeleton crew consisting of the captain, chief mate, chief engineer and a first assistant engineer, two sailors and two oilers. Then in commission there were a crew of 40 people including the officers.
>
> In June of that year a full crew was employed and I was promoted to starboard launch man. This launch was for the owner for transport from ship to shore, etc. The second mate operated the boat. My job was to maintain the boat and help the people on and off the boat.

On the trip through the Mediterranean, around Africa and up to Europe and Scandinavia,

> [a]t 99 percent of the ports we anchored and used the port and starboard launches for shore leave. Port launch was for the crew. There was very little shore leave for crew people as there are watches to maintain. *[See photo 4.16]*

With the return of the ship to the Tebo Yacht Basin, Weston was promoted to quartermaster. He sailed three years on the *Camargo* before leaving yachting. When he went for his Third Mate's license he found he needed steamship, freighter, or passenger ship time so he got a quartermaster job on the *President Harding*, a combination passenger and freight ship. From then on he sailed on a number of ships, passing his various licenses, until he obtained his Master's license and became a ship captain.

Further information on the crew of *Camargo* is sparse. Entries in Gilbert Gross' diary are little more than "one liners." It is apparent that, in calm seas, sailors performed maintenance tasks such as sanding and varnishing the housing. When in port, crew members went ashore to shop, play pool, attend dances, and "have feeds." There are occasional references such as these: January 1: "We helped New Years in with a bang at Menukwari by blowing whistles and firing our one pound gun. Rich is pretty full and happy." January 20 in Java: "Otto gets stewed and is looking for the bosun." January 28: "Rich gets lit up, and is having a great time." References to strong drink, however, are not frequent. More often, it was ice cream that was sought after. Much time, after all, was spent in the tropics. So it was that, when they reached the Suez Canal, Gilbert Gross complained of the cold. The temperature read 64 degrees, which would be a comfortable summer day on Deer Isle. *[See photo 4.17]*

One other shore incident, recounted in Fleischmann's book, is worth mentioning. When in the Marquesan Islands, passengers and crewmen went ashore, where the natives performed traditional dances for their benefit. Feeling obliged to reciprocate, two crew members demonstrated the Charleston, to music provided by George Lufkin on his harmonica. The tune he played is no longer remembered, but the Deer Isle-Stonington

*4.18 Star of Malta, ex. Camargo (right), with Norman Woolworth's yacht Elpetal at Grand Harbor, Malta in 1951. Courtesy of Tinker (Gross) Crouch*

Historical Society has a recording of George on his harmonica made in the 1950s.

## The Last Days of *Camargo*

In 1938, *Camargo* was sold to Rafael Trujillo, the dictator of the Dominican Republic, and renamed *Ramfis*. Four years later she changed hands again, this time to the U.S. Navy. Renamed USS *Marcastle*, she saw service out of Pearl Harbor, escorting merchant ships in the Hawaiian Islands. She then went to Seattle as a patrol and weather station vessel. In 1944, she was decommissioned and sold for commercial use under the name *Commando*. Another name change, to *Westminster*, came in 1947 when she was sold to the Minster Steamship Company.

*Camargo* ended her days in Malta where, in 1952, she was purchased by Paul M. Laferla who put her into thrice-weekly service under the name *Star of Malta* as ferry and mail carrier to Syracuse in Sicily. She was seen in Grand Harbor, Malta, by Arthur ("Dud") Haskell of Deer Isle, who at the time was on a merchant ship in the Mediterranean. As the ferry passed by, he commented to the bridge crew, "That's the *Camargo*." They were not convinced, so that evening in port, he asked the skeptics to "come along." They went aboard the *Star of Malta* and, sure enough, engraved on the engines was the name *Camargo*. *[See photo 4.18]*

In July 1955, the ship came to grief returning from Syracuse in the fog when she ran onto a reef and capsized. Some of the fifty-seven passengers swam ashore or were picked up in small boats, but two drowned. In August, she was refloated and repaired, but in 1966, she was sold for scrap and broken up by an Italian firm. On this melancholy note ended the career of this once elegant Queen of the Sea.

As for the crew, Charles E. Small was, by 1938, 74 years old. He came ashore, and died in 1944. His ashes are buried in a small cemetery at the back of the old Hardy farm beside his mother and father and his daughter, Dorothy Small, who died in 1953. His mother wanted to be buried at the top of the hill which at that time was not surrounded by woods as it is today, so that when her sons sailed through Eggemoggin Reach on coastal schooners she could "see" her boys.

After leaving *Camargo*, Merle Greene went back to the Merchant Marine. World War II found him as commodore of a convoy of merchant ships delivering war material to Europe. When he finally left the sea, he married as his second wife the widow of Delmont Torrey, and took a job as toll collector at the Deer Isle-Sedgwick Bridge. When tourists drove up to the toll house and inquired what there was across the bridge, Merle was fond of replying, "Oh, there's nothing over there but a bunch of pirates and outlaws." He died in 1961.

Norman Gray left *Camargo* upon her return from her around-the-world cruise. For a time he was unemployed, until he found a job as superintendent of an apartment building in Malden, Massachusetts. In 1937, he entered the Light Ship Service, first as Second Mate on the *Nantucket*, then as First Mate on her relief ship, and finally as captain of the Brenton Reef light ship off Newport, Rhode Island. With the outbreak of World War II, the Coast Guard took over the light ships, whereupon Norman was sent to the Chelsea base in Massachusetts. He remained there until he died, in 1950.

### The Big Steam Yachts

As already noted, Weston Small went on to become a ship captain. He sailed for a number of years on Texaco tankers and was torpedoed in World War II on the Texaco tanker *Oklahoma*. He survived this, and in later years became a port captain, fleet superintendent or manager in ports around the world including India, Sicily, Bahrain, Texas and New York.

When Weston retired from Texaco, John Collins, an advisor on labor relations and other subjects to the Texaco Officers' Union, wrote the following:

*4.19 Weston Small, photographed in the late 1970s. Courtesy of Lucy Hopkins*

> When Captain Small was young and fresh out of the State of Maine he was elected to the Executive Committee of the Texaco Tanker Officers' Association when it was about two years old. This was before World War II. His contribution to the association's efforts to improve the lot of officers, and especially to keep them from being "taken over" by national unions, certainly played a part in enabling the Texaco Tanker Officers' Association to continue in existence and accomplish what it has over these many years.
>
> In recent years Captain Small, as a member of management, has been on the other side of the bargaining table but true to his integrity and his basic sense of fairness in matters wherein he had jurisdiction and where there was a legitimate grievance as far as the association was concerned, he always made the right decision. *[See photo 4.19]*
>
> It may be a cliché to say that there aren't many Wes Smalls in the country, but cliché or not, this is a fact. Few that we know of have combined the interest of the fleet officers and the interest of the company (which in a sense are one—although not always recognized as such) to the degree Wes Small has. Maybe it was his even disposition, his commonsense, his ability to relate to the seagoing officers, and his transparent honesty that made him the asset to the fleet that he was.

Weston Small and his wife, Doris, moved from Texas to Florida on his retirement in 1976. He died in July 2005 at age 90.

Various other crew members went into the merchant marine, while some others found employment on other yachts. Gilbert Gross, for example, sailed under his father-in-law on *Hi-Esmaro*. Others came ashore, some sooner, some later, like Myron Shepard, who established an insurance and real estate agency, or Howard Hutchinson and George Lufkin, who worked in the granite quarries.

### *Hi-Esmaro*

Even grander than *Camargo* was this luxury yacht, with its gold-leaf-covered figurehead, whose last captain was Charles Small's brother. Built at Bath Iron Works in 1929 for asbestos magnate Hiram Edward Manville, she was named for the Manville children: Hiram Jr., Esther, Mary and Robert. Her length overall was 267 feet, with a 35-foot 4-inch beam, drew 14 and a half feet and was of 1,062 gross tons. She was powered by two Cooper-Bessemer diesels with twin screws, generating 1,500 shaft horsepower and cruised at 16 knots.

*[See photo 4.20]*

Our knowledge of her interior is limited, but we know that she had gold plated plumbing fixtures, the advantage of gold over brass being that it did not need extensive polishing, as did brass. We also know that the headboards of the bunks bore ivory and gold replicas of the Swedish crown. The reason for this was that one of Manville's daughters had married Count Folke Bernadotte of Sweden. We can only imagine what the rest of the yacht's interior was like. Her cost at the time of launching was over a million dollars—this on the eve of the Great Depression—and the cost of uniforming the crew ran to about $40,000 per year. On the dining room table were menu holders costing $150 each, "pocket change" compared to the $10,000 cost of the china dining service.

*Hi-Esmaro* could carry up to 139 people, including her crew. Her last captain was Grover Small of North Deer Isle, brother of Charles Small. Grover began as First Mate, succeeding to the position of Captain in 1937. Other Deer Isle crew members were Gilbert Gross (husband of Grover's oldest daughter) who had previously sailed on *Camargo*, George Lane Beck, Martin Snowden, Melvin Pickering, Goodwin Eaton and Charles Fifield. Francis L. Gross, an electrician who married Merle Greene's daughter, was part of a skeleton crew on board one winter. The men considered Manville a good man to work for because, unlike many of the moneyed set, he had started out carrying a dinner pail. In spite of his ostentatious display of wealth, he never lost sight of his humble start.

For most of her career as a yacht, *Hi-Esmaro* was based in New London, Connecticut. We know next to nothing about her travels, but presumably most were up and down the East Coast. In September of 1938 she had left Greenwich, Connecticut, on the way to New London when one of the worst hurricanes in New England history hit Long Island Sound. Instead of heading for port, Captain Small kept her out in the sound, knowing it was safer at sea than near shore.

*4.20 Hi-Esmaro. Courtesy of Lucy Hopkins*

## Captain Grover Small

Grover Cleveland Small, the son of George and Lucy A. T. Small, was born in 1882 in the corner of the family living room. He left to go yachting when he was 14 years old. His brother, Charlie, being nineteen years older, was already captain of a yacht and Grover went with him, but he said Charlie did not pay much attention to him. He also told the story that he was always getting punched and picked on by another sailor. When the boat was in Brooklyn, he made up his mind he was going to show his shipmate a thing or two, so he went to boxing school in Brooklyn, learned to box, and the next time the other sailor punched him, he fought back and licked him. After that he was never bothered again. *[See photo 4.21]*

Over the years he went to navigation school, studied, and passed all the merchant marine exams until he attained an unlimited Master's license. He sailed on ships of the Clyde Steamship Company, Puerto Rican Line, and Sword Steamship Company that took him to the Mediterranean and other foreign ports. It may have been on one of these trips that they brought back a load of bananas. He had never eaten a banana before and ate so many that he almost got sick.

When his mother and father grew older and his mother was sick, he came home to take care of them. He married Cecile Powers (older sister

# The Big Steam Yachts

*4.21 George Washington and Lucy Augusta Tower (Hardy) Small with two of their daughters and youngest son, Grover Cleveland. Courtesy of John Melnikas*

of Ruth, who married Grover's nephew, Merle Greene) of Deer Isle in 1905 and returned to yachting after his parents passed away in 1907 and 1910. He sailed on the yacht *Lansi* owned by Arthur Curtis James of New York as sailing master for five years until 1917.

In a letter, Mr. James stated:

> Captain Small is thoroughly familiar with Florida waters, as also with the Atlantic Coast and is fully competent to take charge of any class of vessel. After the war [World War I] is over and it becomes possible to consider yachting again, I should be only too glad to re-employ him, and in the meantime gladly recommend him.

He again returned to the island and went into the herring business by building a fish weir with his cousin Hosea Barbour (who had also gone yachting), married to a sister of the wives of Grover and Merle Greene, and son of the older sister of Grover's mother, who was married to Captain Benjamin Barbour. Grover also farmed and acted as caretaker for Fred Torrey's home at North Deer Isle (Fred Torrey was treasurer of the John L. Goss Corporation, which ran quarries in Stonington). He also had a motor launch called *Paprika* and took out paying parties for trips around the bay.

An anecdote from this period ashore reveals something of Captain Small's willingness to take on any task. At the time, indoor plumbing was a luxury that few families on the island had. Instead, toilet facilities consisted of a "one" or "two holer" out in the barn, or in a separate outhouse. As it happened, the Haviland outhouse had reached capacity, and it was decided to move it to a new location. As told by Tom Haviland, upon hearing of this, Grover offered to bring his ox down to accomplish the move. By the time this was to take place, word had spread around the neighborhood, and a number of people had gathered to watch the operation. Upon his arrival, Grover looked around and declared: "Oh, we don't need the ox, there's enough people here so that we can all grab hold and move it!" *[See photo 4.22]*

After his wife passed away in 1930 he returned to yachting as First, or Chief Officer on the *Hi-Esmaro*. A year later he married Ina Jackson, a registered nurse in Washington, D.C. In 1937, he became captain of the *Hi-Esmaro*, a position he held until it was sold to the U.S. Navy in 1940. Mr. Manville said of Captain Small:

> He was a man of excellent character, absolutely honest and reliable, a splendid navigator, knows how to handle the ship under every condition and in any emergency is well liked and thoroughly respected by his men. *[See photo 4.23]*

In the September 1938 hurricane, *Hi-Esmaro* was in Long Island Sound, and Captain Small refused to take the ship into port, saying it was safer at sea, and the yacht survived the storm. After the storm,

*4.22 Captain Grover Small with his ox, at Haviland's. With him are his two daughters from his first marriage: Virginia (on the ox) and Halga, who would become the wife of Gilbert Gross. Photo by Thomas P. Haviland*

*4.23 Captain Grover Small, aboard Hi-Esmaro. Courtesy of Lucy Hopkins*

the Small family lived on the vessel for a week or so, as an elm tree in front of their house in New London had blown down and broken a gas main. They could not return to it until the main was fixed.

With the *Hi-Esmaro* berthed in New London, Connecticut, the Small family had moved there, but kept the house in North Deer Isle. In the 1930s, Grover was able at times to return to the island and, with Clyde Smith of Pressey Village, added a pantry off the original kitchen, put in a bathroom, a bay window, and a chimney for a fireplace. He also had a Norwegian crew member come up one winter, while the yacht was laid up, to help work on the house. Oscar, the Norwegian, enjoyed being on the island, as it reminded him of his home country. He was later lost at sea when, in World War II, the ship he was on was torpedoed and sunk.

## The Last Days of *Hi-Esmaro*

On October 16, 1940, Mrs. Manville sold *Hi-Esmaro* to the U.S. Navy. Converted to a gunboat at the New York Navy Yard, she was renamed USS *Niagara* and commissioned January 20, 1941. The following month she left New York to tend torpedo boats operating between Miami and Key West and Guantanamo Bay, Cuba. She did not linger long, however, and in March she was back in New York for repairs before service at the naval torpedo station at Newport, Rhode Island.

Nor did she linger long at Newport. By October she was operating as a patrol vessel out of Pearl Harbor. When the Japanese attack came, however, she was at sea escorting a convoy to the Fiji Islands. She subsequently escorted a convoy to San Diego, tended torpedo boats off Panama, and underwent another overhaul in New York. After another stint at Newport, as a school ship for a training squadron of torpedo boats, she returned to the Pacific. Here,

### The Big Steam Yachts

in 1943, she was reclassified as the Navy's first motor torpedo boat tender and redesignated AGP-1. Shortly thereafter, she reached her base in the Solomon Islands. Among the boats tended there was PT 109, on which a young John F. Kennedy served.

The last days of *Niagara* (ex *Hi-Esmaro*) are chronicled in the *Dictionary of American Fighting Ships* (Vol. V, p. 80):

> On 7 April the Japanese raided the Guadalcanal-Tulagi area with 177 planes, of which about 25 were shot down. Two bombs sank New Zealand corvette *Moe*. *Niagara*, in the thick of the fight, was north of the harbor, moored to the west bank of the Maliali River, heading downstream with minesweeper *Rail* (AM-26) tied up outboard well aft. Nine enemy planes came up the river, none of them over 150 feet above the water. *Niagara* and *Rail* took them all under fire.
>
> The first plane, already aflame, crashed into trees about 1000 yards astern of *Niagara*. The next two planes escaped, but the fourth rapidly lost altitude in a stream of white smoke to explode behind the hills to the north. The following two raiders passed within 150 yards and attempted to strafe the ship, but their firing was erratic and they wobbled uncertainly as they passed through *Niagara's* heavy fire before crashing into the woods off her port quarter. The next two planes sheared up and to the right when taken under fire. One trailed light brown smoke as it disappeared close over the hilltops abaft *Niagara's* port beam. The other passed to starboard and crashed in the hills on her starboard quarter.
>
> On 22 May *Niagara*, with Motor Torpedo Boat Division 23, departed Tulagi headed towards New Guinea. The following morning a high-flying Japanese twin-engined monoplane attacked with four bombs. The ship made a tight starboard turn at maximum speed until the bombs were released, then swung hard to port. Three near misses to starboard and one to port damaged *Niagara's* sound gear and the training mechanism of one 3-inch gun and knocked out steering control temporarily. Half an hour later, when steering control had been regained, six more high-flying twin-engine planes dropped a pattern of over a dozen bombs. One hit directly on *Niagara's* forecastle and several were damaging near-misses.
>
> Water rushing through a 14-inch hole 6 feet below her waterline flooded two storerooms, a passageway, and her engine room. All power and lighting failed, and her main engines stopped. Fire below decks forward was out of control, and *Niagara* listed rapidly to port. Her main engine and steering were restored 7 minutes after the attack. But her increasing list and imminent danger of explosion of her gasoline storage tanks necessitated the order to "abandon ship."
>
> *PT-146* and *PT-147* came alongside her stern to take off some of *Niagara's* crew. Others went over her side into rafts and boats to be picked up by other motor torpedo boats. *Niagara* was then ablaze from bow to bridge. Flames were spreading aft, and ammunition was exploding on deck. Yet, despite her damage, not one of *Niagara's* 136 officers and men was killed or seriously wounded.
>
> *PT-147* fired a torpedo which struck *Niagara* in the gasoline tanks. She exploded with a sheet of flame 300 feet high, and went down in less than a minute. The motor torpedo boats landed her crew at Tulagi early the next morning.
>
> *Niagara* received one battle star for World War II service.

Although the original yacht is gone, a working scale model of it may be seen at the Museum of Science in Boston. A color photo of the model is shown here as the frontispiece. According to the museum:

> The scale is 1"=2'8". There are few models of this yacht, and even fewer working models. This working scale model was built by Museum of Science, Boston staff. It is motorized by a 12 volt battery and electric motor and capable of 7 knots (8 mph). The frame is made of white oak throughout, 40 ribs to a side. The planking is white cedar 5/32" thick; 28 planks to a side. The decks are India teak, spar varnished; plexi-glass windows. Fittings are all polished brass especially made for the model, several purchased, die cast. Weight of model is approximately 60 pounds.

As impressive in its own way as the original vessel, the model is a fitting memorial to a grand Queen of the Sea.

After leaving *Hi-Esmaro* in 1940, Grover Small went to sea on a coastal freighter with his cousin, Franklin Hardy (oldest son of Grover's mother's youngest half-brother), who was captain at a time when German subs were sinking ships off the east coast of the United States. He said it was a harrowing time, ships ran with no lights, and he always slept with his clothes on because you never knew what would happen.

He had received an appointment in the Naval Reserve in April 1939 as a lieutenant when he was Master of the *Hi-Esmaro*, and in 1942 he was called to active duty. Now 60 years old, he was assigned to the Maine Maritime Academy in Castine where he taught seamanship in the Deck Department. He was promoted to Lieutenant Commander, went on the training ship cruises with the midshipmen, and became executive officer of the academy before leaving the service in April 1946 after World War II ended. In his history of the academy's early years, James Aldrich remarked:

> Not long after our arrival, Commander Oehmke, our executive officer, was called to other duty by the Navy Department. He was replaced by "Cap" Small, a very able and popular officer. Thus it naturally follows when there is a change in the order of things, and, as we readily learned, the "new order" meant business. When we grew slack, upon occasion, all of a sudden an amazing amount of gold braid firmly lodged itself upon the back of our necks and we were immediately but constructively "spurred" on to new and nobler accomplishments.

Upon reading this, Grover's daughter Lucy commented:

> Commander Oehmke used to come to our Castine home frequently to play Acey Deuce, Cribbage or some other card game with my father. It amused me that Aldrich used the term "gold braid" when he references changes when my father became executive officer. I understand what he was referring to but Dad was never concerned too much by uniforms and gold braid so to speak. I can recall his wearing his galoshes with his uniform when it was snowy or rainy regardless how he looked—his feet were not going to get wet!

While upholding standards, Grover never let it "go to his head."

The Maine Maritime Academy Class of 1945 dedicated their yearbook to Lt. Murray in the engineering department and to Lt. Cdr. Small in the deck department. The following is their dedication to Grover Small:

> Lieutenant Commander Grover C. Small, known affectionately to all as "Cap'n" Small has shown himself to us as both an able instructor and an admirable executive officer; and, always, as a competent and sympathetic friend and advisor.
>
> Commander Small took up his duties as executive officer the first of December, 1944. He will always be

> remembered for his sterling qualities
> so befitting a true seaman and for
> the profound sense of decency and
> fair play he tried to instill in us by his
> own devotion to these principles.

While living in Castine, Grover continued to make improvements to his island home, anticipating living there full time after his time in the service ended. In the summers, he brought carpenters over from the academy to redo the floors, put in central heat, and various other things.

After 1946, the family moved back to Deer Isle full time. Grover, however, worked for a few more seasons as captain of a ferry boat in Long Island Sound, until he became eligible for Social Security. Returning to the island, he tended a vegetable garden, cut wood for the kitchen stove and fireplace, and on the land he cleared, raised wild blueberries. His biggest project was improvement of his water supply. Originally, the house had a dug well accessed through a hatch in the kitchen floor, a feature of several old houses on the island. Because this regularly ran dry in the summer, there was also a laid up granite block cistern in the cellar that collected rainwater off the roof. The family's water problem was finally solved by purchasing an overgrown pasture and woods across the road. Here, in a skunk cabbage patch at the edge of the woods, Grover dug out a spring. He did this all by hand, using a crow bar to loosen hard clay that resisted his pickaxe. Once dug out, he put in concrete sides (mixing the concrete by hand) and built a wooden shed over top. He then proceeded, again by hand, to dig a trench several hundred feet up to and under the main road, and into the house. He installed a pump and pipes himself, and cut cedar poles to run power lines down to the spring. Indeed, there seemed nothing beyond this man's ability to accomplish.

Captain Grover Small, in his last years, still liked to get out on the water. He never missed an opportunity to go out with his friend Tom Haviland in Tom's classic Maine lobster boat. He died in 1965.

## Some Other Hardy Descendants and Yachting

To put the four Smalls and Merle Greene in broader context, it is worth noting that they were not the only descendants of George Campbell Hardy who went yachting. With his first wife, George Hardy had one son, Amos, who achieved the rank of captain before coming ashore to live on a piece of land from the original Hardy farm. From there he went fishing, and took over his father's store. Amos had only one child, Frank, who also rose to the rank of captain. What vessels he sailed on is not known to us, but with his father's death in 1905, he took over his property and, by 1910, in addition to farming, was taking in summer boarders and serving as postmaster. He and his wife had a daughter and two sons, Frank Jr. and Beckwith. Both sons went yachting, although Beckwith (who married a sister of George Lufkin) moved with his family to take a job in maintenance at the University of Connecticut. Frank Jr., who continued yachting and became a captain, acquired a piece of his father's property for his house. The boys' sister married Harry Annis, who, as already noted, was captain of a commuter yacht in New York. Finally, Frank Jr. had five sons and two daughters, of whom at least three sons and one daughter's husband went yachting. Four sons and one daughter all acquired pieces of the old Hardy farm for their houses.

George Campbell Hardy had two other sons with his second wife, both of whom went to sea. The older one, George Leslie (who as a 16-year-old skated across the frozen bay to visit his sister in Camden), by age 29 was captain of several coasting schooners, carrying lumber and freight. His younger brother, William Elmer, sailed with him until taking a position as mess boy on the 1895 America's Cup defender with its all-Deer Isle crew. Around 1900, however, Elmer had come ashore to run his father's farm, which he subsequently inherited. He and his wife had four sons, all of whom went to sea. The oldest son, Franklin, left school at age 15, his teacher having told his father that the boy couldn't learn anything. He got a job with Captain Nathan Lowe (first husband of Franklin's mother's daughter by her first marriage) on a cargo schooner. A year later, in 1906, he got a job yachting, which continued until 1912. In that year, he went as mate on a schooner carrying granite to New York and coal to Deer Isle. The vessel was lost at sea off Nantucket, but all hands survived, except the cook, who froze to death. Franklin continued to go yachting in the summers and on cargo carriers under sail in winters until 1915, when he began on merchant steam ships. He earned his captain's license in 1918, and served on merchant ships from then until retirement, in 1958, to his home across the road from his uncle, George Leslie. One of those merchant ships was the one mentioned earlier, on which Grover Small sailed briefly in World War II. After the war, he carried sugar from Cuba to Japan. Then, on January 18, 1951, the *Island Ad-Vantages* carried this report: *[See photo 4.24]*

> Friends of Captain Franklin Hardy of the SS *Yankee Pioneer* will be interested to hear that after six months in the Korean War zone he is returning to San Francisco. Captain Hardy's ship helped in the evacuation of Hungnam and Inchon, Korea. He writes that he evacuated 5,800 men, women and children and troops from Inchon with no loss of life, in fact four babies were born on the way to Pusan.

Elmer Hardy's second son also began a seafaring career by yachting. Like Franklin, he too became a captain in the merchant marine. The third son began in yachting as well, but settled down in Greenport, New York, to a career in boat and ship building. Although Elmer's youngest son did not go yachting, he too earned an unlimited master's license and went to sea, traversing the Panama Canal about twenty times. But after about twelve years at sea, he returned home to help his aging father on the farm.

*4.24 Captain Franklin Hardy, cousin of Charles and Grover Small. Courtesy of John Melnikas*

# Chapter 5: The Greenlaws of Sunset: An In-depth Look at a Yachting Family, the Early Years

*...we can have some idea of the condition of those who first came here; it required courage to face what they did, and the resolution to go through it...we are enjoying the fruits of their labors, for their hands altered the fields we cultivate and the foundation of our privileges was laid by them.*

Hosmer, *Historical Sketch of the Town of Deer Isle*, page 23.

## Introduction

By tradition, the Greenlaws of Deer Isle are remembered as a seafaring family, yet this is not how it all began.

Against the background of Scotland's flourishing mercantile system in the 1750s and the desire of the British Empire to expand its land holdings and settlements in the colonies, William Greenlaw dared to dream of becoming a landowner. Longing to build a solid future for his family and provide a legacy for his children, an enticing offer of cheap land in a "veritable paradise" across the ocean provided the catalyst he needed to make his dream become a reality.

William emigrated from Scotland with his family in July 1753 and arrived in St. George, near Warren, on the coast of Maine in September. The first few years were a bitter disappointment, but in 1761 the family traveled northward and settled on Deer Isle as a permanent location.

By following a single ancestral line in the Greenlaw family, beginning with William, a fascinating story of one family's struggle for land ownership emerges. In succeeding generations, we will meet Jonathan, William, Richard, Nelson, Edward and, lastly, brothers Edwin and Kenneth Greenlaw. *[See photo 5.1]*

By using the historical material provided in earlier chapters as background and the several generations of the Greenlaw family as examples, we will be able to see how the shift from farming to seafaring impacted and changed the culture of an entire community. Significant attention will be given to each of the brothers, Edwin and Kenneth, and to their lifelong seafaring and yachting careers in the next two chapters.

# First Generation

William Greenlaw was born in Scotland, immigrated in 1753 to Warren, Maine, and died in Deer Isle, Maine, circa 1783. With his wife Jane, he had six children, all born in Scotland. They were: James Greenlaw, born c. 1732, William Greenlaw, born c. 1734, Jonathan Greenlaw, born c. 1736, Ebenezer Greenlaw, born c. 1738, Charles Greenlaw, born c. 1740, Alexander Greenlaw, born c. 1742.

William Greenlaw and his family had made their home in the lowlands of Scotland near Edinburgh. Like many other lowland Scots, William dreamed of achieving middle class stability and a growing middle class lifestyle. His dreams were fueled by the possibility of acquiring cheap and abundant land in another corner of the expanding British Empire; the one man responsible for providing that "fuel" was General Samuel Waldo.

General Waldo was a ruthless entrepreneur who bought out the proprietors of the Muscongus Patent, a huge swath of land west of Penobscot Bay. It derived from a 1630 grant to Sir Ferdinando Gorges, a would-be colonizer of Maine. Waldo's intent was to entice poor farmers and immigrants to settle as tenants, allowing him to sit back and collect rents.

General Waldo traveled to England in 1729 to confirm the grant and consolidate his holdings. As a consequence of these transactions, he eventually owned all of what are now Knox and Waldo counties and portions of current Lincoln and Penobscot counties, the total consisting of almost one million acres of land. He then set about busily recruiting settlers, concentrating on Germans and Scots.

In 1753, while on business in London, General Waldo issued printed circulars inviting emigrants to settle upon his lands "on the great River St. Georges, in the Province of Massachusetts Bay, in the colony of New England." The descriptive material and generous offers of land contained in the circulars were obvious attempts by Waldo to seduce families, like the Greenlaws, for his own personal gain. On the other hand, William Greenlaw saw the possibility of land ownership as a means to improve the welfare of his family and provide a better future for his children.

*5.1 Tombstones in Deer Isle's Old Settlers Cemetery. Many Greenlaws are buried here, including William Greenlaw and his wife, Rebecca Babbidge; Richard Greenlaw and his first wife, Sally Gold Robbins, and second wife, Mehitable Jordan; and Nelson Greenlaw and his wife, Elizabeth Pressey. Courtesy of Deer Isle-Stonington Historical Society*

> The attractive inducements described a veritable paradise and the promise of untold opportunities in a "climate.... as wholesome and safe for British constitutions as any part of South or North Britain." Winters were said to be mild and any hard frost or snow during the three months of winter only helped to "enrich the soil, making it most productive of grass and corn." Moreover, "the sky is so serene that the weather is never prejudicial to health." The ground was promised to be fertile and capable of producing "plenty of Indian corn, wheat, rye, barley, oats, beans,

# The Greenlaws of Sunset: Part I

peas, hemp, flax and roots of all kinds and the rivers and seas were teaming with fish, such as cod, haddock, salmon, sturgeon, mackerel, eels, smelts, bass, shad, oysters and lobsters." In exchange for their emigration, Waldo promised the new settlers land free for the first 19 years; they would only have to pay a yearly quit-rent of between ten and forty shillings per 100 acres thereafter. Further, he promised that all, except Catholics, could freely practice their religion. Lastly, he promised prospective settlers that "if they did not find all things by him stated to be strictly true" he would "pay them for their time, and take them back at his own expense." There is no record that this ever happened. (Cyrus Eaton, *Annals of the Town of Warren*, p. 83.)

Although a consensus is lacking on the name of the captain and the ship on which the Greenlaws sailed, the following notice is indicative of what was expected of them prior to sailing. It appeared in the *Glasgow Courant* on Monday, July 16, 1753:

> The passengers that have engaged or agreed to proceed to Mr. Waldo's Settlement on St. Georges River in New England, are desired to have their Clothes and Baggage, etc. the beginning of the Week on board the Joanna, Capt. Hugh Coulter, Commander, now lying at Greenock.
>
> For the conveniency of the paid Passengers, a Gabart [barge] is freighted to carry their Baggage from the Key of Glasgow to the Ship, and they are desired not to delay in sending the same.

So, it was in response to Waldo's circular that William and Jane Greenlaw, together with their six sons, joined "other persons from Stirling, Glasgow, and other places in Scotland…and entered into an agreement…to emigrate." Sixty adults, in fourteen families, besides ten or more children, sailed from Greenock, Scotland (then the port of Glasgow) in July 1753, arriving on the St. Georges River near the town of Warren, Maine, in September of that year.

Knowing that it would be too late in the year for the new settlers to clear land or construct shelters, Waldo had agreed to have a common shelter ready to receive them. However, when they arrived, the log barracks, partitioned into fourteen rooms designed to accommodate the whole company during their first winter, was minus a roof. Somehow, the roof was never built. As a consequence, "the emigrants scattered round and lived the first winter with the old settlers," those who had arrived previously and were better prepared to weather the coming winter. But, at last, spring arrived and the long winter ended. According to historian Cyrus Eaton (pp. 85-86),

> When the spring opened in 1754 they went out to the place assigned them for a new city and took possession of their half acre lots. This group of new settlers were, mostly, unacquainted with all agricultural operations. Having the promise of lands within two miles of tide waters, they naturally looked forward to the comforts of city life to which they had been accustomed at home. Among the group were two weavers from Glasgow, a brewer, a delft-ware manufacturer, a cooper, a bookbinder, a shepherd, and a slate maker. They had to learn even how to cut down a tree before they could begin building a house.
>
> Their expectations were disappointed, their spirits cast down, and unused to the labors their situation required, they groaned under a load of bodily and mental suffering. They contended with hunger and cold…, till in the following year, the beginning of the French and Indian war compelled them to enter the fort for protection.

## Second Generation

The French and Indian War raged from 1755 to 1760, and the colonists were housed much of that time in the forts garrisoned by British troops, whose muster rolls show that four young Greenlaws, William Jr., Ebenezer, Jonathan and Charles, were enlisted for their defense.

Bitter winters and summer droughts discouraged many, and by 1761 the Greenlaw family had left the proposed settlement and moved to Boston. James relocated to Lunenburg, Nova Scotia, in response to an appeal for settlers, after marrying Catherine Crawford in Boston in 1759, while the rest of the family moved northward. The Greenlaws have been recorded as being the first white family to make a permanent settlement on Deer Isle in 1761. *[See photo 5.2]*

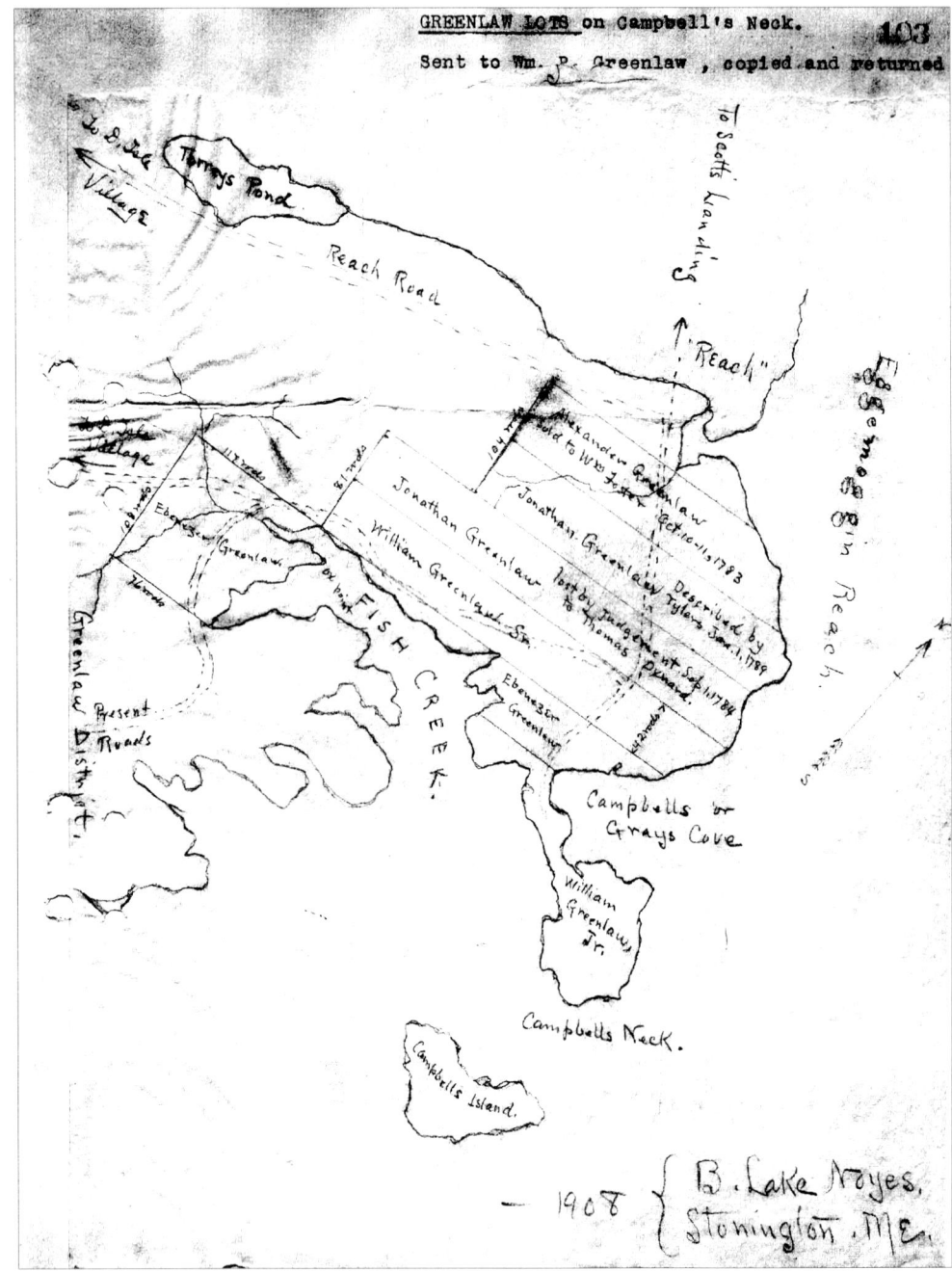

*5.2 A sketch map by Benjamin Lake Noyes depicts original land settled by William Greenlaw and his sons in 1761. Courtesy of Deer Isle-Stonington Historical Society*

In a petition dated August 4, 1762, addressed to the Royal Governor, Council, and Massachusetts General Court, William Greenlaw and his five sons, Jonathan, Ebenezer, Charles, Alexander, and William Jr., with twenty-three other settlers, requested title grants for the land on Deer Isle which they were occupying, clearing and willing to "bring forth a settlement." At that time, the present State of Maine was a part of the Province of Massachusetts and the early settlers, apparently, could get no title to the land they occupied and cleared because it was still deemed "Crownlands." The Greenlaw family continued to work hard and live peaceably, hewing farms out of the forest, comprising a total of more than five hundred acres. (Deer Isle-Stonington Historical Society Collections: Mass. Archives, Vol. 46, p. 458-459)

By the eve of the Revolutionary War the Greenlaw family had a long history on Deer Isle. It was only when the stirrings of rebellion in the colonies increased that their loyalties to the Crown became questionable. Son William's wife, Elizabeth Fossett, died in 1772 and, not long afterwards, he returned to the mainland with his children and remarried, making Georgetown his home.

After the occupation of Bagaduce (Castine) by British forces and the construction of Fort George in 1779, the remaining four brothers made frequent visits there and were suspected of carrying information about their neighbors, who were friendly to the American cause. Persecuted as Loyalists, the Greenlaws were forced to leave their homes and property on Deer Isle and flee to Castine. There, they built homes and lived under the protection of the British troops garrisoned at Fort George. The Loyalists expected that, at the peace, the Penobscot River would be the western boundary of New Brunswick (originally part of Nova Scotia). Under that scenario, Deer Isle and Castine would lie within Canadian borders and not those of the United States. Ostensibly, to their way of thinking, they were already living in Canada. Unfortunately for them, the Treaty of Paris in 1783 changed all that when the St. Croix River, further to the east, became the boundary instead.

The Greenlaws were members of what came to be known as the Penobscot Association, one of the last Loyalist refugee groups. Negotiations with the British government in Halifax resulted in a plan for the establishment of a new township named St. Andrews in the newly created Province of New Brunswick and, in October 1783, the main contingent of Penobscot Loyalists arrived there from Castine. Many of them, including Jonathan Greenlaw, dismantled their houses and took them with them. By this time, William Sr. had died, but three of his sons—Jonathan, Alexander and Ebenezer—were among the original grantees of St. Andrews and each received a town lot and a farm lot of 100 acres, outside of town on the Bayside. Charles followed them later, after the death of his mother in 1789.

Ironically, within a year after the close of the war, the Greenlaw brothers received title to their land on Deer Isle and sold it, in absentia. Ebenezer, Jonathan and Alexander, as original grantees of St. Andrews, made claims to the Loyalist Claims Commission for compensation and each received a minimal settlement. By 1790 Charles was in St. Andrews, but too late to make a claim. He left his wife, Mercy Greenlaw, behind on Deer Isle with power of attorney to dispose of his property. The four Greenlaw brothers lived the remainder of their lives in St. Andrews, died, and were buried there.

## Third Generation

In 1785, Jonathan's eldest son, William (the third of that name), returned to Deer Isle with his wife, Rebecca Babbidge, brought back by his brothers-in-law, Captain Seth Hatch and Joseph Whitmore, who went to New Brunswick to get them in a small sailing vessel. Upon his return William did not occupy the land formerly owned by his father or his uncles because "that passed into other hands." *[See photo 5.3]*.

He was, however, the first settler not far from Fish Creek and received title to the land he occupied under the Act which established "Young Settler's Rights." As described by Deer Isle historian George Hosmer (p. 36), the Act stated that "anyone who had settled after the first day of January, 1784, and before a certain date, was called a young settler and had the right to acquire one hundred acres upon the payment of one dollar per acre."

In his descriptions of early settlers, Hosmer, in speaking of William, goes on to say: "Mr. Greenlaw was one of whom everyone who knew him spoke in praise, as a quiet, honest, and upright man."

William, who was a farmer, and his wife, Rebecca, were the parents of ten sons and one daughter who grew to adulthood, born over a period of twenty-five years from 1781 to 1806. Just as William's sons were coming of age, the "maritime component of Deer Isle's economy was becoming increasingly important" (Chapter 2). Of the ten sons, at least six were identified as seafarers, with four of the six listed as captain or master-mariner. Land and the family farm were still important, offering a valuable resource when shipping fell on hard times, but it

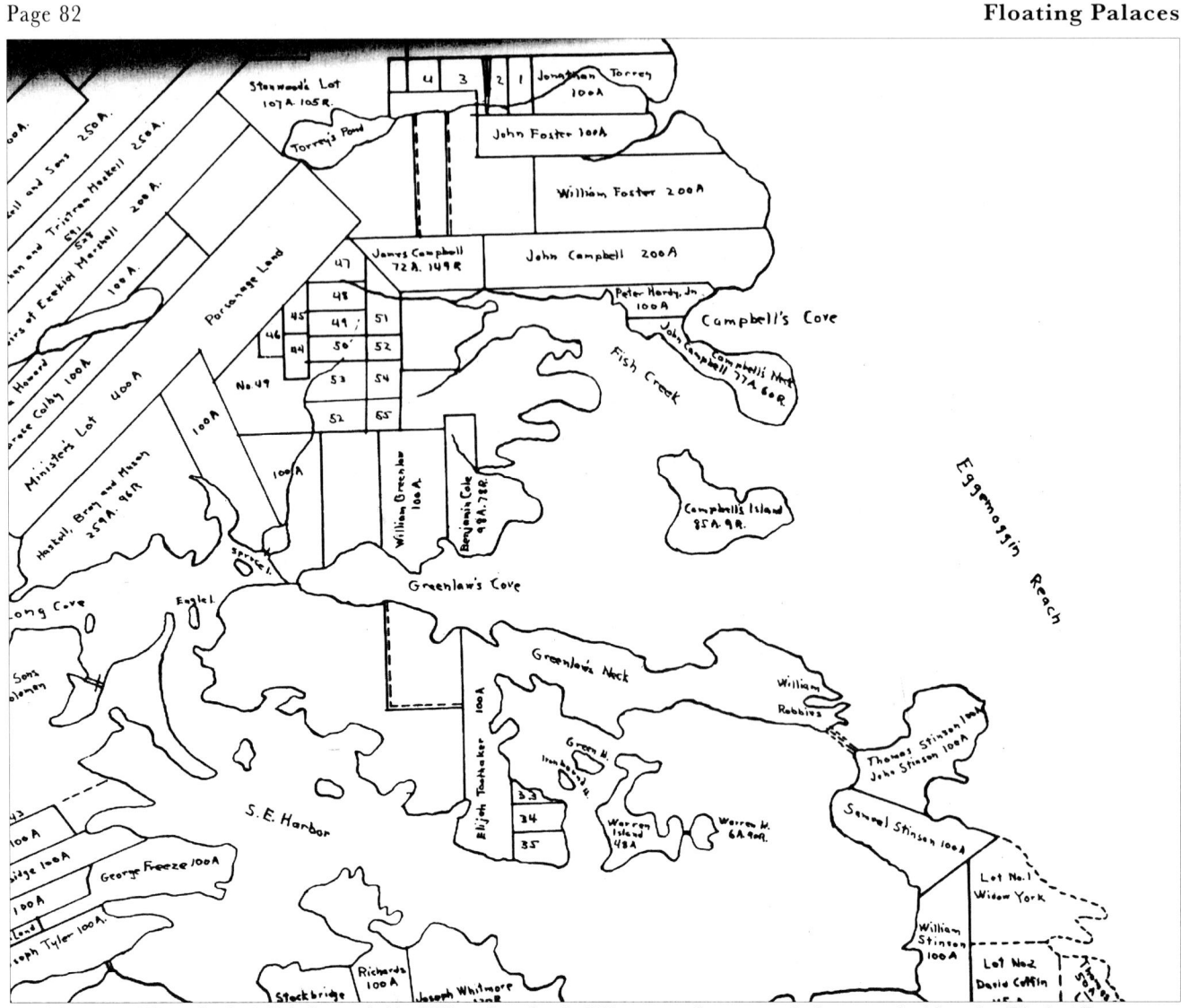

*5.3 Map shows "Young Settlers' Claim" occupied by William Greenlaw in 1785, an area that came to be known as the "Greenlaw District." From a map drawn by John Peters Jr. ca. 1798. Courtesy of Deer Isle-Stonington Historical Society*

was seafaring, for this generation, that assumed primary importance.

Richard, William's younger brother, returned to Deer Isle a few years after his brother, around 1790, but too late to be considered a "young settler." He was a ship's carpenter and never owned land of his own. Later in life, he lived on the farm of one of his sons. Some of Richard's sons (he had six), along with some of William's, ultimately acquired all of the land that became known as the "Greenlaw District." Overall, they exemplify the distinctive mix of farming and seafaring that was the mainstay of the island economy for close to 200 years.

The eldest of the sons of William and Rebecca was another William, who was lost at sea while on a whaling voyage when a young man. Their second son, John, was born on April 23, 1783, married Eunice Stockbridge of Newburyport, Massachusetts, on November 13, 1805, and, by 1813 was master of the schooner *Betsy* of Deer Isle. In keeping with the practice of vessel ownership described in Chapter 2, John also owned shares in the vessel in 1813, along with Samuel Pickering, Nathanial Bray and James Greenlaw, his brother. In 1815, the owners were listed as Samuel Pickering, Pearl Spofford and Frederick Spofford and, in 1816, the vessel was consigned to Henry Lufkin of Deer Isle and Timothy Baines of Castine. Captain John Greenlaw is described by Hosmer (p. 62) "as a capable and intelligent master-mariner, who died in 1870, at the age of 87.

## Fourth Generation

Captain Richard Greenlaw (not to be confused with his father's brother) was the sixth son, in a family of ten males, born to William and Rebecca Babbidge Greenlaw on April 21, 1795. He first married Sally Gold Robbins on September 11, 1817, and, together, they were the parents of eight children, five boys and three girls. Sally died on December 5, 1847, and Richard was remarried on April 8, 1849, to Mehitable Jordan, by whom he had no children.

A look at the 1850 Census of Deer Isle indicated that Richard, age 55, listed as a "sailor," was still going to sea. He and Mehitable Greenlaw, age 46, were married and living together, and only two of Richard's children, Nelson, age 13, and Mary, age 10, remained at home.

A decade later, the 1860 Census of Deer Isle indicated several important changes in the household. Richard, now 65, was listed as "farmer"; Mehitable, 56, was still alive; but Richard's son, Thomas, age 34, listed as "master-mariner," his wife, Lucy, age 40, and their family of six children, ranging in age from a newborn baby (unnamed) to a 16-year-old, now lived with Richard and Mehitable, either on Richard's farm or one owned by Thomas. In either case, it was during this decade that a severe economic depression in shipping took place. Therefore, one can draw the logical conclusion that Richard, who was no longer a young man, returned to farming as a primary resource and the two households were combined, both for economic and mutual assistance reasons. Richard died later in the year, on July 25, 1860, and is buried in Old Settlers Cemetery.

## Fifth Generation

Nelson Greenlaw, the youngest son of Richard and Sarah Robbins Greenlaw, was born on January 30, 1836. As we noted in the previous segment, the 1850 census indicated that Nelson, age 13, and his younger sister Mary, age 10, were the only children remaining at home with their father and stepmother.

By the time of the 1860 census, Nelson was no longer a member of his father's household, having established his own home and family at the age of 20, when he married Elizabeth Pressey on July 6, 1856. Additional information identified him as a "seafarer" and the father of two children, Carrie, age 3, born September 17, 1857 and Fred Richard, age 1, born February 6, 1859.

By the 1870 census, four more children had been added to the family: Mehitable in 1861, George Edward in 1862, Harry in 1865, and Alfred in 1869. Although all six children reached adulthood, Harry died in 1887 from typhoid fever at the age of 22.

Consistent with the shift from farming to seafaring as the primary pursuit for Deer Isle men, it is interesting, but not surprising, to note that in this family not only was the father, Nelson, a sea captain as were his three surviving sons, but both daughters married sea captains as well. Carrie married Captain Winslow Gray and Mehitable married Captain Thomas Lowe. Nelson died, unexpectedly, on November 8, 1880, from "paralysis" (a stroke) at the age of 44.

## Sixth Generation

Born on October 20, 1862, George Edward Greenlaw was the fourth child in the family of six children born to Nelson R. Greenlaw and Elizabeth Haskell Pressey (Betsy), daughter of Captain Frederick S. Pressey and Susannah Haskell. The other five children were Carrie Eva, born September 17, 1857; Frederick Richard, born February 6, 1859; Mehitable, born 1861; Harry, born August 7, 1865; and, Alfred, born December 4, 1869. *[See photo 5.4]*

George Edward never used his first name, only the first initial, and was commonly known as Ed or Edward. He went to sea as a young man and had little formal schooling. In a commentary about his father, written by son Edwin (in our next chapter), it is obvious that Edward valued the importance of an education and regretted the lack of formal training for himself. He writes:

> Father, as a boy, received very little formal education. Grandmother became a widow...and, in order to help support and keep the family together, necessitated his employment at a very early age. He often referred to his few months of schooling, saying that "the teacher was the only person who could afford a lead pencil and the children could not afford paper and had only a slate for writing." Father was an avid reader and could talk on any subject. What he lacked in a formal education, he wanted for his children.

Edward was married first, on August 14, 1884, to Zara F. Thompson born August 31, 1861, the daughter and eldest child of Captain William Haskell Thompson and Mary Ellen Taylor of Biddeford, Maine, who raised a family of four boys and three girls. Married for almost thirteen years, Edward and Zara had only one child, a son, Harold Redman Greenlaw, born July 31, 1893. Shortly before Harold's fourth birthday, his mother, Zara, died on April 4, 1897, and was buried in Mount Adams Cemetery. Harold was brought up by his aunt, Carrie Greenlaw Gray and her husband, Captain Winslow Gray, who had no children of their own. Although Harold never lived with Edward's second family, he visited often and was always considered a beloved older brother.

On October 11, 1898, at the Church of the Redeemer in South Boston, Massachusetts, Captain G. Edward Greenlaw married a second time to Caroline Elizabeth Monnier. *[See photo 5.5]* Born in Neuchatel, Switzerland, on October 30, 1864, Caroline was well-educated. She received her schooling in Berne, the capital city of Switzerland, and was fluent in three languages, English, French and German. She was also trained and became

*5.4 Edward's family members: seated (left to right), his mother, Betsy Pressey Greenlaw and Carrie Greenlaw Gray (his oldest sister). Standing (left to right), the daughters of the younger sister, Mehitable, Carrie Maud Lowe and Bessie (Elizabeth) Lowe Scott. Collection of Barbara L. Britton*

*5.5 Church of the Redeemer in South Boston, Massachusetts. The first service was held here on May 13, 1885. Courtesy of the Library and Archives of the Episcopal Diocese of Massachusetts*

*5.7 On arrival in the U.S. the Monnier family settled in Bridgewater, Pennsylvania. Seated with relatives are Caroline's sister, Ida (front row, left), Caroline (front row, right), and their mother, Catherine Monnier, behind her. Collection of Barbara L. Britton*

*5.8, 5.9 Caroline Elizabeth Monnier and George Edward Greenlaw were married on October 30, 1898, by Albert Beckwith Shields, Rector, Church of the Redeemer, South Boston. Collection of Barbara L. Britton*

*5.6 Charles Monnier, Caroline's father, was a tinsmith by trade. Collection of Barbara L. Britton*

skilled in the needle arts; she embroidered her first sampler in 1869 at the age of five. Her mother, Catherine Gretchman, was born and grew up in Stuttgart, Germany, while her father, Charles Monnier, was from the Alsace Lorraine region of France and a tinsmith by trade. *[See photo 5.6]* Around 1882, having recently lost their son, Albert (age 14), to carbon monoxide poisoning, Caroline's parents decided to emigrate to America with their two daughters, Caroline (18) and Ida (16). The family settled in Bridgewater, Pennsylvania, a town just outside Pittsburgh, where they had relatives. *[See photo 5.7, page 85]* Caroline found employment with the wealthy McClintock family in Pittsburgh as a governess for their children. Later, with the children no longer requiring her services, she was employed as a secretary and traveling companion to Mrs. McClintock for several years before her marriage to Edward Greenlaw. *[See photos 5.8 and 5.9, page 85]*

After their honeymoon, Caroline and Edward returned to Deer Isle and began an immediate search for a permanent home. Edward submitted an offer for a large, comfortable, nine-room house for sale in Sunset, a village near Deer Isle's Southwest Harbor. The land on which the house was built was owned in 1827 by Timothy and James Saunders. In 1895, Timothy Saunders sold 50 acres of the 139-acre parcel to John Smith, manager of the Deer Isle Granite Company, who built a nine-room house on the land, complete with attached barn and woodshed. After only three years, following his transfer to the Quincy Quarry Company in Massachusetts, Mr. Smith decided to sell the property. In response to Edward's offer of $1,500, John Smith wrote the following letter:

> Dear Sir:
>
> It is hard work for us to make up our minds to let the property go at such a sacrifice. Let me show you first how the property stands us.
>
> Land $500.00
>
> Contract for house
> above cellar $1,650.00
>
> Cellar and underpinning 200.00
>
> Cistern 75.00
>
> Fruit trees 25.00
>
> Wire fence for pasture 12.00
>
> Hen House <u>30.00</u>
>
> Making a total of $2,492.00
>
> The above in cash I paid out and does not include my time for one year which I put in making improvements. As near as I can judge, there are about three

# The Greenlaws of Sunset: Part I

*5.10 Captain and Mrs. G. Edward Greenlaw's home in Sunset. Seated on the front steps are Caroline and her mother, Catherine Monnier. Collection of Barbara L. Britton*

hundred cords of wood on the place. I have had a chance to sell part of the wood-lot but did not think it advisable to do so. There is a good cranberry marsh, fine pasture, and good tillage land, free from rocks; all of which I will give you a warrantee deed for the sum of fifteen hundred dollars $1,500.00. Now, Capt. Greenlaw, if you will look the place over, I think you will say you have a bargain. If I had been offered $2,000.00 last Spring for the place, I would not have accepted it. You, of course, know there is a fine stable attached to the house. Hoping to hear from you in a few days, I remain

Yours truly, J. C. Smith (signed)

*5.11 Grandmother Monnier holding baby Edwin Greenlaw, Caroline and Edward's first child. Collection of Barbara L. Britton*

This property on Sunset Road was purchased by Edward in 1898 and remained in the Greenlaw family for almost fifty years, until it was sold in 1946. *[See photo 5.10]*

Edward and Caroline became the parents of three children: Edwin Berger Greenlaw, born August 2, 1899, Lillian Marion, born January 5, 1905, and Kenneth Nelson, born September 27, 1906. *[See photo 5.11]* Other family members included Caroline's mother, Catherine Monnier, a widow by then, who arrived in 1899, just before the birth of Caroline's first child, Edwin; she died in 1903. Mary Berger, Caroline's dearest friend and known as "Aunt

*5.12 Mary Berger, affectionately known as "Aunt Mary" by the family. Collection of Barbara L. Britton*

*5.13 Captain Edward Greenlaw with son, Edwin and young daughter, Lillian, at the wheel, ca. 1907. Collection of Barbara L. Britton*

*5.14 Edward and daughter Lillian, ca. 1912. Collection of Barbara L. Britton*

*5.15 Caroline with Lillian and youngest son Kenneth, ca. 1910. Collection of Barbara L. Britton*

Mary" by the children, lived with the family from 1904 until her death in 1937. *[See photo 5.12]* For many years she had been the cook for the McClintock family and assumed that same role as a member of the Greenlaw household. Both women were buried in the Greenlaw plot in Mt. Adams Cemetery. In each case, they took on important functions in helping to run the house, care for the children and provide welcome companionship for Caroline while Edward was away for six months of the year.

By all accounts Edward and Caroline were disciplinarians when it came to child rearing, but they were loving parents as well and, in turn, were the recipients of love and respect from their children. A few black and white snapshots in a family album also give indications of a father and mother who enjoyed spending time with their young children. *[See photos 5.13, 5.14 and 5.15]*

# The Greenlaws of Sunset: Part I

*5.16 Lillian helps her mother feed the chickens, ca. 1912. Collection of Barbara L. Britton*

*5.17 Vayu, cutter yacht, built 1882 in Lawley Shipyards, South Boston; owner C. A. Welch Jr. Courtesy of Historic New England*

Perhaps the following three letters written to his daughter, Lillian, in 1915, when she was 10 years old, illustrate best Edward's love for home and family:

> For Lillie, my dear little girl
>
> I am a long ways from you, yet you are hardly ever absent from my thoughts and am wishing for the day to come that I may see you again. I am proud to know that my little daughter is so useful in her home and is so willing to help. So keep on, dear, like the ray of sunshine that you are. With love and kisses, Dad
>
> Naponset, Mass. May 9th 1915

> My dear Lillian
>
> I was very pleased to get your nice letter and hope you will send more. You must have my fish shanty decorated with all kinds of stuff. The cherry and pear trees are in bloom here and it is like Summer. You and Kennie must be having a fine time. I would be very glad to see you. With much love from Papa *[See photo 5.16]*
>
> Naponset, Mass. June 3, 1915

> My dear little girl
>
> It makes me very happy to get your nice letters and wish so very much that I could see you, but you know, dear, Daddy must make the dollars. For quite soon now, my Tootsie will be a young lady and I don't know what you will want then, perhaps a piano or something to make you happy, and Kennie, Edwin and Mama like nice things too. Your school report is very good and I am proud of you, dear, that you do so well. How much money do I owe you now? You had best keep account and have your bill made out so that when I come home I can pay you. Then you will have to give me a receipt and a kiss to bind the bargain. I think you must be very busy helping with the chickens and in the house. I guess Mama thinks you are a treasure. Are you going to call the pig Dinah or Topsy? Perhaps Dandelion would be a good name. How does my camp look now? You and Kennie must have it full by this time. I suppose Edwin doesn't take much notice of little girls now that he is wearing long trousers. Well, dear, I will say good night and happy dreams to you. I will write to Kennie next.
>
> With love and kisses from Dad

5.18 *Ranger, sloop yacht, designed by B.B. Crowninshield, built in 1901 by George Lawley and Son, South Boston. Owner Henry P. King. Courtesy of Historic New England*

5.19 *Ranger, schooner yacht, designed by F.D. Lawley, built in 1907 by George Lawley & Son in South Boston; owner Henry P. King. Courtesy of Col. Kenneth N. Greenlaw Jr.*

For many years Edward was in command of several fine sail yachts for wealthy owners. Among them was the *Vayu* owned by C. H. Welsh Jr. of Boston, two *Rangers* owned by Henry P. King of Prides Crossing, Massachusetts, and the *Rusalka* owned by John A. Stetson of Boston, Commodore of the Boston Yacht Club. *[See photo 5.17]*

The *Vayu*, a cutter type yacht, was built and designed by Lawley & Son, and launched at South Boston in 1882. A boat with a broad, square stern for carrying stores and passengers, it was a fore- and aft-rigged vessel with one mast and a jib and forestaysails; the sails were made of hemp. This rig was associated with a hull of extreme length and depth, a heavy lead keel and no centerboard. With a gross weight of 11 tons, the *Vayu* had a length of 33 feet and a beam of 10 feet 3 inches. A brief history of the *Vayu* indicated that C. H. Welsh Jr. held ownership for three years, 1883 to 1885; others followed through 1906.

The *Ranger*, owned by Henry P. King, was a sloop type yacht, a fore- and aft-rigged vessel, with a single mast and sails of cotton. The overall length of the vessel was 55 feet 6 inches, her beam 12 feet 4 inches; her weight grossed 17 tons and she had an 8 foot draft. Designed by B. B. Crowninshield, the *Ranger* was also built by Lawley & Son at South Boston in 1901. *[See photo 5.18]*

A second *Ranger*, this time a schooner yacht, was designed by F. D. Lawley, and built for Henry P. King in 1907, at the George Lawley and Son Shipyard in South Boston. This vessel had a length of 80 feet with a beam measuring 17 feet, a draft of 10 feet 2 inches and a gross weight of 41 tons. *[See photo 5.19]*

*5.20 Rusalka, schooner yacht, designed by George F. Lawley, built in 1896 in George Lawley & Son Shipyards in South Boston; owner Commodore John A. Stetson, Boston Yacht Club. Courtesy of Col. Kenneth N. Greenlaw Jr*

Henry P. King, the owner, was in the fruit export business in Boston, but lived in Pride's Crossing, an exclusive district located in Beverly, Massachusetts. It was there in the late 1800s and early 1900s that grand mansions were built as summer cottages for wealthy business magnates. Notable residents of the time included Henry Clay Frick, steel magnate; Edwin C. Swift, president of Swift meat packing; and Alice Roosevelt Longworth, eldest daughter of former President Theodore Roosevelt.

The *Rusalka* was a schooner type yacht, built in 1896 for John A. Stetson, with an overall length of 63 feet, a beam of 15 feet, a gross weight of 28.8 tons and a draft of 7 feet. She was designed by George F. Lawley and built in the Lawley shipyard at South Boston, Massachusetts. *[See photo 5.20]*

John A. Stetson, owner of the "handsome yacht" *Rusalka*, was president of the Stetson Coal Company in Boston. He took the helm of the Boston Yacht Club in 1892 and held the office of Commodore for ten years. *The Boston*, p. 34 *[See photos 5.21, 5.22 and 5.23]*

Photographs of the three yachts, *Vayu, Ranger* and *Rusalka*, were taken by Nathaniel Stebbins, a noted marine photographer specializing in vessels of all types. Most of his original 25,000 images were on glass plates, the usual method of high-resolution negatives in his time. As previously noted, all the yachts were built in the George Lawley and Son Shipyards in South Boston. *[See photos 5.24, 5.25 and 5.26]*

Although we do not have written evidence of Edward's relationship with any of the yacht owners by whom he was employed, we do know, from the recollections of his daughter, Lillian, that Caroline and Edward received a pair of large, hand-painted Victorian lamps as a wedding gift from one owner. She also related that "every year, at the end of the yachting season, my father received a bonus. And, in addition, at Christmastime he received a lovely gift. One year he received a gold watch, another year he received a brass barometer, and on still another Christmas, he and mother received an entire dining room set which included a table, eight chairs, a sideboard, and a china closet." It appears obvious that these gifts speak to warm and enduring friendships and to the high regard in which Edward was held by his employers.

At the end of the yachting season in 1916, when Edward returned home to the Island, he planned to retire, but he suddenly became very ill and died on October 19, 1916; he was 54 years old. He was buried in Mt. Adams Cemetery next to Zara, his first wife. Caroline, his second wife, was buried next to him when she died, two decades later, on October 17, 1937.

*5.21 Boston Yacht Club, founded in 1866, was the first yacht club in New England. Its first clubhouse was opened at City Point in 1874. Courtesy of Boston Yacht Club*

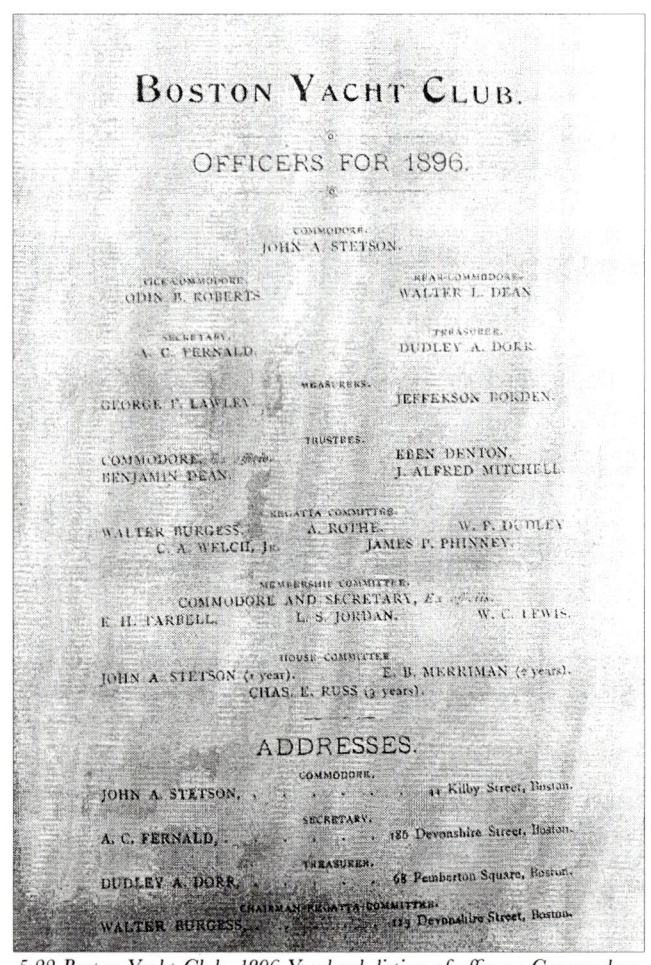

*5.22 Boston Yacht Club, 1896 Yearbook listing of officers: Commodore John A. Stetson. Courtesy of Boston Yacht Club*

# The Greenlaws of Sunset: Part I

*5.23 John A. Stetson and his yacht Rusalka, from The Boston, a history of the Boston Yacht Club written by Paul Shanabrook in 1979. Courtesy of Boston Yacht Club*

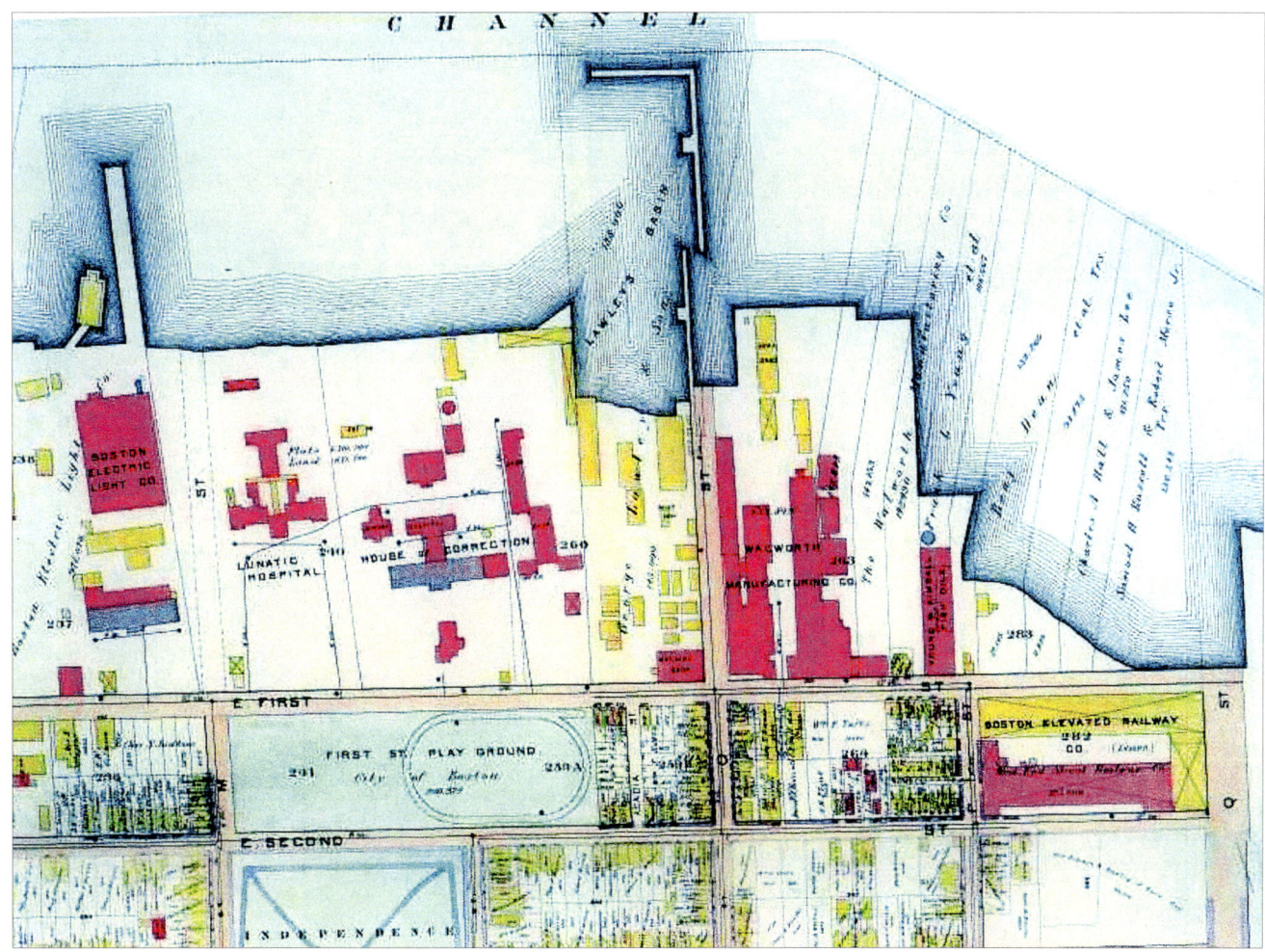

*5.24 Map showing George Lawley & Son Shipyards and Yacht Basin, South Boston, Massachusetts. Courtesy of Dorchester Historical Society*

*5.25 Lawley's Shipyards, South Boston. Early postcard collection, Courtesy of Dorchester Historical Society*

*5-26 Lawley's Yacht Basin, South Boston. Early postcard collection, Courtesy of Dorchester Historical Society*

# Chapter 6: The Greenlaws of Sunset: An In-depth Look at a Yachting Family, Captain Edwin B. Greenlaw

*Whatever it was that caused us to go to sea for recreation rather than for our daily work...the no nonsense business of bringing home the bread and butter...will remain one of humankind's happiest mysteries. All who have gone to sea for pleasure, adventure or competition have been accepted on the basis of their love of the sea.*

Paul Shanabrook, *The Boston*

## The Early Years: Growing Up on Deer Isle

This is the story of Captain Edwin Berger Greenlaw, eldest son of G. Edward and Caroline Greenlaw, presented in his own words. During his retirement, at the urging of family and close friends, he was inspired to write his autobiography, which he titled *Memories and Nostalgia*. His writing provides the reader with detailed, sometimes humorous, recollections of a boyhood spent on Deer Isle in the early years of the 20th century, firsthand accounts of the experience and knowledge he gained from employment on all types of vessels, from a small sailing schooner to luxury yachts, and his rise from the rank of able seaman to captain through hard work and a strong determination to succeed.

In the Preface, he writes:

> The enclosed is a true story of my life. Nothing is fictitious and nothing added to make it more interesting. I have only included a few of my experiences. It would be too much of an undertaking to include them all. My memories and nostalgia pay tribute to my parents who were strict disciplinarians in my early upbringing, guiding me into the proper channels for the safe navigation of my life. One never forgets early training and the guidance received from parents.

As he introduces the narrative, Edwin describes the Deer Isle he knows so well, the family into which he was born, and the house where he grew up. He begins the story:

> Deer Isle is one of the largest islands situated in Penobscot Bay and is not to be confused with Deer Island in Passamaquoddy Bay, to the eastward. Deer Isle embraces approximately one hundred square miles and is connected to the mainland by a long suspension bridge, three-eighths of a mile in length, built in 1939. Deer Isle's coastline is rocky, with numerous

coves and inlets, and is mostly forested. The Island community consists of two towns, Deer Isle and Stonington, with scattered villages on its perimeter. Approximately 3,000 permanent residents populate the Island. During the summer months, the population almost doubles with nonresidents, who own summer homes, and vacationers. Many artists come to the Island for painting and photography, or just to enjoy its scenic beauty. The principal industries are fishing, lobstering, scalloping, shrimping and seining herring; a sardine canning factory is located in Stonington. *[See photo 6.1]*

It was at the turn of the twentieth century that I was born on Deer Isle, August 2, 1899, to be exact. I was the first son of Captain George Edward Greenlaw and Caroline Elizabeth Monnier. My sister, Lillian, was born on January 5, 1905 and my brother, Kenneth, on September 27, 1906. My father was born on Deer Isle, whereas my mother was born in Neuchatel, Switzerland. She attended school in Berne, the capital, where she was educated. Her mother, Catherine Gretchman, was from Stuttgart, Germany and her father, Charles Monnier, from the region of Alsace Lorraine in France; she had one sister, Ida. Her family emigrated to this country around 1880 and settled in Bridgewater, near Pittsburgh, Pa., where they had relatives. My grandfather, Charles Monnier, was a tinsmith by trade. *[See photo 6.2]*

All my Greenlaw ancestors and uncles were seafarers. The original Greenlaw family (a father and mother with six sons) came from Scotland in a sailing vessel in 1753, settling first in Warren, Maine. Later, wanting more land for farming, the parents and four of the six sons pushed northward and were the first settlers of Deer Isle in 1761.

*6.1 Edwin, eldest child of Edward and Caroline Greenlaw, in his baby carriage, 1900. On the back of the photo, his mother wrote: "Prince Edwin - age 10 months." Collection of Barbara L. Britton*

*6.2 Edwin Berger Greenlaw, age two, 1901. Collection of Barbara L. Britton*

My home, where I was born and grew up, was a nine room, two-storied house consisting of four bedrooms upstairs and five rooms on the main floor. The house was connected to a large barn with a floored loft which Father used

# The Greenlaws of Sunset: Part II

*6.3 Edwin with younger brother and sister Kenneth and Lillian, ca. 1910. Collection of Barbara L. Britton*

her writing was in script. She had traveled to many European countries and throughout the United States, having been employed as a secretary to a wealthy lady for several years. On the other hand, Father received very little formal education as his mother became a widow with six children to support. In order to keep the family together, it became necessary for Father to be employed at an early age. He often referred to his limited schooling, but he was an avid reader and could converse on any subject. What he lacked in formal education, he wanted for his children. *[See photo 6.3]*

as a workshop. There was also a large shed attached to the rear of the barn, which was utilized for the storage of fitted wood for the two stoves that supplied the heat for cooking and comfort, one in the kitchen and the other in the living room. The property comprised approximately fifty acres, mostly woodland, which extended for a mile from our home. From this woodland, fifteen cords of wood were harvested each winter, cut to size, and stored for cooking and heating. Aside from the forest land, only about four acres were in grass, but on this were numerous apple, pear, peach and plum trees; all bore abundant fruit. A covered spring of sweet, cool water was also located in the area and was carried to the house daily for drinking purposes. A large rain cistern in the cellar provided water for other purposes.

Mother had the advantage of a good education. She spoke and could read and write French and German fluently;

I have but vague recollections of my Grandmother Monnier who came to live with us shortly after I was born; she died when I was a young child. Soon, thereafter, a very dear friend of Mother's, Miss Mary Berger, retired and came to live with us. She had been employed for years as a cook with the same family by whom Mother had been employed as a secretary. She was the kindest and most generous person that I have ever known. She adored and indulged us children, and I have retained so many happy memories of her. We called her Aunt Mary. She asked so little from life and gave so much. She was a wonderful cook and we all loved her, as much as our Mother. Aunt Mary was of German descent and she and Mother conversed in German, except when Father was home. I was taught to speak German and much of it has remained in my memory to this day.

As Edwin focuses attention on the daily life of the family, he mentions that each member was expected to make his or her contribution toward completing the never-ending daily tasks. In his own case, he writes:

> From the time I was nine years of age, I had certain daily duties to perform. The wood box in the kitchen had to be filled and kindling provided for the start of the morning fire. A pail of drinking water had to be brought from the spring and there were errands to be run, especially during the summer when Father was away. I weeded and hoed potatoes and, periodically, I cleaned the hen pens and hen nests. I hated these jobs but was made to do them.

Throughout the year, the most pressing need for the family was a consistent food supply. It wasn't enough to fill one's immediate needs but something had to be "stored up" for the winter months, or longer, if seafaring fell on hard times. Even on the smallest family farm, such as the Greenlaws', self-sufficiency was a value to be maintained. As we will see a little later on, the farm became a necessity.

> Our Father was a sailing master and, for many years, commanded several large schooner yachts for wealthy owners which took him away from home from April to October. During his absence, Mother planted a large garden, producing a large variety of vegetables for the table and for preservation and storage later during the winter months. Poultry was raised mainly for eggs, which were shipped to wealthy families in Boston. Wild berries were plentiful and were picked and preserved for winter. Cucumbers were pickled and green tomatoes made into piccalilli. A pig and sometimes two were raised and butchered in late fall; everything was utilized except the squeal and the tail. The hams and bacon were sugar cured and smoked. Lard from the fat was rendered and stored in earthenware crocks. The head of the animal was made into hogshead cheese and the feet pickled. The lean meat was kept frozen and eaten during the winter. All surplus fat was placed in a special container and made into soap for washing purposes; it had a strong lye content.
>
> Since we did not have a cow, milk and butter were purchased from a neighbor. I can remember when milk was four cents per quart and butter was twenty cents per pound. When the price of milk rose to six cents per quart and butter to twenty-five cents per pound, my parents considered the price excessive and resorted to evaporated milk and oleo [margarine]. Father, when returning home in the fall, always purchased sufficient groceries to last through the winter season: a couple of barrels of flour (196 lbs. each), 50 lbs. of sugar, a sack of coffee beans that had to be pulverized in a grinder, etc. He owned a boat and would catch fish at the turn of freezing weather. Some he split, salted and dried and some he buried in ice and snow to be consumed later in the winter. On Saturday nights, the evening meal was always baked beans and steamed brown bread; the remains were served at Sunday morning breakfast. Sunday dinner, usually, consisted of roast pork or chicken and a variety of vegetables.
>
> At the conclusion of the Saturday evening meal, with the dishes washed and put away, large kettles of water were heated on the kitchen stove. A large wooden wash tub was brought from the barn and placed in front of the kitchen stove. In this tub, the entire family bathed—first the children, then the parents. This was common practice and a weekly ritual performed by all those who believed that "cleanliness was next to godliness." I can recall that many people had an odor, whether of their own making or contact with barn animals, but it was tolerated and an accepted fact.

# The Greenlaws of Sunset: Part II

> During my growing years, I was always hungry but was not allowed to eat between meals. I would filch cookies or doughnuts, or anything else available, when nobody was visible. Failing in this endeavor, I would resort to eating dried fish or apples.
>
> There was always plenty of good food in our home, but money was scarce and I never had any. A boy could purchase a lot for five cents or a nickel in those days. I'll mention a few: a scoop of ice cream, a cup of coffee, 1 lb. of sugar, two doughnuts, a tablet of paper, five lead pencils, a pen and holder, five sticks of chewing gum (five inches long called O.K.) or a bottle of ink. Carpenters could be hired for $4.00 a day. Those were the prevailing wages at that time. During the winter of 1916-1917, I hired a horse and sled to haul our annual supply of wood to the door for $2.00 a day. Any family who owned their own home and had amassed $10,000 could comfortably retire, but few on the Island had reached this affluence.
>
> Nothing was wasted or thrown away. Newspapers, magazines, boxes, and cans were all conserved. Clothing was mended, patched and repaired. A pair of shoes could be purchased for $3.00 and a pair of boots for $5.00. During my sophomore year in high school, Mother purchased, by mail order, my first all wool suit, a beautiful blue color, for $15.00. And, in 1917, I purchased an all wool, winter coat for $7.00.

Looking back on Maine winters in the early years of the 20th century, Edwin describes them as "extremely cold," with many days of "below zero temperature and dirt roads piled high, in many places, to depths of six feet with drifting snow." At a time when road equipment was non-existent, he goes on to say that "the roads could only be cleared by shoveling or by employing oxen pulling logs or planks to pack down the snow for travel by horse and sleigh." The use of oxen instead of horses was more practical, as the horses were more vulnerable to accidents in the deep snow. He continues:

> During the harsh days of winter, the mail was often delayed for several days. There were days when the mail arrived on the Island via hand-pulled sled or horse drawn sleigh over the frozen expanse of water between the Island and the mainland. A steamboat ran between Stonington and Rockland carrying passengers, freight and mail. When the Island became short of supplies, an icebreaker would be dispatched to break the ice. The vessel could then proceed to within the vicinity of the port and the freight and supplies loaded onto horse drawn sleds.
>
> In spite of below zero temperature, the weather did not keep Father from cutting the year's supply of firewood. It was necessary for him to keep a fire burning nearby for occasional warmth. I should mention that wood cuts more easily and faster when it is frozen and can be split apart with one blow of an axe. After a sufficient supply of wood was cut (sixteen cords in four foot lengths), Father would hire a man who owned a team of oxen, and have it hauled to the door. He spent the winter sawing it, two cuts to a stick, which was the standard size for the stoves. It was left to dry during the summer months, then wheeled into the shed in the fall. I would like to mention that no power equipment had been developed at that time.
>
> There was no socializing during those cold winter days and the women folk stayed indoors. Mother was always busy making clothing for herself and us children—mending, patching, darning, and knitting mittens and long stockings. Aunt Mary would be seated near the stove in the living room during the evening hours making patchwork quilts.

*6.4 Edwin "going skating" in 1911. Collection of Barbara L. Britton*

> I always slept in a cold room and remember, as a little boy, that my bed was a large crib with a mattress stuffed with dry corn husks. When I grew too large for the crib, I was relegated to a regular bed and, in the winter, slept on a regular mattress between two flannel sheets. For covers, I had a blanket, plus a quilt and a goose down comforter, the warmest of all covers with the least weight.

Fond memories of Christmas holidays, filled with anticipation, are remembered as warm family celebrations, bright spots in the dark, cold days of winter. Edwin's word pictures provide the details:

> I remember the Christmas holidays that were observed in our home. A large fir tree, reaching from the floor to the ceiling, had an angel with outstretched wings at its peak. The tree was decorated with popcorn balls, candles, and festoons of threaded popcorn. The wax candles were wired to the outer branches of the tree, as electricity was not one of the luxuries available at that time. Mother would light the candles before we were allowed to enter the room on Christmas morning. Our stockings were hung by the fireplace before bedtime on Christmas Eve and in the morning we found them filled with small gifts, fruit and ribbon candy. Our gifts under the tree consisted, mostly, of new warm clothing. My grandmother (Father's mother), always sent me a pair of woolen mittens that she had knitted herself. On one Christmas I received a sled and on another Christmas, a pair of skates. *[See photo 6.4]*

> I cannot forget the varied colored ribbon candy that was purchased at the country store; it came in large tubs or small casks. Grapes came in boxes and were packed in sawdust. Fruits were very expensive in those days. We were treated to watermelon and ice cream on the Fourth of July. I still remember those treats and how good they tasted! On my birthday, Aunt Mary would give me twenty cents to purchase ice and she would make a freezer of ice cream with pure cream in it.

In the early years of the 20th century, prior to World War I, new inventions were being introduced that changed America's landscape. The automobile and the "talking machine" were considered the new "wonders of the world," so it is no surprise that first time experiences, such as riding in a car or listening to a voice on a round wax cylinder, became exciting events for the young Edwin Greenlaw. In this ongoing narrative, he regales the reader with vivid accounts of these special times:

> One of the great thrills of my early boyhood was my first ride in an automobile, of which there were few on the Island, and mostly steam cars. I was probably about eight or nine years old, and was walking along the road, when a chauffeur driven touring car stopped and the man offered me a ride. My guess was that the car was at least fifteen feet in length, as it could carry seven passengers. It was upholstered

in leather and was equipped with acetylene headlights and side lights. Two spare tires were supported in a frame on the right side, together with a tool box, tire pump and tools for emergencies. It steered with a circular steering wheel; most of the steam cars steered with a lever. The gear shift and hand brake were levers to the left of the driver. The spark and throttle were on the steering wheel, but the choke used for starting purposes was pulled from the dashboard. It had a horn that was actuated by pressing a bulb and a hand actuated windshield wiper. As the self starter had not been invented at that time, it had to be cranked by hand.

The chauffeur wore large sun goggles on a leather cap and a long linen duster, or long coat, over his clothing. Also, he wore leather gauntlets that reached to his elbows to make his appearance look real professional. My opinion of him was that he was nothing less than a genius!

Following this experience and the steam cars, heretofore mentioned, others made their appearance on the Island, but could only be used during the summer months. Fords, Maxwells, Chevrolets, and Overlands, in this order, were later purchased by the more affluent people. The steam cars, except the Stanley, were steered with a lever, had extremely large wheels and were chain-driven. They lacked sufficient power to climb some of the hills on the Island, which made it necessary for the passengers to get out and help by pushing the car up the hill.

I can remember, also, the first "Talking Machine"; it was an Edison product. Later, the name was changed to Graphaphone, Gramaphone, then Phonograph. The local storekeeper, Mr. John Johnson, purchased one and rented it for twenty-five cents a night. It consisted of a square box with a large demountable horn and had a round metal cylinder about 3" in diameter connected and geared to the spring. The records were round, made of hard wax, and were slipped on the cylinder. Later, the flat disc records were invented. Father came home, one evening, with this contraption and a market basket full of records. I recall that one of the records was named The Preacher and the Bear.

In the introduction to his autobiography, Edwin describes the Island community as consisting of "two towns. Deer Isle and Stonington, with scattered villages on its perimeter." The village where he lived as a boy and where he grew up was Sunset, located on the southwestern side of the Island. At that time, the village itself comprised the library (now the Parish House), a one-room schoolhouse (a lovely community garden takes its place today), a chapel (now the Sunset Congregational Church), and a general store (now Olsen Electronics) in which the post office was also located. He goes on to discuss, in more detail, the importance of these buildings to the social life of the community:

> When I was a boy, the building now named the Parish House was formerly called the Library. It was constructed by the Martha Washington Temperance and Benevolent Society, no longer in existence. The building was to be used for lectures and meetings, but also contained a library. It is interesting how this all came about. The Society was formed in the year 1850. At that time the group would go from house to house for their meetings or hold them in the church where they would set up their spinning wheels. Many sheep were raised locally for wool, so the children would be sent out to collect wool from all those who kept sheep. It then had to be "picked" and separated into fibers to fit it for the carding mill. It came back in rolls ready for a spinning bee. The spinning wheels, swifts and reels of all the neighbors were brought to the place where the bee was to be held. Dinner

was served, usually baked beans, brown bread, Indian pudding, cakes and pies, contributed by the members. After the yarn was wound into skeins, it was dyed, and then it was ready for spinning into yarn for knitting into caps, mittens and stockings. Stockings were sold to the seamen for 30-35 cents a pair. I have yet to find a substitute comparable to the warmth to be had from home spun mittens or stockings made from the natural wool of the sheep.

Another way that the Society raised money was by selling Larkin soap, house to house, from a catalogue. The members voted to use the money earned to build a meeting hall. The land on which the building stands was given to the Society by Mr. Johnson, the local storekeeper. Several years later, after the turn of the century, several of the ladies resigned from the Society and formed a Ladies Aid. They met weekly in one another's homes making articles to sell at the annual church fair, with the proceeds being used exclusively for the maintenance of the church. When the Society disbanded in 1943, the former Library became the Parish House.

The store in Sunset, owned by Mr. John Johnson who was also the postmaster, was the meeting place for the men in the community. In the winter, they would congregate at 7:00 p.m. to await the arrival of the mail by horse and sleigh, usually around 9:00 p.m. In the center of the store was a large potbellied stove with several boxes and cases around it on which men sat chewing tobacco, whittling, and conversing about the events of the day. The store sported only one chair, which was occupied by the oldest citizen in the community. In one corner of the store was a large hogshead of New Orleans molasses and in the rear of the store, near the entrance, was a barrel of pickles in brine and a barrel of soda crackers. It was not uncommon for a boy to sneak into the store by the rear entrance and try to filch a cracker and pickle when the storekeeper's attention was distracted; a large pickle sold for two cents.

The store dealt in groceries, cloth, boots, shoes, and a variety of canned foods. The post office was part of the building, but partitioned from the main store, with many pigeon holes for the incoming mail. From the partition extended a long counter with a scale. This, in turn, extended to a long candy counter containing a large assortment of penny candy. The men, from time to time, would help themselves to the candy, placing money on top of the showcase. Tobacco could only be purchased in plug form. Those who smoked cut the tobacco from a plug and rolled it between their hands before filling their pipes. It had a strong aroma and each person smelled from its effect. The store was the local men's club. Women never entered the store in the evening when the men were there. Father seldom missed an evening and occasionally allowed me to accompany him. Owing to the lack of telephones, the store was the news center of the community. When there was a marriage, the groom treated everybody in the store to a cigar.

In his recollections on the fashion of the day, Edwin describes the dressier clothing he remembers. However, in snapshots of his mother and Aunt Mary feeding the chickens or going about their everyday chores, a glance at the photo indicates ankle-length dresses, with perhaps one petticoat underneath. An ample apron, with bib top and strings attached at the waist to tie in the back, always covered the "work" dress.

It was no wonder that clothes had to be kept clean as long as possible when laundry was such an arduous, day-long task. Water had to be heated on the stove. A washtub was filled with water for scrubbing, using a washboard and homemade soap, while another tub was filled with clean water for rinsing. In good weather, clothes were pinned to lines outside with wooden pins, while in the winter or rainy weather, they were dried on large folding racks inside and, when possible, placed near sources of heat. Edwin continues with his review:

> I can well recall how people dressed at the turn of the century. The women wore long, flowing dresses with a couple of petticoats underneath that swept the floor. When traveling outside the home, they wore corsets reinforced with whalebone or steel with drawstrings in the back for lacing and pulling the corset tight. High buttoned shoes were also in vogue. Their hats were decorated with flowers or feathered plumes and, during the cold months, a fur muff and neckpiece were added. Men owned one good suit which they called their "Sunday Go To Meeting Suit", with a vest, and sported a large pocket watch fastened on a gold chain, draped across the vest. The seafarers wore either an anchor or compass suspended from the chain for ornament. Many men wore soft felt hats. The dudes on the Island were few, but their attire consisted of a long, black overcoat, derby hat, and spats over their patent leather shoes.

Recreation and entertainment for young people on the Island were pretty much left up to the individual and what one could create for himself; little was provided by adults. If equipment was required, money for purchase was always an issue. Opportunities for getting together with friends or attending an event at the community house were not common everyday occurrences. Edwin found that singular activities like reading, playing the violin, and hunting were ones that he thoroughly enjoyed and could be satisfied at will in his free time.

> For recreation the boys sometimes got together and played baseball, but there was always a scarcity of equipment. I remember purchasing an old glove from a boy for fifty cents. Baseballs in those days sold for ten and twenty-five cents. Sometimes the boys would pool their meager resources and purchase a twenty-five cent ball. Nobody had any money.

> Many days I spent on the shore but was never allowed to go in the water, therefore I never learned to swim. The water here is very cold; the average temperature during the summer months is fifty-seven degrees.

> During my early years, Mother made me attend Sunday School every Sunday. Prayer Meetings were held on Tuesday evenings. I also attended those as well, as there was nothing better in the way of entertainment for young people. An occasional Medicine Show would arrive and provide a show with a comedian and a couple of dancing girls that were dressed in tights on stage. The shows were patronized mostly by the male population with few women in the audience. At the conclusion of the show the promoter, who also acted as the master of ceremonies, would "pitch" his bottles of elixir as a cure for all human ailments. They could be taken internally and, in addition, could be used as a liniment to alleviate aches and pains; the concoction sold for $1.00 a bottle. The admission fee to attend the show was twenty-five cents. I was never allowed to attend one of these shows.

> Our best season for entertainment was in the winter when there was skating, iceboating and tobogganing. Some of the boys would construct a long toboggan by placing a long plank between two sleds and, loading it with girls, they would slide down the steep hills at a terrific speed on the icy roads. Although the nights were cold, we enjoyed skating on the frozen ponds, and would build a fire on the shore for occasional warmth.

One night during the summer a Chautauqua was held at the local community house. Although I was supposed to return home as soon as it ended, I watched as the floor was being prepared for dancing which I had never seen before. The music was furnished by a fiddler with an organ accompanist. This excited me to the extent that I could not think about anything else. I wanted so much to learn to play a fiddle. I talked about it so much to Mother that she purchased one for me, costing $10.00 from a mail order house in Chicago and Father asked a retired fiddler to give me lessons. I would sit in my room and practice for hours. One of the slow melodies that I would practice was called The Dying Nun. Father would often remark to Mother that he would be so glad when the nun died.

A year later, Aunt Mary presented me with a real violin for which she paid the magnificent sum of $50.00, and which is still in my possession. I continued with my music, taking lessons from a violinist who was the leader of a small orchestra. He charged fifty cents for an hour of instruction. One day the church organist asked me to accompany her in playing a solo in the church; we met for practice in her home. One of the ladies who was a staunch church member learned about it. She informed the church body that although she had been a church member during her entire lifetime and considered herself a good Christian, she would resign her membership and never enter that church again if that boy entered carrying a fiddle box. She said that she would have a vision of the Devil because any music played on a fiddle would only be fit for the Devil. The result: I did not play.

During his boyhood, Edwin developed a passion for hunting. Although one of his anecdotes about hunting is humorous in the telling, the others indicate that, even as a boy, his determination and willingness to accept responsibility and hard work were instrumental in his achieving goals he set for himself. Later, we will see that these same virtues helped him achieve life goals as well.

From the age of ten, I acquired the hunting instinct and spent many hours in the woods hunting small game with a bow and arrow, without much success. My success with projectiles, such as stones and hard green apples, was better. I can well recall the times that I was punished in the woodshed by Mother for breaking a window in the cold frame or hen house. And I remember the one time that my aim was deadly.

Our poultry yard was fenced with a six foot high fence that contained one huge red rooster who was the cock of the flock. It was the largest rooster that I have ever seen and must have had a weight of, at least, eight pounds. He was forever scratching a hole under the fence large enough to exit the yard. Immediately, thereafter, he would be seen in the vegetable garden destroying the young plants. Mother would shout for me to catch the rooster, but I was unable to catch him until he grew tired. No sooner was he confined than he would dig another hole under another part of the fence and return to the garden. It was a constant battle between him and me. One day after he was caught and returned to the yard for confinement, I plucked a hard green apple from a tree and hurled it at the rooster. My aim was true, the apple hitting him atop his big, red head. His feet turned to the sky, as his neck was broken. I picked up the dead bird and carried him to a dense thicket in the woods. Mother always assumed that a fox had captured the rooster; she never learned what really happened.

From the age of ten, I would walk through the woods to visit with Mr.

# The Greenlaws of Sunset: Part II

and Mrs. Benjamin Howard who lived a mile distant from our home. Mrs. Howard would treat me to a glass of milk with a piece of cake or cookies and, upon departing, would give me books to read. My favorites were written by Horatio Alger. They were stories concerning boys who started life without anything to offer their employer but honesty and devotion to duty, which led, ultimately, to promotion and success. I was so inspired that I decided I would follow the pattern of these heroes in my future life.

When I was thirteen Father told me that if I would take care of the garden during his absence, he would buy me a shotgun in the fall when he returned home. I worked hard that summer to earn such a valuable prize and, sure enough, Father presented me with a twelve gauge single shotgun. With the gift came the understanding that all game which I shot had to be cleaned and prepared for the table; it was not to be shot simply for sport. I achieved much success at shooting many partridges and rabbits, and knew each and every woods, road, and path within a two mile radius from our home.

Father was one of the strongest and hardest working men on the Island. He had never known any leisure time and did not believe in sport, it being unproductive. He was a kind man and wanted what he lacked—a good education for his children, hoping that neither of his two boys would follow the sea. However, at times, when I wanted to go hunting, he would make me saw a certain amount of wood from the large pile that required cutting. I decided that this was not going to happen again upon his return home in the fall. So, during the summer of 1915, I sawed fourteen cords of wood and stored it in the woodshed. When he returned home, not a stick was left!

In several places throughout his description of school days spent in grammar and high school, Edwin refers to himself as "not being a good student" and a "slow learner." Although his mother had been well-educated in Switzerland, the methods by which she was taught and, perhaps the subject matter as well, were not applicable to the curriculum being taught in the Island schools, and his father lacked the formal schooling to help him. Edwin refers to the fact that he had a good memory, an asset he relied on to help him pass the examinations required for graduation. Yet, despite his frustration and lack of aptitude for formal schooling, he never gave up. As we will see later in the story, Edwin's perseverance to overcome this "handicap" and adopt improved study habits helped him achieve the success he so desired in his career.

> When September 1905 came, I had just passed my sixth birthday, the age when I must attend school. Mother accompanied me to the school, entered the building, spoke to the teacher and departed. I was alone, amongst a crowd of strange kids who whispered and cast their glances toward me as if a strange animal had suddenly appeared among them. I was dressed differently from those kids and spoke with an accent. They were as strange to me as I was to them. The teacher assigned me to a front desk, rang a bell, the kids ran in and took their seats, and school was officially opened. This was the start of my education in the Sunset Grammar School. *[See photo 6.5]*

All the Grade Schools on the Island were called Grammar Schools, but in later years they were called Elementary Schools. The school had one teacher who taught eight grades. In Sunset, twenty-three students attended. The lower grades were placed and seated in the front row of desks, while the eighth grade pupils had the privilege of the desks in the rear of the room. The teacher's desk was placed in the front center of the room. Two large benches were placed in front of this desk for

6.5 Sunset Grammar School, 1912. Kenneth (first row, right), Edwin (third row, right) and Lillian (fourth row, right). Collection of Barbara L. Britton.

classes called for recitation. In one corner of the room was a potbellied wood stove and in the other corner was a shelf that held a pail of drinking water with a long handled dipper for drinking purposes. It was the duty of one of the older boys appointed by the teacher, each week, to fetch a pail of water from a nearby spring every morning before school opened. Another boy was appointed to bring in the wood for the stove. The toilets were in a shack in the rear of the building, divided by a wall, with one side for the boys and the other for the girls. The school hours were from 9:00 a.m. to 4:00 p.m. with two twenty-minute recesses, one in the morning and one in the afternoon. Lunch period was from 12:00 p.m. to 1:00 p.m. Since the school was only a half mile from my home, I walked home for lunch and was back again when school convened at 1:00 p.m. Fortunately, I had a playmate, Edna Knowlton, who lived close to our home and we always walked to school together. We were the same age and in the same class.

All the teachers demanded the respect due them from their pupils. They kept a ferule on their desk and did not hesitate to apply it on any pupil who disobeyed. Some teachers were more strict than others and made a disobedient pupil remain in school at least an hour at the close of the day. Other pupils, who were deficient in a subject, were made to remain for assistance. I was feruled once for something that I did not do and was made to sit on a stool in the corner of the room, facing the wall, for an hour for whispering. The school did not lack certain pranksters. It was not uncommon for a girl to reach into her desk and have her hand come in contact with a frog or snake, resulting in an uproar from the terrified screams of the girl.

I spent eight years in this school but was only an average student. I can remember the name of each teacher: Mertice Small, Lillian Knowlton, Harry Powers, Florence Trott, Nellie Haskell, Emma Eaton, Emma Damen, Gertrude Eaton, Jane Dane, and Vesta Eaton who was my last teacher. I was thirteen years of age when I graduated and had not seen her since that time, until last year, when I met her at a party. We sat and talked for more than an hour. She told me that her salary, at that time, had been $7.00 a week and it had cost her $5.00 for room and board. I asked her how she managed. She replied that she made her clothes, but never had any money left for anything else.

The school district had a superintendent who was a huge man and all the pupils were afraid of him. His name was William H. Patton and every few weeks he would visit the school and call out one of the classes to interrogate them on what they had learned. We always breathed a sigh of relief when he departed.

All students had to take a written examination each week on the subjects taught. Ten questions were asked and the papers were graded on a percentage basis. Any student who received below seventy-five percent was a failure. The percentages were averaged at the end of each month and the average recorded on a report card, which had to be returned to the teacher with the parent's signature.

Following my graduation from the Sunset Grammar School, Arthur Greenlaw (no relative), who owned a livery stable adjacent to his home, asked if I would work for him during summer vacation for which he would pay me $20.00 per month, plus board. This looked like a small fortune, as I never did have any money. Mother objected to my working in a livery stable but Father, who was at home, said that Mother should let me go because I would be glad to return home in a couple of weeks, as Arthur was a hard taskmaster.

Aunt Mary purchased a second-hand bicycle for me so I could ride back and forth to work, as the stable was located about three-quarters of a mile from our home. I was at work at 6:00 a.m. I had seven horses to feed, stalls to clean, and the horses had be brushed and curried daily. Mrs. Greenlaw was a good cook and there was always plenty of good food served. I drove a surrey that was fringed on top, carrying summer visitors to different parts of the Island. I trucked freight from the steamboat wharf to the local stores and baggage to the hotels. On many days the hours were long, but I learned a lot about handling horses. I became strong and developed muscle so I could handle heavy freight. My services were terminated a few days before the start of the fall term at the High School. One day Arthur Greenlaw met Father in the village and told him, "Captain Ed, that boy of yours is a good boy and a hard worker. He worked hard for me during this past summer." This pleased Father to receive such a good report.

I was fourteen years of age when I entered High School in a class of twenty-seven. The school was located a mile from home; other students had twice this distance. We all walked to school, seldom missing a day, regardless of the weather. In the winter, during the heavy snow, the boys would walk ahead in single file and break a trail for the girls to follow. We boys wore knickers until the age of fourteen. I can remember how happy I was wearing my first pair of long pants. The girls wore long woolen dresses and coats. At noon we ate our lunch in the school basement, sitting close to the furnace for warmth.

As I have always been slow at grasping the fundamentals of a new subject and a slow learner, I was not a good student. I had difficulty with algebra and geometry, but there was nobody to turn to for help. In High School, I deplored studying Shakespeare and English literature, but excelled in bookkeeping and commercial business methods. My Mother's French pronunciation did not coincide with the teacher's, resulting in my loss of interest in that subject. The subjects of algebra and geometry I learned by rote. My average was low but somehow I stumbled through the subjects and managed to pass the examinations.

During my two years in High School, my only achievement was being awarded second prize at the Sophomore Recital, following a bitter controversy between the judges who decided that the first prize should not be awarded to a boy. My cousin, Mae, received the honor of being awarded first prize.

I have always had a good memory, but learned, years afterwards when attending vocational schools, that I did not know how to study. It is quite certain that if my four years of education had been completed at the High School, upon graduation I would have been included among several students who were not expected to have a successful future.

## Life Changing Events Set a New Direction

With the unexpected death of his father, Edwin Greenlaw's world moved from one of familiar routines and unknown plans for the future to one of immediate challenges and responsibilities. With the help of people he respected and trusted, he made decisions that, ultimately, determined the future course for his life.

It was the year 1916, the year Father decided to retire. During the fall, he was at home when he suddenly became very ill and, unexpectedly, passed away on October 19th. I was in my third year at Deer Isle High School and being dissatisfied with the education I was receiving begged Mother to let me quit. Despite her objections, my perseverance finally won her over and I became a dropout. I caught fish for the table, dug clams for which I received forty cents a bushel, seventy-five cents a gallon dressed, and spent the winter cutting, hauling and fitting fifteen cords of wood for our two stoves.

My uncle, Capt. Winslow Gray, was Master of a small schooner yacht. Mother asked him if he would give me a start when the yacht was put into commission, to which he agreed. I became a member of the crew on April 1, 1917. My wages were forty dollars a month. My first experience was when the yacht was anchored in a small cove for protection from an approaching northeast gale accompanied by heavy falling snow. Despite the fact that the vessel was riding to two spreading anchors, at the height of the storm, it began to drag towards shore. The Captain feared the yacht would strike a ledge and decided to abandon ship but, fortunately, the wind changed direction. Meanwhile, we all got ashore in the yacht tender, broke into a fish house, and built a fire. The Captain made a pot of coffee which we drank with some hard tack he brought from the yacht. During the summer we cruised along the coasts of Maine and Nova Scotia; Marblehead, Mass. was our headquarters. I can remember spending a few nights ashore at a movie house, where for a nickel, thirteen reels of pictures were shown and, afterwards, I treated myself to a ten cent ice cream soda. I returned home in October, having saved nearly all the money I had earned, and repeated my work of the previous winter.

The following year, 1918, I obtained a position as a mess attendant on

# The Greenlaws of Sunset: Part II

the Steam Yacht *Nevette* owned by J. P. Morgan, the international banker. Mr. Will Marshall [also from Deer Isle], the chef, took an interest in me, taught me to cook certain foods, mainly pies and cakes, and wanted me to follow his profession. During mid-summer the yacht was commandeered by the government, as World War I was in progress at that time. The crew of the *Nevette* was discharged, but each man was awarded a bonus of two extra months salary. I received $100, as my wages were $50 a month, and returned home.

Soon after my return home, I was called for a physical fitness test by the Draft Board, and was placed in Class IA. The examiners commented that I was a perfect physical specimen. I realized that, sooner or later, I would be called for induction into the Army. I would have much preferred the Navy, but doubted that I would be given a choice in the matter. However, an event occurred that changed my entire future. It was fate that intervened.

It was a Sunday and I was walking toward the beach when a car stopped and the driver offered me a ride, which I gladly accepted. It was Dr. Cecil E. Wascott, the local physician, who was en route to making a house call. When he inquired about my future intentions, I told him that I planned to work and save enough money for an education that would prepare me to be an accountant, as I enjoyed working with figures. Dr. Wascott strongly disapproved of this idea, stating that because I was a country boy, my life expectancy would be about fifty years if I chose an office career. I asked the doctor for his opinion as to what he thought I would be best suited for. He replied, "Edwin, all your family are seafarers. It is in your blood! You should follow the sea! Our government is building a large fleet of merchant vessels and will require crews to man them. It is a good healthy life. Think about it!" I thanked the good doctor for his advice, and he let me out of his car at the turn in the road. I continued my walk toward the beach.

I sat on a large rock and gazed out at the water in the bay, as I pondered the advice the doctor had given me. I thought about it for a long time and, finally decided that becoming a seafarer was what I really wanted to do. Father frequently remarked that he did not want his sons to follow the sea but if it was my intention to do so, after completing my education, then it would either make a man or a bum of me.

## Leaving Home to Follow the Sea

### Life Aboard the Merchant Ships: *SS Lake Winona*

I learned that the government was enlisting young men for training to crew the many merchant ships they were building and, further, that many men with very limited experience, such as barbers and salesmen, were being trained to become deck officers at a Government Navigation School in Rockland, Maine.

I presented myself for an interview with Capt. Charles Magee who was in charge of the Government Navigation School. He was a typical "old sea dog" who had, at one time, served as Chief Mate of the seven masted schooner, *Thomas W. Lawson,* the only one of its kind ever built. I told him of my ambition. He told me that I had insufficient sea experience to qualify for a certificate, but that I could attend the school and, upon graduation, take the examination.

However, my certificate would be withheld pending six months experience at sea on a merchant vessel. I spent a month at the school and passed the examination without any difficulty. After my successful completion of these first two requirements, Capt. Magee gave me a letter to be presented to Capt. Sparks, who was in charge of the U.S. Shipping Board, Sea Service Bureau in Boston, requesting my assignment to a ship.

It was the fall of the year and I was soon on my way to Boston. I had fifty dollars from my previous earnings concealed in a money belt tied around my waist. I registered at one of the cheap, waterfront hotels called the Rossmore. My room was on the third floor and the furnishings consisted of a bed, bureau and chair, for which I paid $1.00 a day. I allowed myself $1.00 a day for food. Breakfast was two doughnuts and a cup of coffee for fifteen cents, lunch was soup and a piece of pie for twenty-five cents, and the evening meal was usually a good helping of stew, pie and coffee. This daily fare never varied until I was assigned to a ship.

I reported to the Sea Service Bureau and presented the letter from Capt. Magee to Capt. Sparks. He told me to "hang around" and he would have an assignment for me. I reported to the Bureau daily. Two weeks passed and I was becoming very discouraged when fate, again, intervened. A huge man, roughly dressed, entered the hiring hall, with a cud of tobacco in his cheek and smoking a black, curved stem, pipe. He cast his eyes around the room, then came over to where I was standing. He greeted me with, "Hello, Sonny, are you a sailor?" I replied, "I don't know, Sir, but I have had some experience in yachts and small boats, and I'm seeking employment as a seaman." He asked me where I was from and what I had been doing. He felt my arm, looked at my hands, and remarked that I had all the appearances of a working man. Little did I know that this man was Capt. Michael T. Greene, from Newfoundland, Nova Scotia, Master of one of the outstanding beam trawlers and Star Captain of the Boston Fishing Fleet. He hired me on the spot and I lost no time in checking out of the Rossmore Hotel. I returned and joined Mr. Greene with other members of the crew he had hired.

My first merchant ship was the SS *Lake Winona*, engaged in transporting coal from Norfolk, Va. to Boston and Portland, Maine. The ship was berthed at a coal discharging pier and was scheduled to sail for Norfolk the following day; Capt. Walter O'Brien was Master. We arrived on board just in time for the evening meal, which consisted of frankfurters and beans eaten from tin plates with tin cups for drinking and steel knives and forks. Our breakfast was oatmeal, ham, two eggs per person, and toasted bread. None of the crew would eat the butter which was a permanent fixture in the middle of the table, it being too rancid for human consumption. The evaporated milk was so diluted that it was merely colored water. It was not uncommon to find cockroaches cooked in with the food, as the ship was infested with them. I filled up with oatmeal at breakfast, as the sight of cockroaches in the fried eggs sickened me. The crew complained, continuously, about the poor quality of food. Although I never made any comment, they had good reason to complain.

The crew quarters, or forecastle, was divided by a partition, one side for the sailors and the other for the engine room gang—oilers, firemen, and coal passers. All ate at the same long table. The deck crew, of which I was a member, was a fine bunch of fellows, all from different parts of the

# The Greenlaws of Sunset: Part II

country and all without sea experience. One outstanding member was Joe Fitzgibbons, a young Irishman from Oswego, New York, who always saw humor in everything and kept the crew in stitches with his Irish wit and humor; he became my best friend.

When the ship was ready to sail to Norfolk, Mr. Harry Lunt, the Second Officer, came to the crews quarters and asked, "How many of you fellows can steer?" Nobody answered. He looked at me and asked, "How about you?" I replied that I had never steered a steamship before. "Well, what have you steered?" he inquired. I told him, "Only small vessels." He told me to follow him to the bridge where I took my place behind the wheel. The Captain entered the pilot house, in full uniform, with four, large, gold stripes on the sleeves of his coat. He looked at me and asked if I knew the difference between port and starboard. I answered, "Yes, Sir." I was petrified at being given this new assignment so suddenly. We sailed out of Boston Harbor under the Captain's directions. He would say either "port" or "starboard," "ease her up," or "steady on your course," etc. After clearing Boston Harbor and with the ship headed down the coast, the Captain turned to me, before leaving the pilot house, and said, "Young fellow, if you can steer as well for the rest of the trip as you did coming out of Boston Harbor, I will promote you next trip to Able Seaman, and your wages will be increased from forty to sixty dollars a month." You can bet your life that I learned to steer a good straight course and received the promotion on our return to Boston.

It was a bitter cold winter and we would come into port with heavy ice on the ship. There wasn't much the crew could do except batten hatches and secure for sea. We all suffered when called out for deck duty. We had four hours on duty and eight off. We had two hours at the wheel and two hours on the bow as lookout at night. If the weather was just too cold or the ship was shipping heavy spray, the officer on watch would ask the bow lookout to stand watch at the corner of the bridge where he had some protection.

When the ship was at dock, in port, the crew would all go ashore, but I preferred to remain on board. Mr. Greene, the Chief Officer, would ask me to do night duty, which meant eight hours on and I would not be required to perform any duties the following day. This gave me the opportunity to study and keep up with what I had learned at Navigation School. When my six months of required sea service was completed, I received my certificate as a Third Officer.

With my certificate in hand, I decided to better my position and told the Chief Officer that I would be leaving at the end of the voyage. When informed about my decision, Capt. Benjamin Smith asked to see me. After seeing my certificate, he did something that very few shipmasters would do. He said, "Mr. Greenlaw, you have been on this ship a long time. Mr. Somers, our Third Officer is resigning and you can replace him with the understanding that because you have never had the responsibility of standing a bridge watch, you must carry out my instructions as you are still a 'green' man." I was elated, as my salary was increased from $60.00 to $124.00 a month, and I was succeeding in my endeavors. The Captain taught me many things, especially practical navigation. World War I was ongoing during the months that I was on the *Lake Winona* and German submarines had torpedoed several ships off the American coast. We were always apprehensive and I can recall the nights, standing watch, when a single porpoise would come streaking toward the ship, my heart would be in my mouth thinking that it could be a torpedo.

We were berthed in Norfolk when we heard the war was over. The day that the Peace Treaty was signed, I received notification to report for indoctrination into the Army. After serving four months as Third Officer, my services were terminated when the operators turned the ship back to the government, and I went home for a brief vacation.

## SS *Lake Narka*

I remained at home for several weeks, then returned to Boston for employment and, upon arrival, I went to the Sea Service Bureau. As I entered the hiring hall, I met Capt. Sparks on his way out. He greeted me with, "Hello, Greenlaw. I have a job for you. I am assigning you as Third Officer to the SS *Lake Narka*, Capt. George Stacey, Master." I reported on board and the ship sailed the next day for Haiti. The trip was uneventful and we docked at Port au Prince, the capital, to load a full cargo of raw sugar for New Orleans. The next day was Sunday and no work was being performed, so with my camera in hand, I visited the native market. I saw scenes that I will never forget. Adults wore clothing that hung in shreds on their emaciated frames; boys and girls were stark naked. Women, sitting cross-legged in the dirt, had a few native vegetables for sale; all were barefooted. While awaiting the sale of their produce, the women were picking lice from each other and cracking them between their teeth. Young children followed me begging for alms. The odors emanating from these unclean people combined with the sight and odor of open sewage is something I can never forget. There was absolutely no visible evidence of sanitation and only abject poverty everywhere.

I walked out of the city and followed a narrow, beaten path which led into the hills. After proceeding for some distance, I noticed a movement in the path ahead of me. I saw the body of a huge snake, which I would estimate to be about four inches in diameter, slowly slithering across the path. I beat a hasty retreat and returned to the ship. The U.S. Marines were in control of the city at that time and I was told, later, that I had endangered my life by walking away from the city into the hills.

The first night after our arrival in New Orleans I went ashore with a couple of the officers and we landed in the well-known Thorn Anderson Cabaret. The place was full of girls soliciting favors from the patrons. I had a glass of beer, although I did not drink anything stronger than coffee. Seeing that my two table mates were seeking a big night on the town, I excused myself and returned to Canal Street, made several purchases and returned to the ship. The year was 1919, and New Orleans was a wide open city, with its large red light district, gambling houses and women soliciting on street corners—a paradise for the seamen.

After discharging our cargo, the ship was chartered to the Puerto Rico Line and Capt. Stacey was relieved of his command by Capt. George Kane. The food on the ship was not up to Capt. Kane's standard. The first night at dinner, Capt. Kane called the Steward and told him that he "always wanted to see plenty of good grub served on this ship because where he came from he was accustomed to good food and plenty of it." I later learned that the Captain was from Surry, Maine. From that time on, there was great improvement in the meals, a striking contrast from that served on my previous ship. I later learned that the Steward on the SS *Lake Winona* fed the crew for thirty cents a day per man in order to make a name for himself with the company. Aside from these "belly robbers" as we called them, the captains and stewards would insist on a kickback for the food supplied by accepting such inferior quality that it was, by modern standards, unfit for human consumption and should have been condemned.

The SS *Lake Narka* was operated by the New York & Puerto Rico Steam Ship Company. Our regular run was between New Orleans and Puerto Rico, outward bound with regular cargo and returning with a full cargo of sugar. On one trip we did not obtain a full cargo of sugar and went to the port of Jucaro, Cuba to fill the remaining space. The crew in the Steward's Department were all Orientals—Chinese, Japanese and Filipinos. Four of them went crazy from consuming cheap Cuban Rum, probably mixing it with some narcotics which they were known to use. They each procured a long bladed knife from the ship's galley and engaged in battle with each other, and anybody else with whom they came in contact. They went berserk and did not know what they were doing. A Japanese had me backed into a corner and was lunging at me with an upraised knife, when our Filipino mess attendant came around the corner and grabbed him from behind. Together, we wrested the knife from his grasp and locked him in a spare room. He was a small, slender man and had started to emerge from the room through a porthole just as the Wireless Operator happened to pass the room. He hit him over the head with a large screwdriver he was carrying, knocking him partly unconscious, and pushed him back into the room. The Chief Officer ran to the bridge and blew distress signals on the ship's whistle and the Second Officer climbed a mast for protection from these berserk Orientals. Three members of the Cuban Militia came on board, disarmed the men, took them ashore and placed them in jail. They were a bloody mess, each having received numerous knife wounds on the upper part of their nude bodies. The Captain and the Chief Engineer were ashore when this happened but shortly after their return to the ship, which had completed loading, we proceeded to New Orleans minus four crew members.

## SS *West Alcoz*

It was January, 1920. We were berthed in New Orleans awaiting a full cargo when a beautiful, new, 10,000 ton ship, the SS *West Alcoz*, tied up alongside. The Third Officer came aboard, told me that he was leaving, and asked if I would be interested in the job. I jumped at the chance! He took me aboard the *West Alcoz* and introduced me to Mr. Carl Hermanson, Chief Officer, who after a meeting with Capt. Thomas Jamieson, hired me. Capt. Kane did not want me to leave the *Lake Narka*, but I told him that I wanted to obtain some ocean going experience. Another personal consideration was that the officers' quarters on the lake-type boats were small, making it necessary for me to share a room with the Second Officer, but on this new ship I would have my own private room. Furthermore, I would be free from fighting bedbugs and cockroaches with a daily spraying of insecticides and washing down the walls of our room with turpentine and kerosene.

The SS *West Alcoz* was the kind of ship on which I had always hoped to be assigned. All the officers were perfect gentlemen and each had his own stateroom. The food was excellent and perfectly served by an experienced waiter. The ship was immaculate, as a ship can be, with a well-disciplined crew. Capt. Jamieson kept everyone on their toes and had the respect of the entire crew. He was one of the finest gentlemen shipmasters that I have ever sailed with during my entire career and taught me much about stellar navigation and new methods that I did not know about. Mr. Hermanson, Chief Officer, was my best friend.

We loaded a part cargo in New Orleans and then proceeded to Galveston, Texas to complete our full cargo of cotton, tobacco and case goods. Our destination was Liverpool and Manchester, England. I will always remember Manchester, a factory town with its coal fired mills, a very dense, smoky city. Except for stormy weather encountered in the North Atlantic on our crossing to England, which is to be expected during the winter, the trip was uneventful. We returned to Norfolk, Va. at the end of April. I had continued my studies during the trip in preparation to take the examination for Second Officer, as I would have acquired more than enough sea time to qualify for the raise in grade. When given my request for time off to take the examination, the Captain approved it. At the end of four days spent writing, figuring navigation problems, etc. in front of the U.S. Steamboat Inspectors in Norfolk, I was granted my Second Officer's license. Meanwhile, although I was unaware of it, the Second Officer on the *West Alcoz* was resigning and Mr. Hermanson had recommended me for the position. The Captain considered me too young for the position on such a large ship, as I was only twenty years of age, but Mr. Hermanson considered me capable and persuaded the Captain to change his mind. I was appointed the new Second Officer and served a year in this capacity.

Our next voyages were made to Antwerp, Liverpool and Manchester. My Christmas holiday spent in Antwerp will never be forgotten. Nobody works and the holiday is extended into the New Year. The Belgians celebrate Christmas with parades, gaiety, and parties. Through an introduction from a friend, I had a second Christmas dinner at the YWCA, which was hosted by a society lady from New York City. After dinner there was dancing, with music furnished by a combo. I did not dance, but at the dinner I was seated next to a beautiful Russian girl who related her experiences during the war (World War I). She told me how she had walked from Poland to Belgium, ahead of the German Army, finally collapsing from malnutrition and fatigue. She was found lying on the roadside by a Catholic priest who took her to his parish house and nursed her back to health. It was 4:00 a.m. when I returned to the ship, but I had spent a most enjoyable evening. We continued on the Liverpool to Manchester run; our future trips were uneventful.

On April 1, 1921, Harris MaGill & Co., operators of the *West Alcoz*, returned the ship to the government for layup in Norfolk and the entire crew was discharged. It was with a feeling of sadness that I said "goodbye" to so many fine shipmates and friendships made.

Since I had acquired sufficient sea time for a raise in grade, I departed by train from Norfolk to Philadelphia where I successfully passed the examination and received my Chief Officer's license. I was twenty-one years old!

## SS *Monomac*

It was early April and I returned home for a visit. Harris MaGill & Co. informed me that they would contact me as soon as a vacancy occurred on one of their ships. In July I received a telegram to report to the Philadelphia office for assignment as Second Officer on the SS *Monomac*. I joined the ship in Norfolk;

# The Greenlaws of Sunset: Part II

*6.6 Edwin aboard the merchant ship SS Monomac as Second Officer in 1921. Collection of Barbara L. Britton*

the ship's Master was Capt. Martin Nugent, an old sea dog. We loaded part of the cargo, consisting of grain, tobacco and case goods, in Norfolk, then completed it in Philadelphia. Our destination was Liverpool and Bristol, England. We encountered good weather crossing the Atlantic and the voyage of thirteen days was fast and uneventful. *[See photo 6.6]*

After discharging our final cargo in Liverpool, we were ordered to return to Norfolk. It was September, the hurricane season. When we were almost in mid-Atlantic, the ship received a radio advisory from the Weather Bureau, alerting all ships in the North Atlantic to a dangerous hurricane crossing the Atlantic with increasing intensity. Only the approximate position of its center was known. The Captain changed course, hoping to avoid the fury of the storm. The date was September 21st—I will never forget it!

At midnight, I relieved the Third Officer on watch. He remarked that it had been blowing and the sea was changing from rough to calm; he thought the worst was over. I glanced at the barometer registering 27.30 and saw it pulsating right to left and left to right over a space of two inches. We were entering the center of a tropical hurricane. I asked the Third Officer if he had ever experienced a hurricane before and he replied in the negative. I told him that he had never experienced anything like what was coming.

Suddenly, the wind velocity increased and the seas grew ferocious. I phoned the Captain who ordered half speed. At 1:00 a.m. we reached the outer perimeter of the storm and all hell broke loose! The wind was screaming like a thousand banshees and increased in intensity. Mountainous seas washed over the ship carrying away everything in its path. The ship lurched and rolled, so far at times, that I was sure it would roll over, since we were without cargo or ballast to steady it in such a severe storm. An American flag passenger liner, the SS *George Washington*, some hundred miles distant, radioed that it was encountering winds in excess of 125 miles an hour.

I noticed that the four ton, spare anchor had been ripped from its deck fastenings and was being catapulted from side to side across the forward deck. It would only be a question of time before the deck plating would be punctured and the forward compartment flooded. During a brief lull in the storm, the Boatswain and I managed to secure the anchor with rope lashings to one of the mooring bitts. For six hours the hurricane continued with unabated ferocity. None of us expected to come out of it alive. We were certain that each time the ship rolled and lurched, we would be taking our last breath. Finally, at 6:00 a.m., the winds abated. Somehow, we had survived the storm.

We inventoried the damage, which was considerable. We found water in the ship's holds and a foot of water in the salon and all the staterooms. At 7:00 a.m. we lost two blades of the ship's propellers; we were now totally helpless. The Captain sent out a distress call, and all ships westbound in the Atlantic were ordered to come to our assistance. The SS *Bellamina*, bound for Baltimore, responded, arrived at our position during the evening, and stood by all night. During the six hours that the ship passed through the storm, we were blown back a distance of over seventy miles, while steaming at half speed into the mountainous and confused seas.

Due to the heavy seas remaining after the passing of the hurricane, it was two days of repeated attempts before the *Bellamina* managed to get a line aboard for connection to our towing hawser. We were towed a distance of 1,760 miles and it had been twenty-six days since we had left England. The Captain radioed for food to be supplied upon our arrival in Philadelphia, as the ship's stores were exhausted. During the final days, part of our meal was from emergency rations taken from the lifeboats. Due to the ship's damaged condition, she was deactivated, the crew discharged and, finally, ended with the ship breakers.

At the conclusion of the voyage, the Master of the SS *Monomac* wrote the following recommendation:

To Whom It May Concern:

This is to certify that the bearer Edwin B. Greenlaw has been employed on board the SS *Monomac* from the 30th day of July, 1921 to the present date, October 6th, 1921 in the capacity of Second Officer.

I do here certify that he is a man of clean habits, decent and respectable, faithful to his duties in every respect, and is a very efficient officer either as Second Mate or Chief Mate. Being a very conscientious man and will work faithfully for the interest of the person that employs him, being a first class navigator in every respect, and I will cheerfully recommend him to any person or persons requiring either a First Officer or Second Officer.

Martin Nugent, Master

## SS *Eastern Sword*

My next position was as Second Officer on the SS *Eastern Sword*, a Japanese built vessel of about the same tonnage as the *Monomac*, operated by Harris MaGill & Co. This ship was on the same run to England as the Monomac, and after a couple of voyages, was decommissioned, returned to the government, and all the crew discharged. It was August, 1922.

I had acquired sufficient sea time on the *Monomac* and the *Eastern Sword* to be eligible to take the examination for my shipmaster's license. I passed the final examination and I was issued a Master's License for Unlimited Tonnage On Any Ocean, my last and final certificate. It was August, 1922 and I was twenty-two years of age.

I had proved by experience and capability that I was qualified, but ship owners would not employ so young a Captain. At the same time, a sudden depression hit the shipping industry. Hundreds of merchant ships were being returned to the government and laid up, thereby leaving hundreds of crew members and officers without employment. I decided to return home for a while and spent the winter cutting twenty-two cords of firewood with the aid of my brother, Kenneth.

# A Career Blown Off Course

In the spring of 1924, still with no job and no change in the economic downturn for commercial shipping, a future in the shipping industry did not appear too promising for the newly licensed Captain Greenlaw. He decided, instead, to investigate the possibilities of a more viable future in the automobile repair business. With that in mind, he went to Detroit, Michigan, where he took an accelerated course at the Michigan State Automobile School. During the next several months, following graduation, he held a job as a garage helper, then a mechanic, and another job installing engines in Model T trucks, all paying no more than $35 a week, and from this salary he had to pay for room and board. Due to a lack of skill, financial constraints, and no real interest in these endeavors, Edwin returned to Massachusetts.

There, with a small capital investment, he decided to open a fish market. Unfortunately, what he discovered was that the business did very well on Thursdays and Fridays, but it was non-existent the rest of the week. Cutting and dressing 1,000 pounds of fish a week netted him a profit of $35. As Edwin put it, "I was not enthused with the fish business; it had not come up to my expectations." So, after several months, he took a 50 percent loss on his $1,000 capital investment, and with "no regrets for the lessons learned," he decided to return to New York and to seafaring, with renewed confidence and more determination.

# Resetting the Compass

## Life on the Oil Tankers: SS *Cedarhurst*

Late one afternoon, shortly after returning to New York, I was still without a job and dropped in at the Neptune Association, where membership consisted solely of shipmasters and deck officers, and where I also was a member. As I entered, the Secretary called out to me, asking if I would accept a Third Officer's position on a tanker. Despite the fact that I had no tanker experience, the Captain hired me on the spot. We departed New York for Tampico, Mexico, at 7:00 p.m. that evening.

The ship was the SS *Cedarhurst* and the master was Capt. Leslie Coffil from Cutler, Maine. It did not take me long during the voyage to familiarize myself with the many valves and pipelines. Our run was from Tampico, Mexico to either New York or Philadelphia. Upon our return to New York, the Second Officer resigned, and I was promoted. The next trip the Chief Officer resigned, and I was promoted again. How lucky can one be!

Just prior to the last voyage, Capt. Coffil was relieved of his command by Capt. Abraham Aasen. It was on that voyage that an accident happened while we were loading cargo in Port Arthur, Texas. It was always the Chief Officer's responsibility to supervise the final loading of the full cargo of oil, a delicate operation. An overflow of the tanks, if it did occur, would mean dismissal. It was a few minutes after midnight when Capt. Aasen returned from ashore and inquired about what I was doing at this late hour. I replied that I was in the final stages of loading the cargo and always attended to this matter, personally, fearing an oil spill. He said that was a "foolish idea" and ordered me to "turn over the final loading to the Second Officer who has had years of tanker experience." I carried out the Captain's instructions and told the Second Officer to watch the incoming cargo, which was rapidly approaching capacity in two tanks. I cautioned him and was told to "mind your own damn business," that it was now his responsibility. I could hear the oil rapidly filling the top of the tank. I remained apprehensive and watched from the upper deck. Again, I warned him. Suddenly, the hot oil shot out of the tanks to a height of six feet. The Second Officer shouted to the two men, standing by, to open the valves on a slack tank to relieve the pressure, but barrels of hot oil had already flowed under their feet causing them to fall into it; they were helpless. Meanwhile, I ran to the bridge and blew the signal to stop the pump in the refinery. By the time the flow could be stopped, the ship's afterdeck was covered with more than a foot of oil. The Captain rushed from his quarters, yelling, "What the hell is going on?" The crew were days cleaning up the oil spill, and it took two trips before the ship was clean and conditions back to normal. The Second Officer left the ship upon arrival in port. I had no further trouble with the Captain.

The recommendation written by Captain Aasen regarding Edwin's performance aboard the SS *Cedarhurst* reflected the renewed confidence he placed in Edwin following the oil spill incident and, in addition, rendered an unspoken apology as well. It read:

Philadelphia, Pa.

To Whom It May Concern:

This is to certify that the bearer, Edwin B. Greenlaw, has served under my command as Second Officer from February 15th, 1924 to March 9th, 1924. Also as Chief Officer from March 9th, 1924 to September 22, 1924.

During the time of Mr. Greenlaw's services in the above capacities, I have found him to be a most capable, energetic, and trustworthy gentleman and officer.

To say I can cheerfully and honestly recommend him as a Marine Officer gives me a chance to congratulate him on service well rendered.

Respectfully yours,

A. Aasen, Master

## SS *Vaba*

In September 1924 the *Cedarhurst* was placed in idle status, awaiting a new charter, alongside the SS *Vaba*, another ship owned by the Italian Steamship Company which had the same run to Tampico, Mexico, and back. Capt. Ferdinand Dohmann, Master of the SS *Vaba*, was a large man of stocky build who had the appearance of a wrestler. He had acquired considerable notoriety as a fighter and enjoyed the reputation of being a tough disciplinarian, so much so that he had a different Chief Officer each trip. One day he asked to see me. He told me that I had made a good reputation on the Cedarhurst and if I would agree to sail with him, he would let me run the ship. I declined his offer and told him my reason. However, Mr. Abatte, the Marine Superintendent, intervened. He asked me, as a favor, to make one trip with Capt. Dohmann and if I did not get along with the Captain, he would return me to my former position on the SS *Cedarhurst*, no questions asked. I sailed as Chief Officer with Capt. Dohmann for a period of thirteen months and found him to be a man of his word. He was a fine shipmaster, a tough disciplinarian, and we became the best of friends.

During this period, one incident stands out in my memory. I had been having considerable trouble with drunken crew members, making it necessary to hire a new crew in each American port, but with the same result. In addition, I was having difficulty keeping the men at work. As soon as my back was turned, they figured they were out of mind. On one trip, after leaving port with a new crew, only two members were fit for duty. Capt. Dohmann

# The Greenlaws of Sunset: Part II

asked me to accompany him to the crew's quarters. He grabbed each drunken seaman and beat him unmercifully. They were a bloody mess! The sight sickened me, but as I pulled him away from further activity, he said, "Mr. Greenlaw, you do not like to fight with your fists, but I love it!" The result was that this was the best crew I had for several trips. The men preferred assault and battery charges against the Captain, but he was exonerated and told not to use such drastic measures in the future.

Capt. Dohmann would fight anyone who challenged his authority. On another trip, one of the engine room oilers let it be known that he was an ex-prizefighter and could beat the Captain because the Captain lacked the science of fighting known to the professional. The Captain learned of the oiler's bragging and decided to challenge him. One day he entered the oiler's room and locked the door. Due to the close confinement, the ex-fighter could not maneuver and was beaten unmercifully. When it ended, Capt. Dohnman's statement to the rest of the crew was, "No man on this ship is better than me."

I enjoyed the time that I was employed on the oil tankers. They were clean and we had good living conditions. We loaded cargo in eight hours and discharged in eighteen, so it was seldom that I could leave the ship for a few hours and, certainly, it was not a life to be pursued by a married man with a family.

Tampico, Mexico was a rough, tough port in those days and I almost got shot twice when we were there. The Mexicans disliked the Americans and would not hesitate to draw a gun or to shoot if the occasion presented itself. General Villa, in charge of his insurgents, was reported to be encamped in the vicinity. The American oil field workers were a rough, tough crowd and would come into the district armed, looking for a big night. They were heavy drinkers and it did not take much to provoke a fight, either amongst themselves, or with the Mexicans.

## Going Yachting

It was in July 1925 when the two oil tankers, the SS *Cedarhurst* and the SS *Vaba*, were again in idle status, awaiting a charter. When the freight rates dropped to fifteen cents a barrel, the American Italian Steamship Company found it impossible to make a profit and decided to sell their two ships; the new owners provided their own crews.

After terminating his services with the American Italian Steamship Company, Edwin decided to seek a yachting position on one of the many large yachts. Supporting his decision were the facts that "salaries were in excess of those paid on the merchant ships, the life was better, and I wouldn't have drunken crews to contend with."

July, however, was the mid season of yachting and, despite placing several applications with yacht brokers and agencies, Edwin had received no results. It wasn't until he was walking down Park Avenue one afternoon that a chance stop at a power yacht showroom provided his next opportunity. During the remainder of the yachting season, he delivered small power yachts to their owners in New Jersey and New England.

### Motor Yacht *Dolphin*

In late February 1926, he returned to New York to seek employment, once again, and was hired by Captain Oscar Christensen, master of the large Motor Yacht *Dolphin*, owned by Mortimer L. Schiff, president of Kuhn, Loeb & Company, International Bankers and a founder of the Boy Scouts of America. *[See photo 6.7]*

According to William Fox (*Always Good Ships*, p. 186)

> The *Dolphin* was built at the Newport News Shipbuilding and Drydock Company and launched on April 8, 1922. Her specifications included a length of 180.82 feet, a beam width of 24 feet, and weight of 496 tons. She was powered by twin screw diesel engines and could attain a speed of 14.75 knots. Two months after the launch this "sleek new yacht," with her crew of 21, left Newport News for her owner's home at Oyster Bay, L.I., New York, where she spent six seasons with Mr. Schiff.

*6.7 The motor yacht Dolphin, owned by Mortimer Schiff, president of Kuhn Loeb & Co., international bankers. Edwin served as Chief Officer for two yachting seasons, 1926 and 1927. Collection of Barbara L. Britton*

Edwin served as the Chief Officer of "this fine yacht" during the 1926 and 1927 yachting seasons. Although he thoroughly enjoyed his time on the *Dolphin*, he felt that employment on larger yachts would enhance his reputation.

> During my final days on the Motor Yacht *Dolphin* I learned that the largest yacht under American registry, the Steam Yacht *Corsair* owned by Mr. J.P. Morgan, the New York banker, was seeking the services of a Chief Officer. I applied for the position and was accepted. The master of the yacht, Capt. W.B. Porter, had the reputation of being a very difficult man with the result that he could not keep a Chief Officer in his employ for long. My feelings were that if I could remain on the *Corsair* for a year, I would be well-known and established in the yachting business. Capt. Porter had been in the Morgan employ for twenty-nine years. He was a loner and played solitaire, in his quarters, for hours. He was autocratic and overbearing and I learned to keep away from him as much as possible.

Captain Porter appears to have exemplified Captain Richard Philips' contention that many mariners "…simply lose the desire to return to their lives on land and just disappear." (Chapter 4). Edwin continues:

> I joined the *Corsair* as Chief Officer on October 6, 1927. She carried a crew of sixty people, and preparations were being made for a Mediterranean Cruise during the approaching winter months.
>
> On December 17, I married and, with my wife, spent a few days with my Mother in Maine. On February 1st, my wife sailed for Oslo, Norway on the SS *Bergensfjord* for a visit with her parents. *[See photo 6.8]*
>
> On February 7th, the *Corsair* departed New York for Bizerte, North Africa, remaining there for two months, before proceeding to Venice, Italy where the owner and his guests joined the ship. The guests were all royalty, Lords and Dukes with their wives and attendants. The winter was spent cruising the Italian, Albanian, Yugoslavian, Greek, and Turkish waters, visiting the various ports of these countries, and the many islands of the Greek Archipelago. We returned to New York in April and spent the summer in short cruises along the New England coast; our final trip was to Bar Harbor, Maine.
>
> I tendered my resignation in August, as the vessel was to be decommissioned and the time I had served had not

*6.8 Edwin married Ada Jacobsen on December 17, 1927, and took her to visit his mother in Sunset a few days later. Collection of Barbara L. Britton*

> been a happy one. The Captain was very complimentary regarding abilities and performance, and recommended me for a future command.

From what Edwin has written thus far, it is obvious that employment on merchant ships, the workhorses of the commercial fleet, was dependent on the financial vagaries of the economy. On the other hand, wealthy yacht owners appeared to have sufficient reserves to insulate themselves against financial downturns (noted in Chapter 4). Owners, like *Corsair*'s J.P. Morgan, took their yachts to tropical climates in the winter and cruised the Atlantic seaboard in the summer, while still others, like E. W. Scripps on *Mirimichi* and W. Wallace Near on *Kallisto*, took extensive trips around the world. For yachting of this magnitude, a full crew was required year-round and an equally large financial investment.

In the past, as a single man, Edwin returned home to Deer Isle for a couple of months when employment stalled on the commercial ships. Even on the small Greenlaw farm, there was always work that needed to be done. Now, as a married man in Brooklyn, New York, where he and his wife had set up housekeeping in an apartment, Edwin found it difficult to be without a job or have productive work to do during the fall and winter months. As a result he sought even short-term employment until the yachting season began in the early spring. Edwin picks up the story: *[See photos 6.9 and 6.10]*

> To my surprise, I was offered the position of Third Officer on the freighter SS *Guayaquil* at the Panama Railroad Steam Ship Company, the first company to which I applied. The next day we sailed for Haiti, Panama and Columbia. The Master was Capt. Spurr, a most eccentric and neurotic man who hated his crew as much as they disliked him. As might be expected, I clashed with him on my first bridge watch leaving New York and he never spoke to me again during the two trips I made with him on this vessel, from New York to Panama and return. After I resigned from the *Guayaquil* and after my departure, I was told by Mr. Erickson, the Chief Officer, that Capt. Spurr had said I was outstanding as a Third Officer and if he had known of my abilities, he would have treated me differently. I later learned that he was relieved of his command.

## Steam Yacht *Saelmoe*

> It was the latter part of January, 1929 when I terminated my service on the S.S. *Guayaquil*. A few days later I learned that Capt. Alfred Nagle, Master of the Steam Yacht *Saelmoe*, owned by Mr. William H. Todd, the shipbuilder, was awaiting my return and wanted to see me. I met with Capt. Nagle, who appointed me Chief Officer on February 1, 1929. *[See photo 6.11]* I served continuously in this capacity until May, 1932 when Mr. Todd suddenly passed away. My three years on this vessel were pleasant. The yacht was laid up for six

*6.9, 6.10 Caroline, Edwin's mother, pays a visit to Edwin and Ada in their Brooklyn, N.Y. apartment in 1928. Collection of Barbara L. Britton*

*6.11 Captain Edwin Greenlaw aboard the steam yacht Saelmo, owned by William H. Todd, where he served as Chief Officer for three years, 1929-1932. Collection of Barbara L. Britton*

months of the year, but I was paid an annual salary and was at home daily. Those of us who were members of the skeleton crew during the winter received three dollars per day subsistence in addition to our salaries. During the summer months, the yacht was used for entertaining business representatives, making short trips around New York and adjacent waters. *[See photo 6.12]*

During this period, my daughter, Sonya, was born. I was a very happy man, as I had hoped so much for a daughter.

The often negative environment in which Edwin found himself aboard the commercial freighters contrasted sharply with the environment he enjoyed on the steam and motor yachts of the wealthy. Apparent in Edwin's reflections are the close and easy relationships he established with the yacht owners which extended, in some cases, to lifelong friendships. One wonders, sometimes, how these transitions were so deftly handled with ease and grace. It is, after all, the character of the man that speaks the same language in all situations, which makes it possible. Edwin continues:

## Motor Yacht *Memory III*

On July 1, 1932, the Motor Yacht *Memory III* was sold to a Canadian industrialist, W. Wallace Near from Toronto, Canada. I applied for the position as Master of his beautiful vessel, but the owner refused the salary I requested and the number of crew members I wanted to efficiently operate the vessel. He appointed a Captain who lacked the experience for one-half the salary I had requested and a minimal crew. The yacht

*6.12 SY Saelmo (ex.Nokomis, Naswind [SP-1233]). Sold in 1921 to William H. Todd, the yacht Nokomis was renamed for his mother, Sarah Elizabeth Moody. Courtesy of Naval Historical Foundation*

departed New York for Nova Scotia but grounded on the rocky shores of Block Island. After several days in a Boston shipyard for repair of bottom damage, the yacht proceeded to Nova Scotia but, unfortunately, collided with a bridge there, doing further damage.

Mr. Near then phoned me and asked me to come to Nova Scotia, take command, and return with the yacht to New York. He agreed to the terms I had previously submitted and I was appointed Captain of the *Memory III*. Upon my return to New York, I discharged the entire crew. The yacht was one of the most beautiful, but it had a reputation concerning frequent breakdowns of the machinery. If possible, I wanted to remedy this situation. I contacted the builders of the engine who recommended a competent Chief Engineer and we encountered no further difficulty. The yacht was outfitted with all kinds of electronic equipment, such as gyros and an automatic pilot. Fortunately, I had previously attended the Sperry Gyro School for instruction in the operation and care of this equipment. With a crew of sixteen, we cruised the Caribbean during the winter months, visiting all the prominent islands, but returned to New York for temporary layup during late spring; we berthed in Troy, New York. *[See photo 6.13]*

*6.13 Captain Edwin Greenlaw, with a crew of sixteen aboard Memory III, cruised the Caribbean with owner, W. Wallace Near and his wife during the winter months of 1933. Courtesy of Alynn Prill, Edwin's granddaughter*

During my final summer as Master of *Memory III*, she was chartered for a month to Mr. J.W.Y. Martin of Baltimore, Maryland. Mr. Martin had just arrived at his twenty-first birthday and had inherited five million dollars and a stable of race horses. He arrived on board with ten guests, nearly all were teenagers or in their early twenties. He changed this entourage with another ten guests every ten days of the

*6.14 SY Kallisto (ex. Miramichi, Ohio) owned by W. Wallace Near, Canadian industrialist, who placed her under British registry. Collection of Barbara L. Britton*

monthly charter. Mr. Martin was very unreasonable and we had frequent disagreements. We cruised the New England coast from New York to Bar Harbor, Maine. It was a great relief to me when this charter was terminated. My second winter with Mr. Near was spent cruising in the Caribbean and Florida waters, after which we returned to New York for layup.

## Motor Yacht *Kallisto*

Mr. Near decided to sell the *Memory III* but, at the same time, he purchased the Motor Yacht *Mirimichi* (ex. *Ohio*) which was idle in Jacksonville, Florida. When Mr. Near took ownership of the yacht, he changed its name to *Kallisto* and its registry from American to British. It was originally built for Mr. E.W. Scripps, owner of the Scripps Howard Newspapers, who died on board and was buried at sea off the African coast. This yacht was 185 feet long and had twice been around the world. It was a fine seagoing vessel, which had a cruising radius of ten thousand miles without refueling, and carried a crew of thirty persons. *[See photo 6.14]*

After several weeks preparing for the winter cruise, we proceeded to the Island of Nevis, British West Indies where the owner and his party met us. We spent the winter off the coast of Panama visiting the famous Cocos Islands, the Pearl Islands in the Pacific, the Galapagos Islands and the countries of Ecuador, Columbia and Panama. Returning through the Panama Canal, we spent several days among the San Blas Indians who live in thatched huts on small islands In the Gulf of Panama. The tribe is ruled by a Chief who had several wives. They make their own laws and punish those who refuse to obey. Small in stature, they live entirely unto themselves and do not marry outside of the tribe. From my observation, the women did all the work and the men, who are fine seamen, spent the day sailing or fishing from their dugout canoes. Some of the women came on board the yacht, bedecked in their native costumes, with hammered gold rings in their noses and plates of gold suspended from their ears. I carried on a long conversation with the Chief, using an interpreter, and was invited to join him for lunch. I, diplomatically,

# The Greenlaws of Sunset: Part II

*6.15 Edwin enjoys a "Crossing the Equator" ceremony with Canadian industrialist W. Wallace Near as King Neptune and Mrs. Near as his queen. On this trip in 1935, the yacht visited twelve foreign countries and cruised 14,000 miles. Later, Edwin asserted, "It had been a perfect voyage." Collection of Barbara L. Britton*

declined his gracious invitation. We had a professional camera man on board with us, who recorded their activities and culture. *[See photo 6.15]*

From the Gulf of San Blas we proceeded to the Island of Jamaica, a very beautiful island, where we spent several days stopping at every port. Our next port of call was Santo Domingo. Upon entering the harbor we were surrounded by two boat loads of soldiers, armed with machine guns, who boarded the yacht and stationed themselves in different parts of the vessel. A General, accompanied by his Aide, came on board and, as I could not converse in Spanish, he sent ashore for an interpreter. The British Minister in charge of Foreign Affairs officiated as the interpreter and I was introduced to the Commander of the Santo Domingo Army. The General informed me that it was fortunate the Fort had not fired a shot across my bow when we entered the harbor as, from all appearances, we were an armed raider with insurrectionists ready to capture the port. I had forgotten that a one pound cannon was mounted on the fore part of the vessel. It was covered with a canvas cover and I had never had it removed, considering it merely ornamental. It was installed at the time the vessel was built and was only to be used for protection in case of attack by pirates in Chinese waters. After a half hour of explanation and negotiation with the General, he recalled his troops and departed ashore. He apologized for any inconvenience or alarm they may have caused but, as he said, "they always had to be on alert for any revolution in their country."

We remained five days in Santo Domingo and were treated with every courtesy. Departing Santo Domingo, we called at several Cuban ports, then to Charleston, S.C. where the owner and his guests left the ship and the *Kallisto* proceeded to New York for layup. We had visited twelve foreign countries and had cruised 14,000 miles. It was the most perfect voyage of my entire career!

It was May, 1935 when we arrived in New York. A couple of weeks later, I received a telegram from Mr. Near's secretary informing me that he had undergone an operation and had passed away. I was deeply saddened by this sudden turn of events and realized that it was but a question of time before the *Kallisto* would be sold. Ultimately, it was acquired by the Brazilian Navy to be used as a training ship.

*6.16 Steam yacht Maria Delores, largest luxury yacht in Texas, owed by Clifford Mooers, president and owner of Shasta Oil Company, 1935. Mr. Mooers and his family made it their home for two years. Collection of Barbara L. Britton*

## Steam Yacht *Maria Delores*

On the first of July, 1935 I was informed that a Captain's position was available on the yacht *Maria Delores* (ex. *Ajax*) berthed in Miami, Florida. I contacted the owner, was hired, and instructed to proceed to Miami and prepare the yacht for a winter cruise. The yacht was owned by Mr. Clifford Mooers, president and owner of the Shasta Oil Company, who with his wife and little daughter arrived on board in early September. The yacht was the largest and most luxurious yacht in Texas and was used, principally, in cruising the Caribbean and the waters off the Florida and Texas coasts; we carried a crew of twelve. *[See photo 6.16]*

Mr. Mooers and his family made the yacht their home, living on board for two years; Houston, Texas was our headquarters. In March, 1937 the *Maria Delores* was sold and I delivered the yacht to her new owner in Los Angeles, California. I must comment that Mr. Mooers proved to be the best yacht owner that I worked for. He was more a friend than an employer and, for years, he and Mrs. Mooers kept in contact with me by telephone or letter. *[See photos 6.17, 6.18 and 6.19]*

## Yacht *Islamorada*

Upon my return to New York, I learned that Mr. John D. Reilly, president of the Todd Shipyards Corporation, had chartered a 90' houseboat cruiser and had inquired if I would consider the command. After contacting Mr. Reilly, I was hired, and took charge of the yacht, *Islamorada*. During the ensuing summer months, we cruised Long Island Sound and the waters of Chesapeake Bay. On October 17th, while in the vicinity of Baltimore, I received the sad news that my Mother had passed away. Mr. Reilly hired a temporary Captain for the few days I was absent to attend the services. Soon, thereafter, we returned to New York and delivered the yacht to its owner.

6.17 Celebrating Christmas, 1936, aboard the SS Maria Delores. Seated (left to right) Clifford Mooers, owner; Maria Delores, his daughter; and Mrs. Mooers (far right); Captain Edwin Greenlaw (second row, right). The governess is in the foreground. Collection of Barbara L. Britton

6.18 Maria Delores Mooers enjoys her gifts under the Christmas tree. Collection of Barbara L. Britton

6.19 Captain Greenlaw gets ready to carve the turkey for the crew. Collection of Barbara L. Britton

*6.20 SS Washington, United States Lines, a transatlantic luxury liner, built at New York Shipbuilding in Camden, New Jersey, in 1933. During World War II, she served in the U.S. Navy as the troopship USS Mount Vernon. Courtesy of Steamship Historical Society*

## Coming Ashore

October, 1937 - It was at this time that Mr. Reilly asked if I would be interested in a position that was becoming vacant in Todd Shipyards Corporation, if I thought I could adapt to a shore position. I informed him that I would not consider a desk job. With that understanding I entered the employ of the Todd Corporation.

During my first year, I was sent to London via one of the luxurious passenger ships, as airplanes had not been developed for transatlantic crossings at the time. I represented the Company in Holland at the beginning of World War II, over a period of three months, but was forced to return home due to the invasion of the German Army. *[See photos 6.20 and 6.21]*

I served the Todd Shipyards Corporation in several capacities during a period of twenty-six years, until I reached retirement age on August 2, 1964. I believe in the

*6.21 Employed as a commercial representative for Todd Shipyards, Edwin was sent to London aboard the SS Washington in 1938. Collection of Barbara L. Britton*

*6.22 The cargo ship Haparangi, owned by Peninsular and Oriental Steam Navigation Company of New Zealand, was built by John Brown Clydebank Shipyards in Scotland. Although Haparangi was strictly a cargo vessel, occasionally she would take "passengers," signed on articles as supernumerary crew. For all intents and purposes, such people were passengers, even though officially they were not. Courtesy of Victor H. Young*

mandatory retirement age of sixty-five years, providing a person survives the stress of our economic and social environment. *[See photos 6.22 and 6.23]*

Since my retirement I have enjoyed communing with nature, watching the birds and the animals in the forest, and I have seen how so many of their habits and traits can be compared to man. Take a walk in the forest or along a deserted beach observing nature, and one will be as close to God as anyone will ever get. Everything in nature is balanced by some Unknown Power.

I believe in the Ten Commandments and that right is right and wrong is wrong, without any in between. People have to have some belief and require a need for spiritual guidance. I believe that whether or not it is revealed, the need is inherent. All religions, regardless of sect, are for the good of the people of that faith.

```
M.V.Haparangi.                              18/2/58.

                    LUNCHEON.

                Creme of Mushroom.

            Curried Prawns au Patna Rice.

                Delice of Turbut Mornay.

                Vol-au-Vent a la Reine.

                    Hawaiian Steak.

        Potatoes, Noisette,  Chateau.

                Sliced Beans au Beurre.

                    Annas Jamaique.

    N.Z.Cheddar, Danish Blue, Processed, Biscuits.

            Saint-Estephe.  Gonzalez Dry Sherry.

                Kummel Liquor.   Coffee.
```

*6.23 In 1958, Edwin traveled on business for Todd Shipyards aboard the New Zealand cargo liner Haparangi. The detailed menu attests to the excellent food, steward service and high standards enjoyed by the ship's officers and supernumeraries who dined in the officers' saloon. Collection of Barbara L. Britton*

*6.24 Reunion in Sunset, 1970. Left to right, Kenn, Lillian and Edwin Greenlaw. When Kenn came home for a visit to Deer Isle, time spent together was cherished and celebrated as a special event. Collection of Barbara L. Britton*

In spite of our many troubles in the present day, I would not advocate a return to the time that is so often referred to as "the good old days." We cannot live in the past. History repeats itself, but we cannot learn from past history. We have to experience life; we have to live it.

In retirement, Captain Edwin B. Greenlaw returned to Deer Isle, Maine, where he purchased property in Sunset and built a modular home, just a mile down the road from his birthplace. He died on September 4, 1991, and, at his request, his ashes were strewn on the waters of Penobscot Bay. *[See photo 6.24]*

# Chapter 7: The Greenlaws of Sunset: An In-depth Look at a Yachting Family, Captain Kenneth N. Greenlaw

*To you who answered the call of your country and served in its Merchant Marine to bring about the total defeat of the enemy, I extend the heartfelt thanks of the Nation. You undertook a most severe task—one which called for courage and fortitude. Because you demonstrated the resourcefulness and calm judgment necessary to carry out that task, we now look to you for leadership and example in further serving our country in peace.*

President Harry S. Truman, White House, 1945.

## The Early Years: Growing Up on Deer Isle

Kenneth Nelson Greenlaw enjoyed a childhood much like the one described earlier by Edwin, his older brother; he was the youngest of Edward and Caroline Greenlaw's three children, born on September 27, 1906. However, Kenn's childhood differed from Edwin's; he had a built-in playmate. With his sister, Lillian, only eighteen months older, Kenn had someone with whom he could share activities, games and childhood secrets. Even their father mentioned the close relationship in a letter written to his daughter, Lillian, from Naponset in 1915; Kenn and Lillian grew up, as siblings, with a warm affection for one another. *[See photo 7.1]*

For young children like Kenn, the rhythm of life on Deer Isle revolved around the home, the school and the church. Since the family owned neither a horse nor a vehicle of any kind, activity was constricted by what was available within walking distance. Home was a comfortable and pleasant place. Although his mother and father believed that discipline was necessary to mold and strengthen the character of their children, they were loving parents. Work was expected to be shared by each member of the family, no matter how young. Kenn remembered that "gathering the eggs and bringing in kindling to start the fire in the stove for breakfast" were two of his chores at the ages of 5 or 6.

Besides their parents, the children in the Greenlaw household had a dear and loving friend in Aunt Mary, who doted on each of them and loved them as her own. She was Caroline's closest friend. Both had been employed by the same family in Pittsburgh, and when Mary retired, she came to live with the Greenlaw family. Mary and Caroline spoke German when they conversed, except when Edward was home, and the children were taught to speak German as well. The year was 1912 when Kenn started school in Sunset at the age of 6. Because he spoke German, some of the older boys called him "the Kaiser's little soldier." He later commented that perhaps it was the teasing or his personal conflict in learning two languages that caused him to stammer during that first year in school. By the time he turned 7, to Kenn's great relief, the stammer disappeared and the teasing was over.

Although the Greenlaw family was far from wealthy, they were comfortable. Like other families on the Island, they practiced frugality as a way of life. Socks were darned and clothing mended or remade as the children grew. Caroline's ability as a seamstress, and her early opportunities for education and travel, gave her clothes and the children's clothes a flair for fashion. Even the beautiful beige wool dress and cape lined in bright pink silk, which she made as her going-away costume when she married Edward, was kept and the seams carefully let out when she became pregnant. Other dresses in her trousseau were similarly redesigned as the need arose.

*7.1 Kenn and his sister, Lillian, holding a beautiful life-size doll with porcelain face and golden curls, a gift from Aunt Mary, ca. 1914. Collection of Barbara L.Britton*

*7.2 McKinley High School, Deer Isle, Class of 1925. Kenn is standing, top row, left. Collection of Barbara L. Britton*

A large garden was planted each year so that fresh produce could be eaten during the summer and vegetables canned in the fall. Berries were made into jelly and jam; sap for maple syrup was tapped from the trees; and apples and root vegetables were stored for the winter months. Chickens and a pig or two were kept for meat, while eggs were used by the family or shipped for sale to Boston. Nothing was wasted.

Kenn's father, Captain G. Edward Greenlaw, was a Master of sail yachts and, for many years, had been employed by wealthy yacht owners in the Boston area. In the fall of 1916, he had come home to Deer Isle, planning to retire but, unexpectedly, he became very ill and died on October 19th. It was a life-changing event for the entire family; Kenn was just 10 years old.

His brother, Edwin, dropped out of high school and went to work digging clams to put food on the table and contribute to the family's financial resources. To increase the family's egg business, his mother added a dozen laying hens to those she already had. More eggs had to be collected, chickens fed and hen houses kept clean. Kenn had to take on additional chores and assume more responsibility. His daughter remembers him saying that the thing he hated most was cleaning the chicken coops.

Despite some financial hardships during the next

# The Greenlaws of Sunset: Part III

*7.3 Steam yacht, Cythera (ex. Agawa), designed by Cox & King, built by Ramage & Ferguson in Leith, Scotland, 1907. Collection of Barbara L. Britton*

*7.4 Kenn, an Able Seaman aboard Cythera on his 21st birthday, September 27, 1927. Collection of Barbara L. Britton*

few years, Kenn completed his education and graduated from McKinley High School in Deer Isle, Class of 1925. *[See photo 7.2]* His sister, Lillian, had graduated in the Class of 1924 and was taking the two-year program at Farmington Normal School, preparatory to becoming a teacher. Kenn worked any number of jobs on the Island for the next two years after graduation, but with limited success. He wanted a more promising future with better pay and greater opportunities. After several talks with friends of his father whom he respected, and communication with Edwin, he decided that, like his father and brother before him, "yachting" would provide the career advantages he was seeking.

## Going Yachting

In the spring of 1927, Kenn began his yachting career as an Able Seaman on the Steam Yacht *Cythera*, (ex-*Agawa*), owned by William L. Harkness of New York. The 215-foot *Cythera* was designed by Cox and King, launched by the Ramage and Ferguson Shipyards in Leith, Scotland, on September 20, 1906, and sponsored by Mrs. C. W. Harkness. Built with a steel hull, *Cythera*'s specifications included a gross weight of 602 tons, a beam measuring 25.5 feet, a draft of 12 feet, and a nautical speed of 12 knots. Newspaper articles at the time described her cabins as "elegant" and her hull lines as "graceful." *[See photo 7.3]*

For the next decade, she was in service as a private yacht and her name was changed from *Agawa* to *Cythera*. Soon, with the onset of World War I, she joined the ranks as one of the U.S. Navy's fighting ships. In his article "Overdue Atlantic—USS *Cythera* (PY 26)," Robert P. Sables provides interesting details about *Cythera*'s service as USS *Cythera* (SP 575) in World War I. He writes: *[See photo 7.4]*

> Shortly after the United States entered World War I on April 6, 1917, William L. Harkness, New York City, a renowned "oil baron" with heavy investments in Standard Oil, leased the *Cythera* for $1 to the U.S. Navy to be used as a patrol vessel. Her gleaming white hull soon gave way to a painted black and white camouflage pattern. After refit, she was placed in commission on October 20, 1917. Sailing from New York on October 27, 1917, *Cythera* arrived at Newport the next day and was assigned to Patrol Force, Atlantic Fleet. Her first commanding officer was

*7.5 USS Cythera (SP 575) in camouflage, serving as a patrol vessel during World War I, 1917-18. Collection of Barbara L. Britton*

Lt. Cdr. Walter G. Roper, a Georgia native, who would later be awarded the Navy Cross for his wartime service. Her second CO, Captain Raymond Jack, USCG, would also receive the same award. *[See photo 7.5]*

On November 1, 1917, the USS *Cythera* (SP 575) departed Newport, Rhode Island, with her squadron for Gibraltar, on the first leg of a journey escorting submarine chasers and other patrol vessels across the Atlantic. Stopping in Bermuda and the Azores while en route, she towed the USS *Margaret* (SP 527) who had suffered several mishaps, and arrived at Gibraltar a few days before the end of the year. Based at Gibraltar during the rest of the war, *Cythera* was employed on escort and patrol missions in the western Mediterranean, encountering enemy submarine activity on at least two occasions. On May 27, 1918, while she was escorting a convoy from Bizerte to Gibraltar, two ships of the convoy were torpedoed. *Cythera* rescued 35 survivors of SS *Ariel* and dropped depth charges. On another occasion, October 3, 1918, en route from Genoa to Gibraltar, SS *Uganda* was torpedoed. *Cythera* searched for the submarine and rescued the crew of the stricken ship, arriving safely at Gibraltar later that month. In December 1918, several weeks after the Armistice ended the fighting, *Cythera* left Gibraltar for home. Arriving at New York City on February 5, 1919, she was decommissioned in mid-March and returned to her owner, William L. Harkness. He died just two months later on May 10, 1919, leaving the *Cythera* to his wife, Edith Hale Harkness of Glen Cove, Long Island, New York.

When Kenn returned home to the Island after his first year of yachting on the *Cythera*, in the fall of 1927, he was introduced to Lyndell Stinson, the new teacher at Sunset Grammar School, the one-room school house in the village. Born on January 20, 1910, she was the eldest child of Harold J. and Edith Belle (Weed) Stinson of Stonington. Like the Greenlaws, her ancestor Thomas Stinson and his family had come early to Deer Isle; they settled in 1765 on what came to be known as Stinson's Neck, on Southeast Harbor. *[See photo 7.6 and 7.7]*

During the next year, Kenneth and Lyndell "kept company," and by Christmas of 1928 they were engaged. They were married by the Rev. Frank

# The Greenlaws of Sunset: Part III

*7.6, 7.7 Just married! Lyndell and Kenn Greenlaw aboard the steamer J.T. Morse, bound for Rockland, October 30, 1929. Collection of Barbara L. Britton*

Judkins in the parsonage next to the Deer Isle Congregational Church on October 30, 1929, Caroline's 65th birthday. The ceremony took place at 11 a.m. to allow ample time, immediately following the ceremony, to get to the landing and catch the boat to Rockland for a brief honeymoon. On their return, they moved into the Greenlaw family home in Sunset. They were needed to continue providing both the financial and physical support necessary for the household and to assist in caring for two aging women, Kenn's mother, Caroline, who now suffered with diabetes at age 65, and Aunt Mary, who was 79.

It wasn't long before the first of Kenn and Lyndell's three children was born, Barbara Lillian on October 2, 1930, followed by Kenneth Nelson Jr. on October 8, 1931. With Kenn away yachting on the *Cythera* from April to October and his return to the Island each fall to seek winter employment, a similar pattern of family life continued for Kenn's young family as it had for his father and mother, Edward and Caroline. *[See photo 7.8]*

During the summers of 1928 and 1929, Kenn was employed on the *Cythera* as Port Launchman, and when new duties were assigned in 1930, he was promoted to Quartermaster. His recommendation for that time period read:

> To Whom It May Concern:
> October 27, 1930
>
> New London, Conn.
>
> This is to say that Kenneth Greenlaw served on Yacht *Cythera* as Port Launchman from April 1st, 1930 until October 27th, 1930. During that time I found him honest, sober, always willing to work and I highly recommend him to anybody that may need a good man. He also took turns on a long run as Quartermaster, and I found him a good man at the wheel. Greenlaw was Port Launchman last year also for the same length of time.
> Walter D. Weed, (Signed) Chief, Yacht *Cythera* *[See photos 7.9 and 7.10]*

*7.8 Lyndell with her two children, Barbara and Kenneth Jr., 1931. Collection of Barbara L. Britton*

*7.9 Port Launch of the Cythera at full speed in Glen Cove, Long Island; Kenn Greenlaw at the wheel, 1928. Collection of Barbara L. Britton*

*7.10 Kenn, Quartermaster, standing on the bridge next to the wheel and binnacle, 1931. Collection of Barbara L. Britton*

*7.11 One of the seven lift locks on the Welland Canal system. Taken by Kenn Greenlaw. Collection of Barbara L. Britton*

# Trip to the Great Lakes and Canada

For the enjoyment and pleasure of the Harkness family and their guests, the Cythera cruised primarily along the Atlantic coast from North Carolina to Bar Harbor, Maine, but in 1931, Mrs. Harkness, with family and friends aboard, took *Cythera* on an extended trip to the Great Lakes and Canada. Black and white snapshots in Kenn's family album highlighted *Cythera*'s trip up the St. Lawrence River to the Great Lakes, from Lake Ontario to Lake Erie through the Welland Canal, with visits to the beautiful cities of Quebec and Montreal in Canada. *[See photos 7.11, 7.12]*

The Welland Canal System, one of the outstanding engineering feats of the 20th century, is about 27 miles in length and includes seven lift locks and one guard lock. The system allows ships to bypass Niagara Falls and moves vessels up the Niagara Escarpment through this series of locks from Lake Ontario to Lake Erie, to account for a difference in water levels of up to 326.5'; it takes 11 hours for a vessel to traverse the canal. *(Welland Canal, Wikipedia)*

Over a dozen individual snapshots of the Welland Canal and the working of its locks, carefully placed in the family album with descriptive captions, attest to Kenn's keen interest in this engineering marvel. *[See photo 7.13]*

*7.12 Mrs. Harkness, with family and friends, took the Cythera on a cruise to the Great Lakes, Montreal and Quebec via the Welland Canal in 1931. Collection of Barbara L. Britton*

*7.13 Guests of Cythera's owner, Mrs. Edith Hale Harkness, on an outing aboard the yacht, ca. 1933. Collection of Barbara L. Britton*

# The America's Cup Races in 1934

No photographs in the family album, however, are more significant than the ones highlighting the America's Cup Yacht Race in 1934 between Great Britain's yacht, *Endeavour*, sponsored by the Royal Yacht Squadron and America's yacht, *Rainbow*, sponsored by the New York Yacht Club. The 1934 race was exciting, dramatic and highly unusual. It was unusual because it pitted the skill of two millionaire yacht owners, Harold Vanderbilt and Thomas Octave Murdoch Sopwith, against each other at the helms of their respective yachts. As sportsmen, each had concentrated on yacht racing and acquired superb skill as amateur helmsmen. Each was, indeed, the "captain" of his fate!

From its beginning in 1851, the international yacht race that came to be known as America's Cup was the sporting event of millionaire yachtsmen. A competition between the rivals of two countries, it tested the excellence of boat and sail design with the extraordinary skill of captain and crew. Such an event attracted enormous interest from the spectators who crowded the shore, but no more than those in seagoing vessels, large and small. The spectator craft, which included hired tugs, ferryboats and other excursion vessels, sought to get the best vantage point and positioned themselves as "close to the action" as possible. So crowded did the race course become that patrol craft had to be sent out to keep order and prevent vessels from intruding into the lanes of the prescribed course.

This period of sail yacht history coincided with the "golden age" of steam yachts. Beautiful, elegant and palatial in every respect, the steam yachts were quite literally "queens of the sea." Their millionaire owners sought every opportunity to show them off, and what better environment than the fashionable mecca of yachtsmen and socialites found at the America's Cup races! Family members and guests were invited aboard these floating palaces for lavish parties and front row seats at the yacht races. In 1934, it was Newport, Rhode Island.

Like so many other yachts, *Cythera* made her way to Newport. Kenn Greenlaw, the quartermaster, carried with him a small Kodak camera and from the deck of *Cythera* took snapshots of other beautiful steam yachts in the vicinity—*Corsair, Kallisto, Eulanie II, Charlinia, Hussar* and *"Old" Caroline*. *[See photos 7.14 through 7.19]*

The snapshot that stood out, however, was the one Kenn took during the race itself. From the book *The Racing Yachts*, we must first recap the exciting elements of this 1934 Cup competition:

> To win the Cup, the two yachts were to compete in six races. The first race on September 15th somewhat relieved the defenders' anxiety. In shifting light breezes. *Rainbow* took the lead from *Endeavour*. Then the breezes died to a near calm, and the race was called off. (But not before the captain of the U.S. destroyer *Manley*, pressing too close to the yachts in order to accommodate newsreel cameramen aboard, received a tart query from another spectator craft, financier Vincent Astor's steam yacht *Nourmahal*: "Are you challenging *Endeavour*?" The signal came from the destroyer captain's Commander in Chief, President Franklin D. Roosevelt, who was Astor's guest that day.)

> The first race was finally completed on September 17th. It was windy, *Endeavour* weather, and *Rainbow*, plagued by foul-ups and accidents to her spinnaker, lost by two minutes nine seconds. To the Americans' consternation, *Endeavour* won again the next day. In fact, she led all the way in a windy, three-hour-nine-minute race, the fastest one thus far in the history of Cup competition. It looked as if this time the Cup really would go back to England. There was no doubt that *Endeavour* was the fastest boat, whether beating to windward or running downwind.

> After the first two races put *Endeavour* two up, New York bookmakers were giving 2-to-1 odds that *Endeavour*

# The Greenlaws of Sunset: Part III

would win. The third race took on an air of more excitement and suspense than any previous contest in America's Cup competition.

It was a two-leg race: 15 miles out to the stake before the wind and then back against the wind. *Endeavour* took off on the first leg well in the lead. *Rainbow*'s crew could not get her troublesome spinnaker to set well and *Endeavour* increased her lead. By the time she reached the mark, 15 miles from the starting line, she led by a commanding 6 minutes 39 seconds. But on the homeward leg, *Endeavour* turned to starboard to escape a soft spot, then tacked back so close to *Rainbow* that the air bouncing off the American's sails backwinded the challenger. *Endeavour* tacked twice more to get clear, but by then *Rainbow* had a commanding lead and went on to win by 3 minutes 26 seconds. *[See photo 7.20]*

The series now stood at two to one in favor of the challenger *Endeavour*. But that race had altered the momentum of the series. Vanderbilt was barely ashore before he was on the phone to Frank Paine, a genius of the spinnaker, asking him to bring his best spinnaker to Newport and join *Rainbow*'s crew. Paine drove through the night to Newport. Next day was a lay day to give the contending yachtsmen a chance to rest,

*7.14 and 7.15. Snapshots of two luxury yachts at the America's Cup Races taken by Kenn Greenlaw from the deck of Cythera: Corsair with Britain's racing yacht Endeavour on the left (above); below is SY Charlinia. Collection of Barbara L. Britton*

*7.16, 7.17 and 7.18 Snapshots of three other luxury yachts at the 1934 America's Cup Races taken by Kenn Greenlaw from the deck of the Cythera: "Old" Caroline (16); Kallisto (17); Hussar (18). Collection of Barbara L. Britton*

# The Greenlaws of Sunset: Part III

*7.19 SY Eulanie, another spectator in the 1934 America's Cup Race, photographed by Kenn Greenlaw from Cythera. Collection of Barbara L. Britton*

but Vanderbilt and Paine used it to rerig *Rainbow* and increase her ballast. By the fourth race, *Rainbow* was ready with a much better behaved spinnaker.

The rest was anticlimax. *Rainbow* won the three final contests closely but conclusively. Yachtsmen on both sides of the ocean agreed that the better boat had lost because of the more skillful helmsmanship of the defenders. On his arrival home in England, Charles Nicholson, designer of *Endeavour*, could not resist saying: "I have learned for the first time that the fastest yacht does not win the race."

In this description, one sentence highlights the lead *Endeavour* held as she rounded the mark: "*Endeavour* increased her lead. By the time she reached the mark, 15 miles from the starting line, she led by a commanding 6 minutes 39 seconds." Now we can take a look at Kenn Greenlaw's snapshot. On the back of the photo, in his handwriting, we read:

"*Endeavour* ahead. *Rainbow* behind. *Endeavour* has just passed the 15 mile buoy."

In the photo, to the left we can see the buoy and in the distance, heading back against the wind, is *Endeavour*, while in the forefront, coming up on the buoy, is *Rainbow*. Truly, an historic photograph!

*7.20 "Endeavor ahead. Rainbow behind. Endeavor has just passed the 15 mile buoy." The buoy is to the left in the photograph, with Rainbow in the foreground. This snapshot was taken by Kenn Greenlaw from the deck of the Cythera, 1934. Collection of Barbara L. Britton*

7.21 Roger Lee at three years, born October 12, 1936, the youngest child of Lyndell and Kenneth Greenlaw. Collection of Barbara L. Britton

7.22 Cythera in winter quarters at Shaw's Cove, with the "house" on. Kenn (right) sitting on the car's running board with friends. Collection of Barbara L. Britton

# From Deer Isle to New London

In 1935 Kenn's status on the *Cythera* changed from being a summer employee to becoming a member of the permanent crew with full-time steady employment. It was then that he moved his family from Deer Isle to New London, Connecticut, where the *Cythera* laid up for the winter in Shaw's Cove. It was in New London that Kenn and Lyndell's third child, Roger Lee, was born on October 12, 1936. During the next two years, having acquired the necessary experience, Kenn studied and passed the examination for his Second Mate's license. *[See photo 7.21]*

## The Hurricane of 1938

September 21, 1938, is a date never to be forgotten in New England. The full force of a monstrous hurricane, after coming along the New Jersey shore, struck Long Island and the New England coast with relentless fury, creating a path of complete destruction. At the height of the gale, the winds were estimated at 186 miles per hour. Hurricane winds and the storm surge made kindling wood out of miles of shore property. In addition, New London experienced the horror of a fire when the five-masted school ship *Marsala* pushed its bow head-on over The Shoreline Railroad tracks, and was believed to have started the $2,000,000 conflagration by demolishing the corner of a building and bursting a boiler. The fire, spreading from the waterfront and a good portion of the business district to residences nearby, was "the worst conflagration since Benedict Arnold burned the city in 1761. (Brochure: *Hurricane and Flood*, p. 4)

The *Cythera* was in its winter quarters at Shaw's Cove. The crew had just completed the work of "putting on the house" when the hurricane struck the waterfront. (The "house" was a covering of boards which acted as a protection over the deck of the ship when laid up.) *[See photo 7.22]* In relating the story to his children, Kenn told them: "Pieces of the house were picked up like matchsticks and blown all over Shaw's Cove and beyond, some to be found more than a week later." The yacht itself stayed secure at its anchorage. During the melée of howling wind and water rising, the launch was lowered from the hoist on the side of *Cythera*. With Kenn's experience as Port Launchman, he became the man in charge and, with the help of other crew members, several people were rescued from their homes and taken to safety as the water rose. *[See photo 7.23]*

In the evening as Kenn made his way home on foot across New London, through the chaos of downed trees and wires the hurricane had left behind, he could see the fire still raging as the coal company building burned out of control on Bank Street. On the way, he assisted other people wherever he could. Finally, at about 10 p.m., he reached his own front door. Filled with anxiety, bone tired, and soaking wet, he pushed open the door and found, to his utter relief, his wife and children safe inside.

*7.23 The hurricane of 1938 that swept the New England coast, and the fire that followed in New London, brought devastation to its waterfront and ravaged its business district. Collection of Barbara L. Britton*

His daughter spoke afterward about the emotional trauma the family had experienced that day as her mother huddled to protect the three children in the center of their small house, fearing at any moment that either one of the two large trees, in the front or the back of the house, would come down on top of them. Remembering the feeling of joy and relief at the moment of her father's safe return, Kenn's daughter said, "My mother, my two brothers and I ran to him, hugging and kissing him. That was the first time I ever saw my father cry."

## USS *Cythera* (PY26) in World War II

On December 31, 1941, following more than two decades of renewed use as a private yacht, and three weeks after the Japanese attack on Pearl Harbor, *Cythera* was purchased by the U.S. Navy from the Harkness family. She was one of seventy-three private yachts acquired for coastal patrol service by the Navy during World War II.

The formal Change of Command ceremony for *Cythera* occurred in New London, Connecticut, on January 10, 1942. That was the day when America's involvement in World War II became a heartbreaking reality for the Greenlaw family. Kenn's children, Barbara and Kenn Jr. tried not to cry. *Cythera* was like an old and dear friend, and saying "goodbye" wasn't easy. As they grew older, they had often spent Sunday afternoons on the *Cythera*. When their dad had to stand watch, it was a special treat for them to take the two-mile walk from their home on Raymond Street to the familiar pier in Shaw's Cove, *Cythera* tied up on one side and *Hi-Esmaro* on the other. Kenn always bought the Sunday papers on the way to the ship in the morning, but the "funny papers" were saved until the children arrived. There, in the fo'c's'le, the enjoyment was so much greater when the "funnies" were read together. At other times, Kenn taught his son to play chess, while his daughter curled up on a leather cushion to read a book. Then, all three would make the hourly circuit to inspect the ship, from the engine room to the bridge. There, Barbara and Kenn Jr. took turns at the wheel, steering *Cythera* safely through another imaginary voyage. As the afternoon drew to a close, walking home, hand in hand with Dad, still remains, in memory, the end of a "perfect day." *[See photo 7.24]*

At the Change of Command ceremony, Captain Walter D. Weed, the officers and entire crew of SY *Cythera*, together with their families, were assembled on the dock, with the U.S. Navy personnel standing at attention. The Navy captain presented his orders to Captain Weed and then saluted. Captain Weed returned the salute and wished him "Good

*7.24 Second Mate Kenn Greenlaw on the deck of the Cythera. Collection of Barbara L. Britton*

luck and Godspeed." The Navy captain dismissed the Navy crew to take command of the ship and, shortly thereafter, USS *Cythera* pulled away from the dock and left New London for the last time, sailing out into the ice-filled Thames River and down Long Island Sound to Philadelphia. In his article, "Overdue Atlantic" *Cythera* (PY 26) Robert P. Sables continues the story of *Cythera*'s return to naval service and, ultimately, her sinking by a German U-boat less than four months later:

> The vessel was delivered to the Philadelphia Navy Yard where she again underwent a refitting for naval service. Three 3"/50 gun mounts were installed plus two stern depth charge racks. Upon completion of the refit, the *Cythera* was placed in service as a patrol yacht on March 3, 1942—designation PY-26. Her tonnage now was 1,000 gross tons and the complement she carried numbered 71, which included the Naval Armed Guard. *[See photos 7.25 and 7.26]*
>
> Lt. Cdr. Thomas Wright Rudderow, age 56, was assigned as commanding officer. He had served aboard the transport USS *DeKalb* during the First World War and afterwards remained active in the reserves. When recalled to active duty in January 1942, he was the superintendent/commanding officer of the Pennsylvania Nautical School Ship, *Seneca*. Joining him aboard the *Cythera* were Lt. Casper L. Zacharias, USNR, Ensign Robert Earl Brister, USNR, Ensign William Logan Bunker, Jr., USNR, and Ensign Stratton Christensen, USNR. New recruits, sprinkled with some "old hands," were assigned to the various departments on the USS *Cythera*. A substantial number of men were from the greater New York area. *[See photo 7.27]*
>
> Finally, the USS *Cythera* received orders assigning her to the Pacific Fleet at Pearl Harbor. At 0300 hours, 1 May 1942, she departed Norfolk, Virginia, and set course for the Panama Canal.
>
> On the evening of 1 May 1942, the U-402, commanded by Baron Siegfried von Forstner, was cruising on the surface some 100 miles off Cape Fear, North Carolina. She was on her third war patrol—with negative contacts— and was shortly due to leave station for St. Nazaire, France. The bridge look-out, around midnight, spotted a small warship zigzagging on a southerly course. Forstner performed an "end around run" on the spotted craft, submerged, and proceeded to launch a torpedo attack. Two torpedoes struck the USS *Cythera* splitting her in half. As she sank, the depth charges on her stern exploded causing casualties. The U-402 shortly surfaced and rescued two survivors, Sea2/c James Monroe Brown

*7.25, 7.26 USS Cythera, under U.S. Navy command, moves away from the dock at Shaw's Cove and out into the ice-filled Thames River and down Long Island Sound to Philadelphia. Collection of Barbara L. Britton*

and PHM1/c Charles Harold Carter. They were taken aboard the U-boat for the return trip. *[See photo 7.28]*

Regarding their care, Captain John Waters Jr., USCG, Ret., in his book *Bloody Winter*, quotes portions of a letter from Forstner to his wife. The Kapitanleutnant related:

> We should really have kept them locked up and all that, but a U-boat is not spacious, as you know, and they were nice chaps and friendly—and they joined us in our meals, and we brought them home in our own way, and nobody the worst for it. At our arrival, they were met by an escort and taken away in the usual manner thought fit for prisoners of war, much to the consternation of my crew, whom they had invited to come and see them

back home in the States after the war.

Sea2/c James M. Brown later provided a written statement about the sinking (dated July 4, 1945):

> On 1 May 1942, at 0300 the *Cythera* departed from Norfolk, Virginia. According to the scuttlebutt, we were proceeding to Hawaii to take up duty there.
>
> At approximately 0045, 2 May 1942, the *Cythera* was struck by a torpedo. Just previous to that time, I was standing watch as a trainer on the forward gun mount. I was looking out to starboard and saw two flashes of white in the water. The full moon was off the port quarter at the time. It was a very clear night and the sea was calm. As soon as I saw the flashes, I gave the warnings

*7.27- USS Cythera leaves New London for the last time on January 10, 1942. Collection of Barbara L. Britton*

to the man on the telephone just aft of the gun mount. Immediately after giving the warning, I saw a torpedo wake passing under the bow. I then saw another wake directly approaching the ship. A couple of seconds later the ship was struck about amidships and there was a terrific explosion. I was thrown in the air and landed on my knees on the gun mount. I couldn't see the stern but in my opinion the ship broke in two immediately, just aft of the bridge.

The forward part of the ship started to sink and heel over to port. The gun was useless and I found it impossible to get to the point of damage. I heard a sound which I took to be machine gun fire, and crowded behind the solid railing (about 2-1/2 feet high) on the deck. At this time I saw the legs of two men going over the side near me. Very shortly thereafter, I heard two muffled explosions. I then went over the side myself. As soon as I broke water, two large waves swept over me.

After the waves passed, I looked around and saw the last part of the ship, the bow-sprit, sink from sight. A minute or so later, I saw Carter, PHMl/c, USN, sitting in a life raft about fifty feet away from me. I shouted to him and when he answered, I started to swim towards him and on the way picked up a life ring which was floating in the water. When I reached the raft, Carter was sitting on part of a hatch cover he had laid across the raft. With Carter's aid, I climbed partially into the raft and then we looked around in the water to see if we could see any other survivors. We could see none, and only a very small amount of debris. After a couple of minutes, we heard the submarine surface. We saw it slowly circle around toward us. We attempted to hide in the water but the moon gave away our position and the submarine closed and picked us up. While on the conning tower, Carter and I again looked around for other survivors before we were taken below. The German submarine personnel later told us that they had seen no other survivors or bodies.

We were put ashore at St. Nazaire, France, on or about 21 May 1942.

*7.28 Cythera underwent a refit for naval service in World War II and was recommissioned as a patrol yacht, USS PY26, on March 3,1942. She was torpedoed by German U-boat 402 and sunk in the Atlantic Ocean on May 1,1942. Courtesy of D.M. McPherson, 1975, Naval Historical Foundation*

The lack of communication with *Cythera* and her failure to appear in the Canal Zone forced the Navy to announce the ship lost "due to suspected enemy action." Accordingly, on June 2, 1942, a notice was sent to family members advising that their husbands/sons had been placed in a "missing status." It was policy to hold personnel in this status for one year before declaring them dead.

However, a few weeks later an article appeared in the German newspaper, *Deutsche Zeitung in Den Niederland* announcing that two American sailors, "Charles and James," had been brought back from Atlantic coastal waters. It was noted that their ship had been a "Coast Guard cruiser formerly luxury yacht owned by Mister Harkness."

The two POWs were shortly writing to their families back in the States, Sea2/c Brown to his parents, Mr. and Mrs. J. M. Brown, New York City, and PHM1/c Carter to his wife, Willie Irma Carter, Corsicana, Texas. These families soon learned that there were no other survivors from the sinking. Within a short time, families of the other missing crew members were contacting the Browns and Mrs. Carter to obtain information about their loved ones. Not knowing what to say, they contacted the Navy Department for guidance. After review, the Chief of Naval Personnel, on January 23, 1943, sent a second letter to the families acknowledging that two enlisted men from the USS *Cythera* were being held "as prisoners of war at Marlagmilag, Nord, Germany." It noted that no other prisoners were reported from the patrol vessel and "as time passes, the hope of your son being found necessarily becomes more remote." The letter concluded by stating that the crew would be "carried as missing for a period of one year."

In May 1945, the two survivors were released and returned to the United States.

Baron von Forstner retained command of the U-402 for the rest of her career. He was awarded the Knights Cross on February 9, 1943, and subsequently promoted to Korvettenkapitan. The U-402 had participated in the wolf pack attack on Convoy SC-118 in February 1943. In that attack she sank the American tanker, *R.E. Hopkins* and the transport *Henry R. Mallory*. On October 13, 1943, the U-402 went to a watery grave north of the Azores after being struck by an MK.24 homing torpedo dropped by Lt. Cdr. Howard M. Avery, squadron commander VC-9, USS *Card* (CVE-11). There were no survivors.

## In Memoriam

In keeping with the U.S. Navy tradition of retaining the names of lost warships, the yacht *Abril*, purchased on July 14, 1942, was commissioned as the USS *Cythera* (PY-31) on October 26, 1942. She spent her war career at New London, Connecticut, conducting training exercises with submarines. She was transferred to the Maritime Commission on November 6, 1946. Further, the Navy named two destroyer escorts after officers lost on the USS *Cythera*. They were the USS *Brister* (DE-327) launched on August 24, 1943 and sponsored by Mrs. Blanch Brister (the mother of Ensign Robert Brister, USNR), USS *Rudderow* (DE-224) launched on October 14, 1943, and sponsored by Mrs. Thomas W. Rudderow (wife of Lt. Cdr. Rudderow). The USS *Rudderow* was the class leader of twenty two destroyer escorts whose armament was upgraded to 5"/38 cal. dual-purpose guns.

As *Cythera* left New London on January 10, 1942, she took with her all that the words "going yachting" represented. World War II had intervened and, in effect, "sounded the death knell for the big yachts" (Chapter 4). Sadly, the sinking of *Cythera* was the symbolic end of the very way of life her beauty and grandeur epitomized.

Unlike his brother, Edwin, who moved from vessel to vessel during his seafaring career, Kenn was a member of *Cythera*'s crew for fifteen years, extending from 1927 to 1942. His final recommendation, written by Captain Walter D. Weed on January 10, 1942, read:

## Steam Yacht *Cythera*

> To Whom It May Concern:
> New London, Conn.
>
> January 10th 1942
>
> This is to certify that Kenneth Greenlaw has been on Yacht *Cythera* as Quartermaster from February 15th 1937 to October 31st 1940. He also served as 2nd Officer on Yacht *Cythera* from November 1st 1940 to January 10th 1942, the day that Yacht *Cythera* left in charge of the Navy crew for Philadelphia. He was a very good Quartermaster.
>
> He also was a very good 2nd Officer, sober, honest and a good worker and Watch Officer and it gives me great pleasure to recommend him as such.
>
> Walter D. Weed (signed)
> Master, Yacht *Cythera*.

# Moving on to Electric Boat

Now, Kenn had to pursue a new direction. From January 1942 to February 1944, he worked as a rigger at Electric Boat, located in Groton, Connecticut, just across the Thames River from New London.

> The term "rigger" comes from the days of sailing ships, where a rigger was a person who worked with rigging or ropes for hoisting sails. Sailors could put their rope skills to work in lifting and hauling, in an era before mechanical hoists and cranes were available. In time, rigging became a trade in itself. Riggers tend to be highly specialized in moving jobs that cannot be accomplished by ordinary means and use equipment especially designed for moving and lifting objects weighing hundreds and even millions of pounds in places where ordinary material handling equipment cannot go. Because of the highly specialized nature of the work riggers do, it is one of the few remaining occupations that can only be learned by apprenticeship. Because of the potentially dangerous nature of rigging, men who choose this occupation must learn to work together as a cohesive team and to trust one another. (Rigger-Industry, Wikipedia)

For Kenn, the skills that had become "second nature" aboard ship were quickly and easily

### The Greenlaws of Sunset: Part III

transferred to the new job onshore. It was January 1942; the shipyards at Electric Boat were a hub of activity. As soon as America officially entered the war on December 7, 1941, just a month before, employees began to leave their jobs to volunteer for one of the armed services, and peacetime conscription into the military began in earnest for all men between the ages of 18 and 45. Many hundreds of employees, both men and women, were needed to fill their places. Recruitment and training were challenges confronting the company immediately. Experienced workers, like Kenn, were an important and valuable asset to Electric Boat for the task that lay ahead.

With a growing national reputation for excellence in the development and building of submarines, Electric Boat was already expanding its facilities to meet the production required to shore up the country's defenses. The company's annual production of submarines went from six in 1939 to twelve in 1940 and in early 1941, Electric Boat announced even more expansive plans for new shipyards and ship ways. Employment, too, had more than doubled, with workers numbering 2,300 in 1939 compared to 4,783 in March 1941. In his book, *The Legend of Electric Boat*, Jeffrey Rodengen (pp. 83-84) summarizes the tremendous production effort achieved:

> By 1942, Electric Boat launched sixteen submarines annually, in 1943 twenty-five, and in 1944, it launched twenty-three submarines, or nearly one every two weeks at the peak of production. By the time the war ended in 1945, Electric Boat had delivered seventy-four submarines to the Navy from the Groton shipyards, more than any other yard in the country.
>
> The quality and efficiency of construction at Electric Boat was so impressive, that it was awarded the Navy "E" pennant with four stars for "its outstanding performance in the design, construction, and delivery of Submarines for the United States Navy.

Although Kenn had an active role in the huge wartime production effort at Electric Boat, as the war continued he felt that his heart and his skills were better suited to life on the deck of a vessel rather than building one. He had also prepared himself for the future by studying and passing the examination for his Chief Mate's license.

## United States Merchant Marine

In the mid-1930s, the Merchant Marine of the United States was in a state of decline. The country's merchant fleet was aging. Most cargo and passenger ships were over twenty years old, becoming obsolete and fewer in number. It was at this point that Congress took action and passed the Merchant Marine Act of 1936.

This key legislation established the United States Maritime Commission to oversee

> "...that the United States shall have a merchant marine...to provide shipping service essential for maintaining the flow of such domestic and foreign waterborne commerce at all times, capable of serving as a naval and military auxiliary in time of war or national emergency, owned and operated under the United States flag...composed of the best-equipped, safest, and most suitable types of vessels..., and supplemented by efficient facilities of shipbuilding and ship repair." The fleet of ships responsible for this mission is called the U. S. Merchant Marine. (Setting the Stage, *Liberty Ships and Victory Ships*, p. 1)

Under the newly established Maritime Commission, the original plan was to build fifty ships a year for ten years; however, this plan was grossly inadequate to meet the changing world situation. With war looming in 1939-1940, an intensified shipbuilding program became critical.

*7.29 Kenn, leaving home in New London, as a deck officer in the Merchant Marine, 1944. Collection of Barbara L. Britton*

Under the Lend Lease program, signed into law by President Roosevelt in March 1940, the United States agreed to build commercial ships for Great Britain, already at war with Germany, and in dire need of food and supplies, while increasing its own merchant fleet at the same time.

The new emergency cargo ships, known as Liberty Ships, were built using a common design and assembly-line techniques, pioneered by Henry J. Kaiser, in eighteen newly established shipyards along the West, East and Gulf coasts of the United States. Parts were manufactured in every state in the country. In this manner, 2,000 ships were constructed by the end of 1943, a total of 2,710 overall. At peak production, three Liberty Ships were being launched every day. The speed of construction allowed the U.S. to build cargo vessels faster than German U-boats could sink them. In his article, "World War II: The Liberty Ship Program," Kennedy Hickman details the "cookie cutter" specs for these "workhorses of war":

> The Liberty Ships were steamers, propelled by two oil-fired boilers, triple expansion steam engine, single screw, 2500 horsepower. All were made with the same cookie cutter specs: length–441' 6"; beam–56' 10.75"; displacement–14,245 tons; draft–27' 9.25"; and a speed of 11 knots. Their complement included a volunteer crew of 44 and 12-25 Naval Armed Guard.
>
> The armament for the Liberty Ships, typically, consisted of one 5-inch gun on the stern, a 3-inch gun on the bow, and a total of six machine guns on the flying bridge and after steering station. Navy Armed Guard units were trained and placed on board the Liberty Ships to provide defensive firepower to merchant ships because of the constant danger from enemy submarines and fighter aircraft and because there was a shortage of Allied escort vessels to provide adequate protection. The naval units helped to train the crews of the merchant ships so that reinforcements would be available and ready at the time of attack.
>
> Liberty Ships were designed to be the workhorses of the war and were capable of carrying 9,000 tons of cargo in the hold, plus airplanes, tanks and locomotives lashed to the deck. They were neither sleek nor beautiful and, in fact, they were referred to as "ugly ducklings" by President Roosevelt. But, as he was quick to acknowledge, looks didn't matter when the sole purpose was "to get the job done." *[See photo 7.29]*

Kenn Greenlaw joined the Merchant Marine in February 1944. Unlike the other services, however, a man who wanted to join the Merchant Marine simply didn't go to a recruiting office to sign up. Instead, he applied to a commercial cargo company which, during wartime, had its shipping fleet nationalized under the Merchant Marine Act of 1936. There, he presented his application, his papers, and his recommendations noting his competence and experience. In conversations with his brother, Edwin, then employed by Todd Shipyard in New Orleans, Louisiana, and with Randall Haskell, his friend from Deer Isle, Kenn had heard that cargo shipping companies were actively recruiting seasoned men to man their ships; both officers and crew were hard to find. Not only did a company have to staff the fleet of cargo vessels already under its flag, but a number of the newly mass-produced Liberty Ships that were coming off the production line every day as well. In addition, Kenn learned that Isthmian Steamship Company enjoyed an estimable reputation among mariners, thus Isthmian Steamship became his career choice. *[See photo 7.30]*

The first ship listed in Kenn's "Continuous Log Book" was the SS *Frank Wiggins*, a Liberty Ship, loaded and ready to embark from New York on February 24, 1944, for a "foreign port." During wartime, no specific destination was ever listed but, in reality, the *Frank Wiggins* rendezvoused with other cargo carriers and traveled in convoy to England. The ship returned and discharged in Boston on April 26, 1944; Kenn served as Second Officer on his first voyage as a merchant seaman.

During the ensuing months of the war, Kenn made three additional trips across the Atlantic to England, in convoy. On his second trip in 1944, he sailed again on the SS *Frank Wiggins*, loading and discharging cargo in Boston, but this time he was employed as Chief Mate. *[See photo 7.31]*

In October 1944, he served as acting Chief Officer on the Liberty Ship SS *James McCosh*, and his final two trips in 1945 were as Chief Mate aboard the SS *Annniston City*, a cargo carrier built in 1922, which had sailed under the Isthmian Steamship Company flag before the war. *[See photo 7.32]*

Originally, Liberty Ships were to be named for prominent (deceased) Americans starting with Patrick Henry and the Signers of the Declaration of Independence. However, it wasn't long before the job became exceedingly difficult as liberty ships were being launched by the hundreds. One way of dealing with the issue was to offer a proposal which stated that any group raising $2 million in War Bonds could suggest a name for a Liberty Ship. Following are two examples,

> The Liberty Ship *Frank Wiggins* (1849-1924) was named for a man instrumental in the development of Los Angeles Harbor and the establishment of a steamship line between that port and Hawaii. (Walter W. Jaffee, *The Liberty Ships from A to Z*)

> The Liberty Ship *James McCosh*, (1811-1894) was named for a Presbyterian clergyman and president of Princeton University for twenty years beginning in 1869. (Jaffee, *The Liberty Ships...*)

With Germany's surrender, victory in Europe was declared on May 8, 1945. Although the war was over in the Atlantic, the *Anniston City* made another trip to England, embarking with foodstuffs and much needed materials for a war-torn nation on May 17, 1945. Some part of the cargo was also taken to Norway, a country whose people had suffered deprivation under German occupation.

With easy access to shops in both England and Norway, Kenn took great pleasure in being able to buy small gifts for his family back home. For his wife and daughter, he bought two lovely pieces of wool tartan material which were transformed, with Lyndell's sewing skill, into beautiful pleated skirts, envied by all. For his sons, he bought steel-bladed knives in Norway, one with a leather sheath and the other with a sheath of bone, made by the Inuit. And, for the family, he brought home the best gift of all—a small, tan-colored, Norwegian husky dog. Already named Judy by the crew on the Anniston City, for whom Judy Garland was a favorite, the dog became an instant member of the Greenlaw family and lived a long, happy and comfortable life.

It wasn't until August 15, 1945, that Japan finally surrendered, but only after nuclear bombs had been dropped on two Japanese cities, Hiroshima and Nagasaki. After four months away, the Anniston City returned to the U.S. and discharged cargo at the port of Baltimore on October 1, 1945, in a country and a world at peace.

The War Shipping Administration, created by

7.30 Copy of Kenn's "Continuous Log Book." Courtesy of Col. Kenneth N. Greenlaw Jr.

7.31 A Liberty Ship, representative of Liberty Ships SS Frank Wiggins and SS James McCosh, that carried military supplies, cargo and personnel vital to our Allied forces in Europe during World War II. Courtesy of American Merchant Marine at War, www.usmm.org

**THE ISTHMIAN STEAMSHIP COMPANY
71 BROADWAY, NEW YORK, N.Y.**

*7.32 House flag of the Isthmian Steamship Company; "the Blue for the ocean and sky - the White Cross of Peace - and the Red Diamond for the glow of the sunrise and sunset of the mighty oceans." From a brochure of the Isthmian Steamship Company, collection of Barbara L. Britton*

President Roosevelt in 1942 as an emergency war agency of the U.S. government, was given the task of purchasing and operating the ships that America needed to fight the war. At the same time, the men who manned those ships were all civilians, had volunteered for duty in the wartime Merchant Marine and had become, in effect, government employees. Still, they were not recognized as government personnel during the war nor as veterans after the war. More than 8,300 mariners were killed at sea and more than 12,000 were wounded. One in twenty-six mariners serving aboard merchant ships died in the line of duty, suffering a greater percentage of war-related deaths than all other U.S. services.

It wasn't until forty-three years later, on January 21, 1988, that Merchant Mariners who had served during World War II finally received the recognition as veterans they so richly deserved, but so long overdue. Now, all mariners are entitled to the benefits of receiving health care in a veterans hospital, burial in a veterans cemetery, and a fitting gravestone to commemorate their service.

## The Isthmian Steamship Company

The war was over! There was no return to the peacetime job Kenn had known; it no longer existed. Going forward, he saw the possibility of a career with Isthmian Steamship Company. Certainly, Kenn's familiarity with large, ocean-going cargo vessels had become commonplace, and in the wartime Merchant Marine, he had gained experience in proper cargo handling and stowage. There were other options, of course. One could always look for a job ashore. New London itself, as well as Groton and Mystic close by, held many possibilities. But, for Kenn, having been a seafarer throughout most of his adult life, the final decision was not a difficult one!

The war was over for the commercial shipping lines as well. The hectic, war-weary days of World War II were difficult, but the outstanding results achieved by Isthmian Steamship Company in its contribution to the Allied victory were worthy of its longstanding reputation for dependability and service. Both were noted by author, Skip Lewis, in *The History of the Isthmian Steamship Company* when he wrote:

> During WWII Isthmian acted as general agent for 132 War Shipping Administration (WSA) vessels which made 872 voyages, carrying 50% of all supplies to the Red Sea and the Persian Gulf. These ships were instrumental in setting the stage for the turning point of the European theater at El Alemein in 1942. The total amount paid by the U.S. Government to Isthmian for vessel chartering from 2/1/1942 - 9/2/1945 was $37,000,000.

> With peace restored, Isthmian was appointed General Agent for the U.S. Government for transportation of all goods for the reconstruction of Europe, known as the "Marshall Plan." It was time for a new beginning.

Marking the day when Kenn began his career with Isthmian Steamship Company was the entry in his Continuous Log which gave the date of embarkation for his next trip on the SS Anniston City as October 18, 1945. Within a few short months, however, beginning in 1946, the older vessels were being sold or scrapped and the names of Isthmian's new peacetime fleet of ships began to appear in Kenn's log.

A large photographic brochure, titled The Isthmian Steamship Company, published in 1954, provided the following detailed information about these ships, their facilities and trade routes in a peacetime round-the-world economy:

> By 1947 Isthmian had sold or scrapped all its outdated vessels and purchased a fleet of twenty-four cargo vessels of the C-3-S-A2 type. Eight were constructed in San Francisco, California, by the Western Pipe and Steel Corporation, and sixteen at Pascagoula, Mississippi, by the Ingalls Shipbuilding Corporation. All twenty-four were built during the years 1943 to 1945. Seven were used as attack transports by the U.S. Navy and the others served in the wartime years under the direction of the War Shipping Administration. Owned by U.S. Steel, Isthmian's fleet had the word "Steel" preceding the name of each vessel, such as *Steel Seafarer, Steel Vendor* or *Steel Ranger*, to list a few. *[See photo 7.33]*
>
> Each vessel was 492 feet in length with a beam of 69 feet, 6 inches and a depth of 42 feet, 6 inches; each had a gross weight of 8,500 tons. All vessels were equipped with an 8,500 horsepower single screw type, modern turbine engine, could travel at a speed of 16.5 knots and were equipped to steam 30 days without refueling. The latest cargo handling equipment was essential to an efficient and cost-effective operation. Cargo booms, usually four at each hatch, were rigged to handle loads from 5 to 10 tons, and one or two cargo booms were rigged to handle heavy weights from 10 to 30 tons; the cargo winches were electric. *[See photo 7.34]*
>
> The goods that Isthmian's vessels carried were diverse and almost limitless. In the Persian Gulf Service, for example, the principal commodities carried outward were: asphalt, automobiles and trucks, drugs, oil refinery equipment, iron and steel products, refrigerated products and tobacco. On the return trip, the principal commodities carried homeward were: carpets, crushed bones, dates, frozen fish, gums, hides, and iron ore in bulk, pepper and edible nuts.
>
> One important aspect of Isthmian's reputation was its "duty to cargo" which demanded "close control over every detail of operation and procedure which could affect the safe transport of cargoes from loading port to port of destination." Proper stowage was critical to protect against damage due to shifting, contamination, pilferage or moisture due to atmospheric conditions en route.

The task of loading and unloading was a demanding one; nothing could be left to chance. With various types of cargo destined for several ports in any given region of the world, proper stowage was essential to insure the safe delivery of the material, and sequencing for loading and unloading cargo at its appropriate destination was equally important. The responsibility for this critical task was usually that of the Chief Mate and/or the Captain and could take long hours, stretching over several days. Depending on the ship's schedule, sometimes there was little time left for Kenn to spend at home with his family.

However, Kenn's youngest son, Roger, remembered one period in 1950 when his father remained at home for three months to study for his Master's license. At the same time, Roger had joined the Boy Scouts and was studying to get his next merit badge. Together, they learned Morse code, quizzing each other to achieve proficiency. The final result? Kenn

# The Greenlaws of Sunset: Part III

7.33 SS Steel Seafarer (ex. Katharine S. Holmes), a cargo-passenger ship of the Isthmian Fleet. Courtesy of Victor H. Young

7.34 A model of the Steel Seafarer made by the ship's carpenter was presented to Chief Mate Kenneth N. Greenlaw, ca. 1954. Courtesy of Roger L. Greenlaw

went to New York, took the grueling three-day examination, and received his Master's license, for Unlimited Tonnage on Any Ocean. Roger passed the requirements for the Morse code merit badge and, with it, gained Star Scout status, the next rung on the ladder of achievement in Scouting. With more study and hard work he went on to reach the top and the following year, at age fourteen, he received his Eagle Scout Award. *[See photo 7.35]*

A typical complement of men on an Isthmian vessel, which included the captain, officers and crew, was forty-six. Although there were twenty-four vessels in the Isthmian fleet, there were thirty Masters of the Fleet and an equal number of Chief Officers and Chief Engineers; the extras in each category were available to cover vacations and illnesses. The man who held the position with the title of Commodore was the highest ranking officer of the fleet.

The motto of Isthmian was: "The flag that sails and serves the seven seas." And, so it did! Isthmian was known for round-the-world service. Its trade routes, circumnavigating the globe, were divided into six distinct voyages: Westbound 'Round the World Service; Eastbound 'Round the World Service; India, Pakistan, Ceylon Service; Persian Gulf Service; and Hawaiian Islands Service. *[See photo 7.36]*

For many years, Kenn was Master of Isthmian ships that traveled to the Far East, either to ports in the Persian Gulf or to others in India, Pakistan and Ceylon. On one such voyage in 1965, as his ship, the *Steel Vendor*, headed for New York, he encountered a fellow seafarer in a very small boat in the middle of the ocean. To Kenn's amazement, neither the boat nor the captain showed any signs of distress. For the captain, Robert Manry, the *Steel Vendor* was simply a floating post office to take his mail. He and *Tinkerbelle* had been on the high seas for a month, having left Falmouth, Massachusetts, on June 1st and there had been much to write home about. Six weeks later, following the chance meeting with the *Steel Vendor* and Kenn Greenlaw, *Tinkerbelle*, with Manry aboard, reached her destination at Falmouth, England, amid the cheers of thousands of spectators and the whistles and horns of hundreds of little boats. Both he and *Tinkerbelle* had made it, nonstop across the Atlantic. In writing a book about his odyssey later, Manry mentioned his fortuitous meeting with the *Steel Vendor* and an affable, but concerned, Captain Greenlaw. He wrote:

> Monday, July 5th. We made good time. The fine weather, the blue beauty of the sea and the easy, smooth rolling of the swells put me into a wonderfully happy frame of mind.
>
> "The only thing that could make the day more perfect," I said to myself, "would be for a ship to come along and pick up my mail."
>
> About twenty minutes later I took my eyes off the compass and looked around the horizon and there, over my right shoulder, steaming toward me like the answer to a prayer, was a ship. It turned out to be the 12,640-ton cargo vessel SS *Steel Vendor,* bound from India and Ceylon to New York.
>
> Its master, Captain Kenneth N. Greenlaw, maneuvered the big ship very well, making it easy for me to bring *Tinkerbelle* in close to within fifty feet of my starboard beam. The day was so calm, and the 492-foot *Steel Vendor* and the 13'6" *Tinkerbelle* were so close to each other that Captain Greenlaw and I had no difficulty making ourselves understood. He wanted to know if I was lost and I assured him I wasn't, but that I'd appreciate a check on my navigation, so he gave me our position.
>
> "Do you need any provisions?" he asked.
>
> I assured him I had all the provisions I needed, and yet he looked skeptical, as though he just couldn't believe it. He seemed to be a big man, and he had a friendly face and a warm manner about him.
>
> He readily agreed to take my mail aboard and soon a crewman heaved

# The Greenlaws of Sunset: Part III

*7.35 Masters of the Isthmian Fleet, Captain Kenneth N. Greenlaw in the first row. From a 1954 brochure of the Isthmian Steamship Company, collection of Barbara L. Britton*

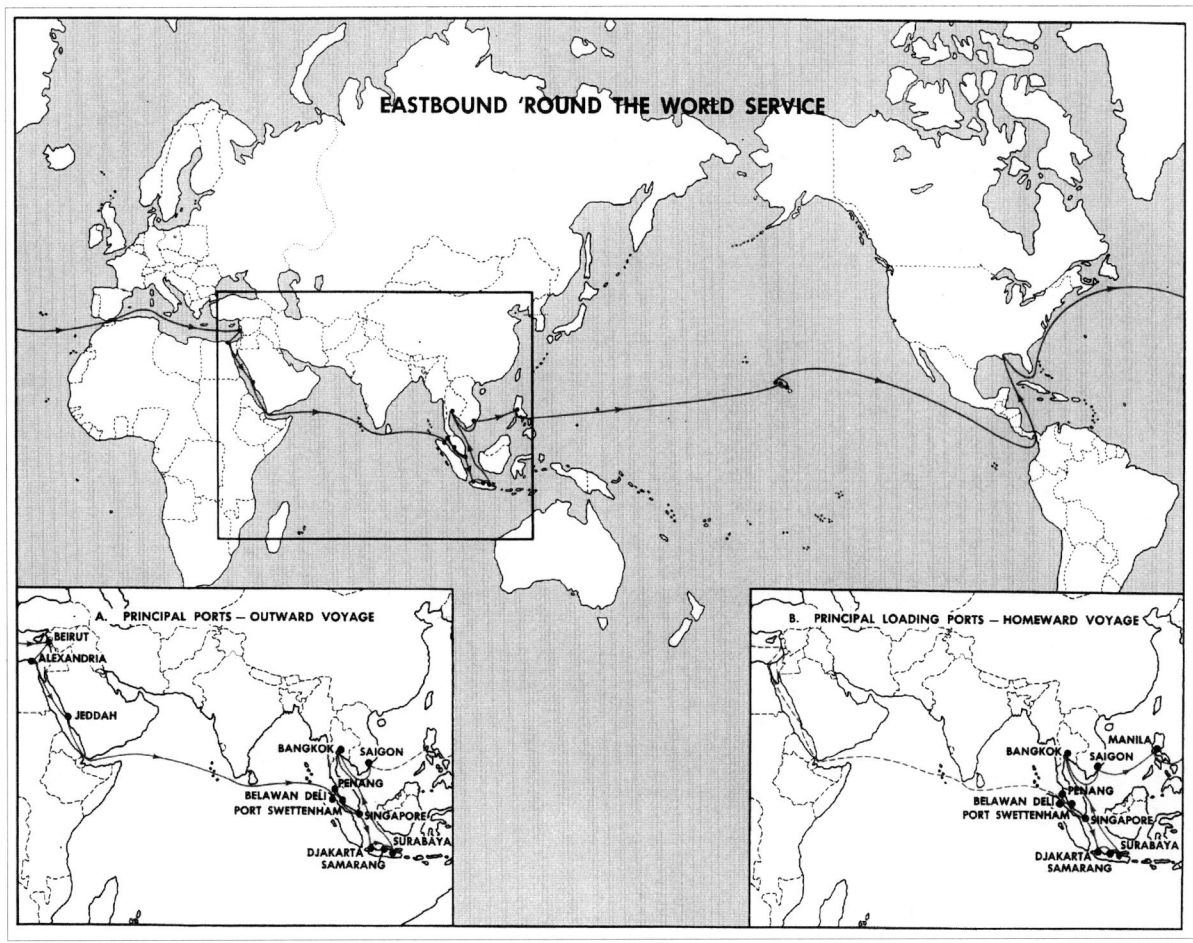

*7.36 Map indicates trade routes for Isthmian's Eastbound 'Round the World Service. From a 1954 brochure of the Isthmian Steamship Company, collection of Barbara L. Britton*

a line to *Tinkerbelle*. I had a bundle of ten letters all ready in a waterproof plastic bag and attached it quickly to the end of the line. Then the crewman hauled away. The letters were aboard the ship in a jiffy, on their way to my family and friends ashore.

"Thanks!" I yelled, waving to the captain and all the crew. "Have a nice trip."

"You have a nice trip!" the captain shouted back.

We all waved again, slowly drew apart and then turned stern to stern and resumed our separate courses. In a few minutes I was alone again on the restless sea. *[See photo 7.37]*

*7.37 The Tinkerbelle and her captain, Robert Manry, nearing Falmouth, England, and the end of their epic journey across the Atlantic Ocean nonstop. Courtesy of the Robert Manry Project*

Isthmian also carried paying passengers. Twenty of the twenty-four Isthmian vessels had four three-berth bedrooms, each with a private bath. One ship had six two-berth bedrooms, with private bath. The remaining three ships had two two-berth bedrooms, each with a private bath and sitting room. Kenn related to his family that many of the people who chose this type of ocean travel were missionary families who were on assignment to a foreign country or returning to the U.S. for vacation and found it a more economical way to travel, as did others who were working for companies abroad. Some simply chose the cargo liner with its comfortable accommodations and good food as an interesting way to see the world rather than travel in the high-priced, socially conscious environment of the expensive luxury liner. "And," Kenn added, with a laugh, "no one gets an engraved invitation; *everyone* eats at the Captain's table on my ship."

Financial problems plagued the Isthmian Company in the decade after World War II. Although the company, at first, gained huge profits, the postwar shipping boom came to an end in 1948. In *The History of the Isthmian Steamship Company*, Lewis points out the following conditions that were contributing factors:

By 1953 economic conditions were changing in shipping and U.S. Steel, as Isthmian Steamship's owner, began to have doubts about keeping its own fleet of vessels. Because many countries were back on a strong postwar footing, setting up their own steel mills and supplying other countries as well, cargoes were declining.

In 1956, the name of Isthmian Steamship Company was changed to Isthmian Lines, Inc. and the company was sold by U.S. Steel to States Marine Corporation. Although its ownership changed, Isthmian's management remained the same.

In retrospect, U.S. Steel had made a good business decision in disposing of its obsolete fleet, thereby avoiding altogether the problem of replacing its break-bulk vessels. Although it would take over twenty years to become fully operational, containerization was poised in 1956 to revolutionize the shipping industry and, ultimately, change the face of world trade as well.

Rather than loading, storing and unloading goods and material one piece at a time, cargo could be grouped into standardized containers, significantly

# The Greenlaws of Sunset: Part III

*7.38 Captain Kenneth N. Greenlaw takes a sighting with his sextant aboard the Steel Seafarer, ca. 1960. Collection of Barbara L. Britton*

increasing efficiency and reducing shipping time and the associated costs of excessive handling, pilferage and theft. In the early days, surplus tankers from WWII were converted into container ships. Although Isthmian's fleet of traditional cargo vessels could accommodate containers on deck, conversion of the cargo holds was not possible. Thus, it was only a matter of time before new, fast (21 to 25 knots) container ships were designed and built, leaving aging Isthmian vessels in their wake. *[See photo 7.38]*

The scrapping of Isthmian's fleet began in 1971 and was completed in 1973. Captain Kenneth N. Greenlaw sailed with Isthmian, in wartime and peacetime, for twenty-nine years and he was there at the very end: his last trip was documented in his Continuous Log Book. On July 6, 1973, he sailed from New Orleans, Louisiana, aboard the SS Steel Executive and arrived on September 30, 1973, at Kaohsiung, Taiwan, where the ship was scrapped. Three days later, Kenn flew home. By the end of October, the two remaining Isthmian vessels had also been scrapped and, with them, Isthmian Lines, Inc. ceased to exist.

*7.39 This tribute, in memory of Captain Kenneth N. Greenlaw, honors his twenty-nine years of dedicated maritime service, including active duty in the U.S. Merchant Marine, in war and in peace. The awards are as follows: The eagle on top is the U.S. Navy Reserve emblem. The round disc is the emblem of the Merchant Marine, designed by Walt Disney early in the war. The six ribbons are, top row, left to right: the Atlantic War Zone Ribbon, the Mediterranean and Middle East War Zone ribbon and the Pacific War Zone Ribbon. The bottom three ribbons are, left to right: the WWII Victory Ribbon, Korean Service Ribbon, and Vietnam Service Ribbon. The medals are the actual awards. The brass plate identifies Captain Greenlaw's service and dates of birth and death. At the bottom is the Merchant Marine identification award. Courtesy of Col. Kenneth N. Greenlaw Jr.*

In retirement, Kenn lived in California. He died on April 19, 1988, and, at his request, his ashes were scattered over the Pacific Ocean.

In the summer of 2013, a gravestone in memory of Kenneth N. Greenlaw was placed in the G. Edward Greenlaw lot in Mt. Adams Cemetery, Deer Isle, Maine, marking his service as a World War II veteran in the Merchant Marine. A similar gravestone, in memory of Lyndell L. Stinson, was placed beside it. Both memorials were given by their children. *[See photo 7.39]*

# Chapter 8: More Yachts with Deer Isle Men Aboard

*The steam yacht Shada, owned by Mr. Darling of Boston and commanded by Capt. Whitney B. Lowe, was in the harbor over the Fourth. The yacht is on a cruise east with the owner and party aboard and Mr. Darling kindly stopped over that the crew might enjoy the Fourth at home.*

*Deer Isle Messenger*, July 8, 1921

A popular pastime of the yachting set was to cruise along the coast northeastward, with Bar Harbor as a favored destination. As can be gleaned from the news items reviewed at the start of Chapter 4, it was not uncommon for them to put into Northwest Harbor on Deer Isle, providing sailors an opportunity to visit friends and families ashore. Sometimes owners themselves would go ashore for special events, such as a Fourth of July celebration or gunning. Even if the yachts did not stop over at Deer Isle, they often did so at a port near enough for at least a captain to get home for a quick visit.

The *Shada*, mentioned above, was a wooden vessel built in 1908 by George Lawley and Son of South Boston. Of 66 gross tons, she was 96 feet long, with 15-foot 5-inch beam and 5-foot draft. She had two gas, rather than steam engines. Owned by J. A. Dowling (the paper didn't have his name quite right) of South Boston, her captain was a son of Captain Samuel Lowe, who ran a store and acted as steamboat agent at the North Deer Isle landing. His house is now the Inn at Ferry Landing, and attached to it was a substantial farm, run by the son of Samuel's wife by a first marriage. Besides Whitney, Samuel fathered three other sons, one of whom succeeded him as steamboat agent, another who went yachting before settling on the family farm with his older half-brother (Samuel's stepson), and one who ran a livery stable. The family continued to operate the farm into the early 1950s, whereas Whitney, after he was done with yachting, went on in the Merchant Marine. *[See photo 8.1]*

## Steam Yacht *Akela*

One regular visitor to Deer Isle was the yacht *Akela*. This wooden-hulled vessel, which went into the water in 1899, was built for Massachusetts Governor Oliver Ames by the Gas and Engine Power Company and Charles L. Seabury Company of Morris Heights, New York. Of 72 gross tons displacement, her length was 117 feet 6 inches overall, with 14-1/2 foot beam and 4-foot 8-inch draft. She was powered by two triple expansion steam engines driving twin screws and cruised at 12 knots. She carried a crew of fifteen, and for eighteen years her captain was William ("Willie") Scott Greene of Deer Isle (brother of Allie Greene, Merle Greene's father; see Chapter 4). *[See photo 8.2]* Her crew,

*8-1 Captain Sam Lowe's house, where Whitney Lowe grew up. Now The Inn at Ferry Landing, its appearance is much the same as when the Lowes had it, except for a new connection to the barn. Photo by William A. Haviland*

*8-2 The steam yacht Akela; note the open-air helmsman's position on the boat deck forward. Courtesy of Deer Isle-Stonington Historical Society*

too, was made up of islanders, including Ernest H. Pickering as mate. She had several owners over the years, the last of whom (from 1904 on) was Henry A. Bishop of Bridgeport, Connecticut. As described by Captain Greene, he was a

> ...financier and a noted member of the New York Yacht club. For many years his father was president and purchasing agent of the New York, New Haven and Hartford railroad. He owned private sporting camps in northern Maine, and I made many hunting and fishing trips with him into the Maine woods.

Each season, while Willie Greene was captain, the *Akela* would put into Northwest Harbor, at which time an "Akela Ball" would be held at the Deer Isle town hall. As reported in an August 2, 1907, island newspaper:

> The steam yacht *Akela*, commanded by Capt. W. S. Greene, of this town, came in Monday night and will make this her headquarters for several weeks. The *Akela* is owned by Mr. Henry E. Bishop of Bridgeport, Conn., who with Mrs. Bishop, Miss Bishop, Miss Henriette and Master Henry E. Bishop, Jr., and several guests, is on board. To-night Mr. Bishop will give the officers and crew of the yacht a complimentary ball in the hall. The "Akela Ball" has come to be quite an annual affair to which our citizens look forward with much pleasure.

Besides putting on the Akela Ball, on one of his visits to the island, Bishop organized an impromptu basketball contest between Deer Isle and Stonington, putting up a trophy for the winner. The game was won by Deer Isle, and the trophy cup was exhibited

### More Yachts with Deer Isle Men Aboard

around town for some time. Eventually, though, it disappeared.

Bishop's tenure as *Akela's* owner was briefly interrupted by World War I, when the yacht was taken over in 1918 by the U.S. Navy and commissioned USS *Akela* (SP-1793). It was used to transport armed guard detachments to merchant ships in the New York City region, but with the end of the conflict, was turned back to the owner, one year to the day she was taken over. She was ultimately scrapped in 1935.

Captain Greene, who was born in 1873, got an early start on seafaring. His father, John W. Greene, was skipper of a coasting schooner, and began taking his son fishing from her at the age of 10. A year later found Willie as cook on the schooner *Sunnyside*. A year after that, at the ripe old age of 12, he was captain of a 27-ton packet making regular runs between Northwest Harbor and Belfast. In a 1936 interview with journalist Henry Buxton, Willie Greene reflected on this:

> My mate on the packet was Isaac Dow, who was only 11 years old. How we managed to run that packet at our tender ages is more than I know, but we did it and never had an accident. Sometimes we ran into some rough weather, too, but we must have been natural sailors, for we kept out of trouble. We would transport lumber and fish to Belfast, and return with groceries, grain, and other items of the average general cargo. I was skipper of this packet until I was 15, and then I started yachting on the steam yacht *Nowthen*, which at that time was the fastest steam yacht in the country. It was owned by J. Edward Addicks of Boston. For two years I served as an able seaman, and then I was mate of the vessel for two years.

Reflecting on his yachting career, Captain Greene continued:

> One summer we were racing another steamer called the *Republic* in Delaware Bay when our boiler exploded, killing two of our crew. That was 49 years ago, but I remember it as if it were yesterday.
>
> After leaving Mr. Addick's boat I was given command of [actor] Bill Daley's 30-foot racing sloop, the *Harbinger*. It will be recalled that Daley was a great sportsman and often refereed prize fights. He was a jolly good fellow, and entertained the leading lights of the stage and sporting world aboard his boats. Every time we passed Buoy 9 in Boston Harbor he would always pipe all hands to grog. He had the superstitious belief that if we toasted Buoy 9 we would have all kinds of fair weather and good luck. In Daley's sloop I raced and won in 1893 the celebrated Commodore Cup, a gift of the commodores for the different yacht clubs of the New England coast. Winning this cup, which contained more than $200 worth of silver, established us as champions of the New England coast. Mr. Daley expressed his appreciation of the victory by giving me a gold watch. The next season we defended the title, and when we won again Mr. Daley gave me a gold-headed cane. He was a man of great generosity, and his friends were legion.
>
> My next command was the steam yacht *Colante*, owned by Frank Waterman of Boston. This was a 60-foot pleasure craft, and I was with him for two seasons. After that in succession I commanded the steam yacht *Cloelia*, owned by Henry F. Ross, the architect of Newtonville, Mass.; the sloop *Alletta*, owned by H.F. Swift of Chicago; the *Apache*, owned by Governor Oliver Ames of Massachusetts; the English-built yacht *Gundreda*, owned by W.S. Pierce, New York lawyer; and other craft.
>
> The yacht *Gundreda*, owned by W.S. Pierce, was 225 feet long, and we cruised her to the Virgin Islands, Windward Islands, and South

American waters. We enjoyed some tall fishing in these waters, and in the jungles of South America we hunted for jaguars and other big game.

My last command was the yacht *Kehtoh*, 185 feet over all, owned by Roswell Eldridge of New York. I retired from yachting in 1924 because of ill health, and since then have had charge of small craft at Bar Harbor and other places. For three years I was on the yacht *Nada*, owned by William Rhinelander Stewart of New York and Bar Harbor. Mr. Stewart inherited a vast fortune from ancestors who bought large lots of land in New York from the Dutch and held on to it until it was almost priceless.

Apparent from these reflections is Willie Greene's easy relationship with his employers, in keeping with the egalitarian values of the culture in which he was raised on the island. Speaking of H.F. Swift, of Chicago meat packing fame:

> H.F. Swift was a fine man to work for, being considerate of his employees. While we were sailing he often told me of his struggle towards success. He was born on Cape Cod a poor boy, and worked his way to a high position in the financial world by sheer grit and ability. I was very close to the Swift family, and taught his daughter, Mabel, how to swim, shoot and sail a boat.

After more than 40 years around boats, Captain Willie Greene turned to a variety of other pursuits. Besides hunting in the woods of northern Maine, at age 63,

> I now own a launch which I use to take out parties of summer folks, and in the winter I get a great kick from racing ice boats which I built myself. I do most of my racing on Branch Pond and Graham Lake and on Blue Hill Bay. It is a thrilling sport, and I never tire of it. *[See photo 8.3]*

Another hobby was building bird houses:

*8.3 Captain Willie Greene at the Salmon Pool in Bangor. In 1939, he caught the largest salmon of the season after a great fight in a spring snowstorm with ice cakes floating all around. Courtesy of Deer Isle-Stonington Historical Society*

> We have built comfortable little homes for them all around the place, and we feed them regularly every winter. Life would be a dreary thing indeed without the cheerful notes of our feathered songsters.

Finally, he maintained a small museum behind his house. As described by Henry Buxton:

> I followed him to a little building which he explained was his curio shop. On the walls were the mounted heads of moose and deer which he had shot himself, and there were numerous decoys for different kinds of game birds which he had carved from blocks of wood. He showed me a fine piece of lacy fancy work which he had made himself under the tutelage of a Scandinavian sailor, and explained that it was done with the aid of the teeth and two hands, all working at

the same time. On a shelf I saw a lighthouse fitted with a dozen little clocks which showed the exact time of day in the principle [sic] capitals of the world, and in a corner were stacked ancient flintlocks and navy pistols of the period of Captain Paul Jones. But the relic in which he takes the greatest pride is the weathered sea chest of his sea-going grandfather, Captain William S. Greene. *[See photo 8.4]*

*8.4 The modest house at the head of Main Street in Deer Isle village, which Captain Willie Greene built in 1941 for himself and his wife Cora. She herself was the daughter of a well-known mariner, Captain George Dudley Haskell, from Deer Isle. Photographed in 2014, the house looks much the same as it did in Greene's day. Photo by William A. Haviland*

In 1952, Greene was annoyed by some disparaging remarks in a Bangor newspaper relating to the seamanship of Deer Isle yacht captains. As Clayton Gross described his reaction,

> Monday morning found him onboard the bus (which then ran to Bangor; to the best of the writer's knowledge he never owned or drove a car). The result was the first retired skippers race held in the Reach and won handily by Capt. Phil Haskell.

A veteran of the all-Deer Isle crew of the 1899 America's Cup defender *Columbia*, Haskell's crew consisted of two other master mariners from the island: Captain Irving Eaton and Captain Avery Marshall. The retired skippers race continues to this day as an annual event.

Willie Greene died in 1954. In his last years, on a warm summer day, he was frequently to be found down on Main Street in Deer Isle village. Always interested in people, he would walk up to any visitor or summer person from away, and say, "Welcome, welcome to our island," followed by, "And what did you say your name was?"

## The Yachts *Tarantula* and *Ara*

Although she is not known to have stopped off at Deer Isle, the yacht *Tarantula* did visit nearby ports. She was an unusual craft, in both appearance and power. One of the earliest turbine yachts, she had a pair of steam turbines driving nine propellers on three shafts. Her top speed under optimal conditions was an impressive 23.3 knots, but her usual cruising speed was 18. Measuring 153.6 feet in length with a 15-foot beam and 7-foot draft, she was built of steel on the Isle of Dogs in London, England, to a design by Cox and King, for the U.S. millionaire Colonel Harry MacCalmont. She was launched in 1902, and purchased by William K. Vanderbilt Jr. when her original owner died in 1904. Her original cost was a mere $200,000, but she underwent extensive alterations as soon as she reached the United States.

As for her unusual appearance, she looked exactly like a small torpedo boat destroyer. Upon her arrival in Rockland Harbor in 1905, one observer commented that it had to be a steam yacht or "a young torpedo boat." Nothing like it had been seen in the harbor before. Another onlooker opined that it was "the homeliest" thing he had ever seen. In reaction to such comments, as reported in the *Rockland Courier-Gazette*, "Vanderbilt, the man who could buy Rockland at ten times its assessed valuation, only smiled."

*Tarantula* carried a crew of 18 officers and men. Her captain at the time of her Rockland visit was Albert Love Haskell of Deer Isle, who claimed that he could go from Rockland to Bar Harbor in two and a half hours, or even two if he pushed it. But with a bunker capacity of only 35 tons, she had a limited cruising range. She had to take on more coal every 300 miles. For this reason, she was towed from England, where she had been built, to within 100 miles of the U.S. coast before she could proceed under her own steam to New York. Most of her cruising was in the New York area, where she was frequently the subject of complaints. At high speeds, she threw up a huge wake, and on trips through the East River, it caused considerable damage along both banks.

Captain Haskell, who was held in high esteem by Mr. Vanderbilt, said that he "learned the ropes" of seamanship while living on Deer Isle. He was the twelfth of thirteen children of Edward Young and Martha Washington (Haskell) Haskell. The 1850 census lists Edward as "sailor," but his descendants remember him as a fisherman. Born in 1851, Albert was raised in the house his father had inherited from his father, Nathan Haskell, who built it around 1785. It is a New England cape on Gilmore Lane, which passed to Albert's older brother, George Dudley, after his mother's death. All of Alfred's brothers followed the sea, four as master mariners. George Dudley (one-time skipper of the schooner *H Curtis*, discussed in Chapter 3) and his brothers, Caleb and Edwin, all were masters of vessels in the southern and West Indies trade, with George Dudley and Edwin later

*8.5 Steam yacht Tarantula, soon after conversion to a torpedo boat as HMCS Tuna. Courtesy of Directorate of History and Heritage, National Defense, Canada*

*8.6 Steam yacht Ara, partially sunk after running aground in 1928 on Little Duck Island off Mount Desert. The accident ended her career. Courtesy of Deer Isle-Stonington Historical Society*

turning to steam yachting. Thus, Albert grew up in a family with a strong maritime focus. Besides his brothers and father, his maternal grandfather was a master mariner, and his other grandfather (Nathan) was a sail maker. It would be surprising had he not "learned the ropes" of seamanship!

A yachtsman all his life, Albert died at his home in Port Jefferson on Long Island, New York, in 1935. He is not listed in the *1910 Register*, although Caleb, George and Edwin are, so Albert must have moved off-island by the time he became captain of the *Tarantula*.

Both of *Tarantula's* owners used the yacht to commute from their homes into Manhattan. Vanderbilt kept

*8.7 Motor yacht Moana in New Haven. Courtesy of Tinker (Gross) Crouch*

the yacht until he sold it to George Lawley in 1913. A year later it was sold to J. K. L. Ross and renamed *Tuna*. With the outbreak of World War I, she was sold in 1916 to the Canadian Navy, becoming HMCS *Tuna*, based out of Halifax. Her days were numbered, however, as she was sold for scrap by the navy in 1918 owing to an irreparable engine mount fracture. *[See photo 8.5]*

Another yacht owned by Vanderbilt ("Willie K", as his family called him) was the *Ara*. Built of steel in 1917 by Camper and Nicholson, Ltd. of Gosport, England, she was of 896 gross tons, 211 feet 9 inches long, 31 feet 3 inches in the beam, and had a 14-1/2 foot draft. She was powered by two Polar diesels which moved her at 14-1/2 knots over a 6,000 mile range. She was also equipped with sails to steady her.

Originally built as a sloop-of-war for blockade duty, she was well suited to Vanderbilt's needs. He liked to cruise to distant ports, and spent much of his life doing so. Along the way, he carried out oceanographic studies, and dredged for ancient artifacts. Thus, *Ara* was not so much fitted out to impress, but rather was selected for her construction and seagoing properties. Her interior was fitted out comfortably, but not ostentatiously. She still carried armament—several "three pounder" guns as protection against pirates. *[See photo 8.6]*

On board as Third Mate in the 1927-28 season was Merle Greene of Deer Isle. In that season, she cruised from New York to the Galapagos and back. At the end of that cruise, Vanderbilt wrote of Greene:

> I found him a most reliable watch officer and only too glad to recommend him to any one who may desire his services in that capacity. I have always found him willing, courteous, honest and sober and he leaves my employ of his own accord as he has an opportunity to become a first mate on a yacht of about the same tonnage as ARA.

Over the summer, until the large yacht was ready, Greene served as master of a small gasoline yacht *Moana*. It was in the fall that he took up his position as First Mate on *Camargo*. *[See photo 8.7]*

## Steam Yacht *Viking*

This elegant craft, built by Newport News Shipbuilding and Drydock Company of Newport News, Virginia, slid into the water in 1929. Built of steel, she had a classic clipper bow with, in her case, a beautifully carved Viking figurehead. To complete her clipper-like appearance, she also had masts with yards and a counter stern with elegant, hand carved and gilded tailboards. For heavy weather, she was equipped with steel shutters to protect her large windows. *[See photo 8.8]*

The vessel's displacement was 1,720 gross tons, her length 272 feet, with 36 foot beam and 14-1/2 foot draft. She had turbo-electric propulsion, powered by steam, with twin screws. Built for George F. Baker

*8.8 Steam yacht Viking. Courtesy of Deer Isle-Stonington Historical Society*

Jr., her cost was $1.5 million. Baker's father was at the time one of the three or four richest men in the United States, and is said to have remarked, "My son can afford it. He has a rich father." Junior, who loved deep sea fishing, used the yacht to follow the fish for about eight years, but generally his cruising fell into a pattern: up to New England, Nova Scotia and the Saint Lawrence in summer, down to the West Indies and west coast of South America in the winter. In between, in January and February, the yacht would lay up for maintenance work. In addition, in the fall and spring, the yacht would often sail to the Mediterranean.

Men from Deer Isle who served on *Viking* included her captain, Edwin ("Eddie") Thompson. Born in 1886, he was one of ten children, five girls and five boys, of Frederick E. and Clara J. (Small) Thompson, who married in 1871. Their father was a mariner who lost his life twenty-two years later in 1893 on the schooner *Brave*, off Plum Island, as described in Chapter 3. How his mother survived with a houseful of children is not known, as she did not remarry. Presumably, her two older sons,

*8.9 Viking officers Captain Eddie Thompson (left) and Chief Engineer Kimball Eaton. Courtesy of Deer Isle-Stonington Historical Society*

who were 20 and 22 when the tragedy struck, helped support the household. At the time, Eddie was all of seven years old. Three of Clara's sons went to sea, two of whom became captains. One was Eddie Thompson, who by 1910 is listed in the *Register* as "Yachting Officer." By then 44 years old, he had moved to New London, Connecticut, where many of the big yachts were berthed, as did many islanders. Thus, there was quite a collection of people from Deer Isle living there. *[See photo 8.9]*

Chief engineer was Kimball Conary Eaton. His wife was Edith Pond Haskell Greenlaw, a fourth

### More Yachts with Deer Isle Men Aboard

*8.10 Family picture of Captain Farrington Powers (left), his wife Hattie (second adult from the right), her mother and father (between her and Farrington), Michael and Hannah Snowman, and the Powers children, Maurice the youngest on the right. The woman on the far right is Hattie's sister, Grace Grindle. Courtesy of Tinker (Gross) Crouch*

*8.11 The house of Captain Farrington Powers, in which Maurice Powers and the wives of Captains Grover Small and Merle Greene grew up. Photographed in 2014, the house looks the same today as it did 100 years ago. Photo by William A. Haviland*

Serving on *Viking* along with its captain and chief engineer were islanders Maurice Powers, Chief Mate; Randall Haskell, Second Mate; Robert Thompson, Radio Officer; Allen Smith, Second Engineer; Percy Joyce, Launchman, and about twenty more. Of these, Maurice Powers was a brother of Merle Greene's wife. His father was Farrington Collins Powers of North Deer Isle, himself a yacht captain. *[See photo 8.10]* All three of Farrington's brothers went to sea, two of them going yachting, but farming as well. The other brother is listed in the *1910 Register* simply as mariner. Farrington himself as a youth sailed with his father aboard a Grand Banks fishing vessel, before going on to command the yachts *Irene* and *Evelyn*. His seafaring ended in his 50s when he went totally blind. At least two of Farrington's sons went yachting, one briefly before turning to masonry work. Maurice was the only one of Farrington's three sons who made a career of it. All four of his daughters married yachtsmen, including Grover Small, profiled in Chapter 4, Grover's nephew, Merle Greene, and Grover's cousin, Hosea Barbour. *[See photo 8.11]*

After service on the earlier *Ventura* (see below), Maurice went on to become Chief Mate on *Viking*. Others who served as mates on *Viking* at one time or another were Martin Billings, Ernest Smith and Norman Gray. Among the deck crew were Carroll Joyce, Howard Haskell and Lowell Kent. Percy Joyce was promoted to Quartermaster as well as captain of Baker's commuter yacht (*Little Viking*), Lyle Cleveland and Ira Allen also served

generation descendant of one of the two Greenlaw brothers who returned to Deer Isle after the Revolution. She and her husband took up residence in the house built by her grandfather, on land carved out of his father's original hundred-acre farm. The house still stands on the north side of the Greenlaw District Road, just beyond its intersection with the Sunshine Road.

Kimball Eaton served as engineer on several steamboats, including the Penobscot Bay steamboat *Westport*, and tugboats of the Crotch Island, Stonington, granite quarries. Born in 1892, he died in 1955.

as quartermasters. Seamen were George Lufkin (when not on *Camargo*), Gilbert Marshall, Perley Kent, Merle Greenlaw and Clarence Sawyer; Henry Haskell was in the steward's department, and Ted Pickering was oiler. An article in a June 1932 *Deer Isle and Stonington Press* reported that the yacht was manned "from Captain to cabin boy, by Deer Isle sailors."

In 1937, owner Baker embarked on a round-the-world cruise. From Panama to Tahiti he ran under one engine alone, so as to have sufficient fuel. At Tahiti, he refueled, taking on 76,000 gallons from nearly 1,500 oil drums, all managed by hand. From Tahiti, he headed for Australia, but shortly became ill. With this, *Viking* diverted to Honolulu, but instead of getting better, George Baker Jr. died. His estate then sold the yacht, in 1938, to Norman Woolworth, cousin to the heiress Barbara Hutton and related to descendants of the founder of the F.W. Woolworth five- and ten-cent stores. His father had made a fortune from real estate, sugar and other investments. Norman and his family lived on a 65-acre estate in New Canaan, Connecticut, but spent summers on a 1,750 acre family estate in Winthrop, Maine. Under his ownership, *Viking's* name was changed to *Noparo*, for his children, Norman, Pamela and Robert. Remaining in her crew were islanders Randall Haskell, Perley Kent and Ernest Smith; newcomers were Beckwith Hardy and Leroy Eaton. Woolworth's ownership was brief, as the ship was purchased in 1940 by the U.S. Navy.

With yet another name—*St. Augustine* (PG-54)—the old *Viking* was converted to a patrol gunboat and commissioned in 1941, just in time for World War II. She served first as a patrol ship out of Boston, then went to New York in 1942. From there, she escorted convoys to various Caribbean ports. This was a dangerous run, owing to the operation of German submarines (recall the torpedoing of *Cythera*, noted in Chapter 7), but in 1942, she led a successful depth charge attack on U-701. She was still doing escort duty in 1944 when, one dark and stormy night off Cape May, New Jersey, she met her end. She was escorting a convoy under radio silence and no lights—standard operating procedure at the time, despite poor visibility—when she was hit by the bow of a merchant tanker, slicing her open. She sank within minutes, with the loss of 115 of her 145 crew.

For several years, the wreck lay undisturbed beneath 250 feet of water. Then, in the 1990s, she was discovered and has since been visited by a number of divers. Now officially designated as a war grave, it is illegal to remove any objects from the wreck.

## Other Yachts of George F. Baker Jr.

The *Viking* just discussed was not the only yacht owned by the junior Baker. There was an earlier *Viking*, built of steel in 1909 by Pusey and Jones Company of Wilmington, Delaware. Considerably smaller than her later namesake, she was of 301 gross tons and measured 180 feet overall. Her beam was 23-1/2 feet, and she drew 9 feet 9 inches of water. She was steam powered, with twin screws.

There were Deer Isle men aboard this early *Viking*, including in the 1922-23 season Edward Young Haskell as captain and Merle Greene as second mate. E.Y. Haskell, named for his grandfather, was born in 1879, son of George Dudley Haskell, brother of Captain Willie Greene's wife and nephew of Albert Love Haskell, captain of the *Tarantula*. Edward was a commander of yachts when he was barely out of his teens, and came to be one of the most widely known captains on the Atlantic coast. He married the daughter of Captain Ed Richardson (see Chapter 3), and the couple moved to New London, Connecticut. By 1915, he had been appointed captain of the early *Viking*, which turned out to be his last command. He died in 1928, at the age of 48.

In addition to his yachting, Edward was something of an inventor. He held a patent for an instrument used in connection with a mariner's compass to sight a moving object at sea, recording automatically its true bearing. The device, known as the "Locator," was soon installed in all the major trans-Atlantic ocean liners.

We do not know how many other islanders were aboard, or who they were, with two exceptions. One lost his life in a tragic accident, as reported in the *Deer Isle Messenger* on May 16, 1913.

### More Yachts with Deer Isle Men Aboard

*8.12 George Baker's yawl, Ventura, in Biscayne Bay, Florida. Courtesy of Tinker (Gross) Crouch*

The community was saddened Monday when it was learned that Brainard Bray, son of the late Sargent Bray, was drowned on Saturday afternoon by falling from his launch on board the yacht *Viking*. He was a very worthy young man and had just arrived at the point where he was a much needed help to his widowed mother who has had, since the death of her husband, something of a struggle in the rearing of a fatherless family. Bray was launchman on the *Viking* and the accident happened while the yacht was proceeding through Hell's Gate. The launch had but shortly been hoisted to the davits; Bray got into her to wipe her off, and by some means, unobserved, lost his balance and fell overboard. His cries attracted attention, the yacht was stopped; a boat lowered and every possible effort made to rescue him; but in the strong tide, he was unable to keep above water until assistance came and sank before they reached him. Up to this time the body has not been recovered, although it is said the yacht's owner has offered a reward of $500 for its recovery. Sargent Bray, a younger brother who was on the yacht at the time of the accident, arrived home Monday, bringing the first news of the sad event.

Another of Baker's boats was the *Ventura*, built in 1922 in the Herreshoff yard at Bristol, Rhode Island. Built of wood, she was a sailboat, rigged as a ketch, with an auxiliary gas engine. Of 25 gross tons, she was just over 60-1/2 feet overall, with a 14-foot beam and drew 4 feet of water. She cruised up and down the east coast to Cuba and into the Bahamas and, among other things, followed the fish, including swordfish. Her captain after 1923 was Merle Greene (discussed in Chapter 4); on board with him were Deer Islanders Maurice Powers (brother of the captain's wife), Charles Hutchins, and a cook from Newfoundland. *[See photo 8.12]*

When not in the water, *Ventura* was hauled at the Electric Boat shipyard in Groton, Connecticut. It is said that work on her over one winter is what kept the yard "afloat" in that year. After Baker was through with her, the vessel was renamed *Adventure*, and sank going south under Captain Ed. Billings of Little Deer Isle.

George Baker had not just one, but two yachts named *Ventura*. The second was a 45-foot sloop, on which Merle Greene served in 1922 before moving on to the *Viking* and larger *Ventura*.

## Yet Another *Viking*

One of the frustrations in trying to find out about the big steam yachts is that the same name was frequently used for several vessels. Evidently, there were not just two named *Viking*. Consider the following news item, dated before either of the *Vikings* just discussed was launched; it is from the July 25, 1902, *Deer Isle Messenger*.

> The fine steam yacht *Viking*, recently purchased by Franklin Haines of Yonkers, N Y, and commanded by John C. Greenlaw, one of Deer Isle's most efficient yacht captains, entered this harbor on Sunday, leaving Monday for Castine, en route to Bar Harbor. The *Viking* is 138 feet over all, 20 feet beam, and 10 feet in draught. She carries fifteen men. Of these, Jason Greenlaw, first officer, J.E. Smith and L.E. Pickering, Quartermasters, are from Deer Isle.

## Steam Bark *White Heather*

In command of this yacht was another Deer Isle captain, George Dudley Haskell. This handsome vessel, built by J. Reid and Co. of Glasgow, was of 443 gross tons, had a length of 168 feet, beam of 28 feet 2 inches, and drew 13 feet. Though she had steam power, she also had three masts rigged to carry square sails. She went through a number of owners: from 1880 to 1899, Cecil Leigh; 1900-01, C. G. Millar; 1902-03, H. L. Drummond; and 1904-10, Edward Randolph, with a new name, *Apache*. Heir to a Wall Street banking fortune and a member of the New York Yacht Club, Randolph raced her in the Kaiser's Cup Great Ocean Race of 1905. And therein lies a tale. The race itself was from Sandy Hook, New Jersey, to the westernmost tip of Cornwall, England. Eleven sailing yachts participated: the Kaiser's, two from Britain and eight from the United States. The trophy was a cup put up by Kaiser Wilhelm II of Germany, and was said to be solid gold, worth $5,000. The cup was not won by Randolph (he came in last), but by the American schooner *Atlantic*, owned by Wilson Marshall (the Kaiser's boat finished second).

With the outbreak of World War I, the trophy became a symbol of this country's hostility to all things German, so its holder presented it to the Red Cross, to be auctioned as a fund raiser. It brought in $125,000 and then, as a final statement, it was smashed on the stage of the Metropolitan Opera House in New York City. For the privilege of doing this, another $2,500 went into the Red Cross coffers. It was then discovered that, far from being a "golden cup," the trophy was made of pewter with a thin gold veneer, of very little worth!

In 1910, *White Heather* went to a new owner, L. Legru, then in 1915 to the French Navy, and in 1919 into commercial service.

George Dudley Haskell was an older brother of Albert Love Haskell of the *Tarantula*, whose family history was summarized earlier in this chapter. Originally named George Henry Clay Thompson Haskell, he did not like this, and so changed his name to the one by which he is remembered. He was not the only one disliking his given names; his brother (who also became a yacht captain) changed his from Walter Leroy Haskell to Edwin Leroy. As noted, this family had a strong maritime tradition. George, Edwin and one other brother began their careers in merchant sail, carrying cargoes to and from the southern states and West Indies. Later, George and his brother Edwin turned to steam yachting.

In the crew were other islanders, including the captain's son, Judson T. Haskell. He served as Second Mate, with Charles Pressey as First Mate and Herbert Bray as Third Mate. In 1899, both Haskell and Bray left *White Heather* and were part of the all-Deer Isle crew on the America's Cup defender (as Bray had been also in 1895). They then signed on as quartermasters aboard the *Sapphire*, under Charles Small's command (photo 4.11). Haskell, at least, was still aboard in 1904. An item in the *Deer Isle Messenger* for July 7 of that year reported that:

> Mrs. Charles A. [sic] Small and Mrs. Judson T. Haskell have been spending the past week at Islesboro where their husbands have been for awhile in the yacht which Capt. Small commands.

*8.13 Steam yacht Narada. Courtesy of Rena Day*

It may be recalled that later, on *Camargo*, Small's engine room crew was largely from Islesboro.

## Narada

Another steam yacht that sported a spread of canvas as well was *Narada*. In 1889, this wooden-hulled vessel slid down the ways at Ramage and Ferguson in Leith, Scotland, with the name *Semiramis*. She underwent two subsequent changes of name, first *Margarita* and then *Narada*. This last name was for a Vedic sage important in Hinduism. The vessel's displacement was 505 gross tons, with a length of 224 feet, 27-foot beam and 15-foot 9-inch draft. Though she was steam powered, cruising at 15 knots, she was rigged to carry a set of square sails on her foremast, with a fore-and-aft rig on her main. *[See photo 8.13]*

It was in 1896 that *Narada* was acquired by Henry D. Walters, who became a member of the New York Yacht Club in that year. Although born in Baltimore in 1889, at the age of 41, he removed to Wilmington, North Carolina, and subsequently to New York City. His father had amassed a fortune from the creation of the Atlantic Coastline Railroad, of which Henry became manager upon his father's death. Both men used their fortune to acquire important works of art, which Henry donated for the creation of the Walters Art Museum in Baltimore. Nevertheless, he seldom returned to the city of his birth, and in New York, served after 1903 on the executive committee of the Metropolitan Museum of Art, and later as a vice president.

Though not the largest of the thirteen yachts owned at the turn of the century by members of the New York Yacht Club, *Narada's* elegance was such that she was regarded as one of the premier "show boats" of the fleet. Walters used the yacht as his summer mailing address, hosted many parties aboard her, and made weekend jaunts to Newport, Rhode Island. Other cruises were up the Hudson River, or to various European and Mediterranean ports. For these, Walters would send the yacht ahead, crossing the Atlantic himself on one of the big ocean liners. At Southampton, England, he would join his yacht and cruise along the coast of Europe and around the Mediterranean, or into the Baltic Sea. *[See photo 8.14]*

When the U.S. entered World War I, the *Narada*, like so many other private yachts, joined the Navy. As SP-161, still with her civilian name, she became a patrol boat from 1917 to 1919. Based at New London, Connecticut, she was used for experimental submarine signal work. Once the war was over, the ship was returned to her owner, who was then 71 years of age. A year after his death in 1931, his widow sold the yacht to Louis Lubchansky of Connecticut Iron and Metal Co. for $5,000. It seemed a bargain, considering her original cost of $80,000, plus another $30,000 to refit her after her service in the Navy. Her new owner toyed with the idea of using her as a floating night club or an excursion boat, but in the end, scrapped her and sold off various parts.

It was in 1914 that Lawrence Burton Gross of Stonington took command of *Narada*. Born in 1877, he was the fifth child of James Edwin and Helen Marr (Webb) Gross. The family, which ultimately included five sons and one daughter, lived at Green Head. James, who died in 1894, was a fisherman, and three of his sons followed in his footsteps. The other two, Lawrence and his younger brother Seth, became yacht captains. Seth, captain of the *Whileaway*, moved off island to Brooklyn, New York; Lawrence to New London, Connecticut.

Lawrence married a girl he met in New London, whose family had emigrated from Ireland when she was 8 years old, but they had no children. Though living away, the two of them returned to the island periodically. When not needed on the yacht, they had a summer home in Stonington. This was a house built by Lawrence's father who when he retired, put up a house at Sand Beach, soon taken over by one of his older sons. He then built a second for himself, and it was that one which Lawrence inherited.

When *Narada* was returned to her owner after the war, she needed work to convert her back to civilian use. This was done in New London, and Captain Gross oversaw the work. Upon its completion, in November of 1920, he hosted a luncheon for 150 employees of the Thames Towboat Company in the loft of the company plant. His co-host was Thomas Riley of the yacht, and it was to express their appreciation of the work done on the craft. *[See photo 8.15]*

On board *Narada* with Captain Gross was Randall Haskell of Deer Isle as Second Mate, a position he

*8.14 Narada's figurehead. Courtesy of Rena Day*

also held on *Viking/Noparo*. He was the youngest of five children—4 boys and a girl—born to Jasper W. and Martha Flavilla (Haskell) Haskell. She was a daughter of Edward Young Haskell, who we have previously encountered. Jasper was the grandson of Ignatius Haskell, whose family came to Deer Isle in the late 18th century from Newburyport, Massachusetts. There, they had important shipping interests. In 1772, Ignatius' father Mark acquired the land on which Deer Isle village now stands, and by 1778 he and his family had taken up residence here. With his sons Ignatius and Solomon he went into business as Mark Haskell and Sons, building a saw and grist mill, of which the milldam in the village is all that remains. The firm also built some stores, as well as several vessels used in the family's trade. When his father died, Ignatius inherited the business, and was a big promoter of vessel construction. For his part, Solomon saw to the family's affairs in Newburyport. It was Ignatius

## More Yachts with Deer Isle Men Aboard

8.15 Unidentified members of *Narada's* crew from Deer Isle. Courtesy of Rena Day

who built what is now the Pilgrim's Inn, as a house for his bride. It was intended to make life livable for her, on the frontier far from the bustle of the town where she grew up. The pieces of the house were fabricated in Newburyport, and shipped Down East in one of the Haskell vessels.

Although Jasper's father Aaron became a tanner, Jasper himself followed in his grandfather's footsteps. He is listed in the *1910 Register* as a sea captain, but he owned several vessels as well. For several years, he lived with his family in New Haven and went yachting. Later in life, however, he came ashore and ran a grist mill and tannery where the Lily Pond brook enters the Mill Pond at Deer Isle village. Jasper died in 1914; nine years later, the building was moved up onto Main Street, where it became the White Front Sweet Shop. It is still there; most recently, it was the Deer Isle Photo Studio.

Jasper's oldest son is also listed in the *1910 Register* as a sea captain. His first command was at the age of nineteen; his last command was the schooner *Hesper*, familiar to travelers on Route 1 in Wiscasset, near which it lay abandoned (photo 3.13). Another son is listed as yachting, and later became a captain. The third son was listed in 1910 simply as mariner. Randall at that time was still in school, but with his father and brothers all seafarers, it is not surprising that he, too, would take to the sea. After yachting, he served as a captain in the Merchant Marine before coming ashore in the 1950s. With his own children then in school, he ran a grocery store and meat market in Deer Isle village.

Another Haskell on board was Randall's second cousin Ralph (their grandfathers were brothers). Ralph's grandfather was a tradesman, and his son ran a tannery (as did Aaron and later, Jasper). Ralph, however, returned to the sea, and after his time on *Narada*, became a yacht captain himself. In the 1920s he commanded the *Ocalagua*, owned by the inventor of the Locomobile. Unfortunately, the yacht fell victim to the Depression, and Ralph found himself beached. His career ended as janitor of the Deer Isle high school.

Many other island men served aboard *Narada* as crewmen. We do not have all their names, but among them were Emaron Eaton, along with George Washington Trundy and Francis Marion ("Frank") Trundy. The latter two were brothers, sons of Thomas and Julia Trundy. Born in Sunshine, the family moved to Oceanville when George (born in 1859) was 4 years old (Frank was older by three years). The boys' father was a sail maker, a profession taken up by George after his early years at sea. George also worked later on the granite quarry. His last years were spent living with his sons, one in Stonington, the other in South Deer Isle. He died in 1941. Frank, who lived until 1940, became a captain. His last years were spent at Sailor's Snug Harbor on Staten Island, New York, a home for aging seamen.

Also on board was Frank (Francis Packard) Saunders of Sunset. He was the son of Edwin L. and Martha (Packard) Saunders. Edwin was a mariner who went on ships from age 13, having fled school to avoid punishment. He became captain of the *Anita*

*Berwin* and *Warren Sawyer*, the latter wrecked off Nantucket. His last days were spent at Sailor's Snug Harbor on Staten Island.

For a time, Frank lived on the Dow Road and did some fishing. Family lore has it that he married a prostitute named Mary and taught her to read. They later separated, and he became blind. At that point, he went to live with his sister and her family on their farm in Litchfield, Connecticut.

*8.16 J. P. Morgan's yacht Corsair II. Courtesy of Rena Day*

## The *Corsairs* and Other Yachts of J. P. Morgan, Sr. and Jr.

Over the years, the financial tycoon J.P. Morgan and his son had a series of big yachts, all named *Corsair*, as well as smaller commuter yachts, to take them from their estates into New York City. Although not exclusively manned by Deer Isle sailors, islanders did serve on several.

The first *Corsair* was a relatively modest craft, built in 1880 to carry its owner from his estate on the Hudson River near West Point to lower Manhattan. Her builder was William Cramp and Sons in Philadelphia. Measuring 185 feet overall, she was 23 feet in the beam and drew 9 feet 3-1/2 inches of water. Twin engines of 760 horsepower each drove her twin screws, giving her a speed of up to 15 knots.

She was replaced in 1891 by a vessel built by Neafie and Levy of Philadelphia, which set the pattern for her successors, with her dark hull and buff-colored masts and stack. Her displacement was 786 tons; she was 240 feet 8 inches long with a beam of just over 27 feet, drew 12 feet and cruised at 17 knots. Morgan had her in almost-daily use, to commute to Manhattan and to live on while there, and also for business conferences as well as summer cruises.

Seven years after her launch, the U.S. Navy purchased her for service in the Spanish-American War as a gunboat under the name USS *Gloucester*. The price was $225,000, but the Navy got their money's worth. She participated in the blockade of Cuba and the Battle of Santiago de Cuba, entered the harbor of Guanica, Puerto Rico, ahead of the fleet, capturing it, and helped capture Arroyo. From 1899 to 1902 she served as a schoolship at Annapolis, and after that, as tender to the Commander in Chief of the South Atlantic Squadron. Later, she was on harbor patrol at New York City. Finally, in 1919 while doing survey work in the Gulf of Mexico, she struck a reef and sank.

Meanwhile, Morgan commissioned a new yacht, built in 1899 by T.S. Marvel of Newburgh, New

York, and finished by W. and A. Fletcher in Hoboken, New Jersey. At the time, Morgan had just been elected Commodore by the New York Yacht Club, and with his old boat sold to the Navy, he needed a new flagship. Larger than her predecessor, this third *Corsair* had a displacement of 1,132 gross tons, was 304 feet overall, with a 33-foot 4-inch beam and 15-1/2 foot draft. Her speed was 19 knots, provided by two vertical triple expansion steam engines driving twin screws. On her lower deck were ten state rooms, a large library, six bathrooms and a dining saloon. On the saloon deck was the galley, chart room and deck state room. She carried a crew of 55 officers and men, and their quarters were forward. On board were three launches, one gig, one lifeboat and one cutter. *[See photo 8.16]*

No expense was spared on furnishings. Morgan wanted the new *Corsair* to resemble its predecessor, and so he sought out carpets identical to the earlier ones. Because that pattern was no longer available, he paid to have it set up again in the factory. Food was served on priceless china: custom-made hand-painted French porcelain and hand-painted Minton china, all emblazoned with the burgee of the New York Yacht Club, and Morgan's personal house flag. The latter was embroidered on the ship's linens as well. The sterling silver included such items as two salters, with urn bowls atop reeded columns and engraved with "S.Y. Corsair" and a silhouette of the yacht, and a Tiffany and Co. cigar cutter designed in the *Corsair's* crescent and star motif. For entertainment there was a mahogany poker set with ivory chips. Guests entertained aboard included Theodore Roosevelt, Thomas Edison and Mark Twain.

When J.P. Morgan senior died in 1913, *Corsair* was inherited by J.P. junior, who was Vice Commodore of the New York Yacht Club (he became Commodore in 1920). He chartered her to the Navy in 1917 for service in World War I. As USS *Corsair* (SP-159), she went on anti-submarine patrols off the coast of France, also escorting other vessels. In the course of her duties, she rescued survivors of two Army transports, and towed a disabled Norwegian freighter into port. After the armistice, she went to Britain, serving as flagship for the Commander, U.S. Naval Forces in European Waters. She then was returned to Morgan and refitted for civilian use. Now known as *Corsair II* (peculiar, as she was actually the refurbished third), she was then the largest yacht under U.S. Registry.

In 1927, when Edwin Greenlaw was First Mate (Chapter 6), *Corsair II* had a crew of sixty. In that year, she sailed from New York on February 7 for the Mediterranean, where her owner and guests boarded in Venice. It was Morgan's practice to cross the Atlantic on ships of the White Star Line, in which he had a financial interest, as the big liners were more comfortable in the unpredictable Atlantic storms than *Corsair*. Once aboard his own ship, he visited Adriatic and Aegean ports, returning in the spring to the New England coast, with a visit to Bar Harbor, before lay up in New York in late summer.

In 1930, Morgan considered scrapping *Corsair II*, but instead turned her over to the U.S. Coast and Geodetic Survey in exchange for a token payment. From then until 1942 she was used as a scientific research ship under the name *Oceanographer*. As such, she carried out extensive surveys, producing 15 charts. With the outbreak of World War II, she was converted to a gunboat for the Navy as USS *Natchez* (PG-85) and sent to Alaska to carry out surveys. As conditions there proved too harsh for her, she was redirected to the South Pacific under her previous name *Oceanographer*. In June 1944 she was sent to San Pedro, California, for repairs, but was found beyond fixing, and so was scrapped. *[See photo 8.17]*

When Morgan Jr. rid himself of *Corsair II*, it was to take delivery of an even more grandiose yacht, *Corsair IV*. *Corsair IV* was built by Bath Iron Works, and for the launching, the Morgan family and friends traveled to Bath in two private train cars. Despite a request for no publicity, in a small town, an event of this sort was bound to attract notice, and a crowd of onlookers turned out for the occasion. Of 2,181 gross tons, the overall length of the new vessel was 343-1/2 feet, with a 42-foot 8-inch beam and 18-foot draft. She had the traditional *Corsair* black hull touched off by gold trim, with two raked masts and funnel painted buff. Her cabins and bulwarks were all paneled in teak. Power was provided by four oil-fired boilers and two General Electric turbo-electric

*8.17 The launching of J. P. Morgan's Corsair IV at Bath Iron Works. In spite of Morgan's desire to avoid much notice, a close look at the photo reveals throngs of spectators on the bridge. Collection of Maine Maritime Museum, courtesy of Maine Memory Network*

systems. Speed capability was 17 knots. Total cost for this queen of the sea was $2.5 million.

Each year, Morgan would meet the Archbishop of Canterbury at Marseilles for a cruise to the holy land. On the earlier *Corsair*, the Archbishop found an after skylight handy as a table for his after-breakfast cup of coffee. For His Grace's continuing comfort, a special skylight, like one on the earlier yacht, was installed on the main deck of the new one for him to use. For ten years, the yacht made numerous ocean cruises, with a crew of fifty, including a physician and laundry staff. Then, in 1940, she was leased to the British Admiralty for one dollar a year.

During World War II, *Corsair IV* went on patrol duty out of Bermuda. Afterwards, she was sold to Pacific Cruise Lines, under Panamanian registry. Her interior was completely redone to create elegant surroundings for passengers on what was intended to be the most luxurious cruise ship ever. Her forty-two rooms could accommodate eighty-two passengers, and her crew of seventy-six included more than forty in the steward's department, as well as top European chefs. For a price of $600 per person, passengers could go on two-week cruises out of Long Beach, California, Acapulco, Mexico, or (in 1948) up the inside passage along the Alaska coast from Vancouver. Alas, in 1949 she struck a rock and beached at Acapulco, although with no loss of life. So ended the career of *Corsair IV*. Her generators were salvaged, however, and used to power the resort town of Acapulco.

In addition to the *Corsair*s, J.P. Morgan Jr. had two commuter yachts for use between his Glen Cove, Long Island, estate and New York City. The first was the *Mermaid*, about which we have been able to learn little. According to Lloyd's Register of American Yachts, she was a wooden vessel, built in 1902 in the Herreshoff yard at Bristol, Rhode Island. With a length of 89 feet overall and a 10-1/2 foot beam, she drew 3-1/2 feet of water. She

*8.18 J. P. Morgan's commuter yacht Navette. Copyright Mystic Seaport, Rosenfeld Collection, #2180F, used with permission*

was powered by steam. Whether Deer Islanders served on her is not known.

Built as a replacement for *Mermaid* in 1916 was the better-known *Navette*. She was aptly named, being French for "Shuttle." Launched at the Herreshoff yard in 1917, she was the last of the steam commuter yachts. Her length overall was just over 114 feet, with a 14-foot 3-inch beam and 3-foot 6-1/2-inch draft. For power she had two triple-expansion, coal-fired steam engines with 9-inch stroke. She was quite fast, cruising around 30 miles per hour. *[See photo 8.18]*

The vessel's crew quarters were forward, with a raised steering section amidships, a galley and dining area next aft, the latter being quite sumptuous. Aft of this was an elliptical, roomy cockpit, and a flat, wide stern. The cruising accommodations were ample for a party of six. With her hull designed for speed, *Navette* was only once passed by another boat. Morgan immediately ordered the crew to "pile on the steam," overhauling and passing the other yacht. So great was the stern wave that it washed over the other craft, drenching its occupants.

Morgan discontinued use of *Navette* in 1931, about the time he acquired *Corsair IV*. The smaller yacht remained in lay up at Hempstead, Long Island, until 1938, when she was purchased by inventor Edward Christopher Warren. An associate of the better-known Nicola Tesla, his intent was to use her to test a rotary steam engine he had designed. To do this, he removed *Navette*'s original engines (but not the boiler), which still survive—one at Mystic Seaport, the other at the Herreshoff Marine Museum in Rhode Island. Warren and some of his children lived aboard the boat, but with the outbreak of World War II, the vessel was without a licensed steam engineer. To rectify the problem, Warren's daughter Marjorie obtained a license, becoming the first woman in the United States to do so. Another daughter, Dorothy, got a master's license and the two of them, with a brother, worked their way along the coast to Florida and up a canal to La Belle and Lake Okeechobee. There they tied up and continued to live, in the galley and dining area, with a sitting room and bedroom under a shelter added to the original cockpit.

Since then, the engines were removed, the hull deteriorated, and gradually the old boat sank. Sometime after 2006, the remains were removed.

The only islanders we know that served on any of the *Corsairs* are Madison Torrey from the Reach, who was a chef on the original yacht, and as we saw in Chapter 6, Edwin Greenlaw as First Mate on *Corsair II* for a year. There surely were others, as one of the island newspapers reported in 1932 that one third of the men on J.P. Morgan's yachts "signed on from this island." The three yachts were probably *Corsair II* and *IV*, and *Navette*. On the year of her launch, as told in Chapter 6, Edwin

Greenlaw served on board as Messman, along with chef William Marshall of the Greenlaw District. A list of Deer Isle men on *Navette*, as of 1921, were Charles Greenlaw, Arthur Eaton, Lewis Sylvester, Gordon Scott, Ernest Pressey, and Courtney Bray. The latter was the older brother of Sargent and the ill-fated Brainard, who perished on the older *Viking*. He is listed in the 1910 *Register* as "farmer." What turned him to yachting may have been the need for household income to replace that which was lost with the death in 1913 of his brother Brainard.

Captain of the *Navette*, at least for some of her career, may have been Monty Haskell, an " old salt" who we met in Chapter 3. His grandson recalls that he was captain on one of J.P. Morgan's smaller yachts, that it was fast, and had unusually large engines. This suggests *Navette*. It will be recalled that Monty began his seafaring under sail, moved to yachting when commerce shifted to steam, but ended his career on schooners carrying vacationers.

## The *Gem* and Captain Alton Torrey

Another yacht on which Deer Isle men served was the *Gem*, owned by William Ziegler Jr. Built by George Lawley and Sons of Neponset, Massachusetts, in 1913, she was of 201 gross tons, 146-1/2 feet in length, with 18-foot beam and 7-foot draft (quite a contrast with *Corsair IV*). She was powered by two 1,100-horsepower oil-fired steam engines and cruised at 15 knots.

In 1917, the yacht went under charter to the U.S. Navy as USS *Gem* (SP-41). Her first service was to patrol the entrance to the harbor at New Haven, Connecticut. Subsequently she was taken by the Submarine Defense Association to test camouflage schemes, submarine detection devices and other types of equipment. She was also used to experiment with specially processed (pulverized) coal. In 1919, the Navy was through with her, and she was returned to her owner.

Captain of the yacht after the war was Alton Torrey, son of Roland B. Torrey, also a mariner. A news item in the *Deer Isle Messenger* from 1901 informs us that Roland was on the yacht *Athene*, which stopped over in September in Northwest Harbor. This provided an opportunity for a short visit to his family on the Reach. Their home was on or near the 200-acre farm that was established by pioneer Jonathan Torrey in 1763. Another reference to *Athene* in the local paper mentions Lester Gray in 1901 on the yacht with her captain, Charles Gray. Both had previously sailed as part of the all-Deer Isle crew aboard the 1895 defender of the America's Cup.

Alton Lawrence Torrey was born in 1894, and was yachting as early as the age of 16. In 1915, he was aboard the yacht *Wakiva* on a cruise to France. Owned by Lamon V. Harkness of New York, this steel vessel was built in 1907 by Ramage and Ferguson Ltd. of Leith, Scotland. Of 853 gross tons, she was 239-1/2 feet long overall, with 30-1/2 foot beam and 13-foot 10-inch draft. Her travels ranged from the North Sea to the East Indies. Steam powered, she cruised at 15 knots. She seems to have replaced an earlier smaller yacht of the same name from the same builder. On board with Torrey were islanders Morris Powers and Franklin Hardy (briefly profiled in Chapter 4). *[See photo 8.19]*

*Wakiva* went into the Navy in World War I as SP-160, escorting convoys in European waters, sometimes in company with *Corsair*. Her career ended in 1918 in much the same ways as *Viking's* did later. In heavy fog, one of the ships being escorted sliced into her, sinking her in the depths of the Atlantic.

After service in World War I as a senior Lieutenant, Torrey served as captain on two other yachts besides *Gem*—*Contessa* and *Cigarette*. The latter was one of the early commuter yachts, built in 1905 of steel by the George Lawley firm. She was 126 feet long overall, with a 14-1/2 foot beam, 4-1/2 foot draft and a displacement of 99 gross tons. With twin screws, she would move right along at 22 knots. From 1917 to 1919, she was taken by the U.S. Navy for patrol duties off Boston, Provincetown and Bar Harbor, as USS *Cigarette* (SP-1234). Her original owner was C.A. Wood of Cambridge, Massachusetts, but when the Navy was done with her she was sold (in 1920) to a new owner. For ten years, she steamed under the name *Pocantino* until scrapped in 1930.

Several yachts had the name *Contessa*; we suspect the one Alton Torrey commanded was a vessel designed by John Alden, built in Norway in 1939.

### More Yachts with Deer Isle Men Aboard

*8.19 Steam yacht Wakiva, on which Franklin Hardy, Morris Powers and Alton Torrey sailed in 1915. Courtesy of Deer Isle-Stonington Historical Society*

*8.20 Photos of Alton Torrey are hard to come by, as he did not like to be photographed. Courtesy of Almont Haskell*

It was of wood, 11 gross tons, 30-feet 2-inches in length with a 6-foot 1-inch draft. For power, she had a gasoline engine. *[See photo 8.20]*

With the outbreak of World War II, Alton Torrey served as a pilot in the Merchant Marine. After the conflict, he and his wife Marion (Greenlaw) returned to Deer Isle, having lived most of their settled life in Ridgewood, New Jersey. Their house (no longer there) was on the Reach Road a short distance from Route 15. Back on the island, he took up lobstering in a small boat he kept moored at the old ferry landing. Then, in 1950, he took charge of Nelson Rockefeller's yacht *Nirvana*, with Elmer ("Mike") Dow as deckhand. Another John Alden design, she was the largest wooden boat ever built at Hinckley's yard on Mount Desert Island. Of 35 gross tons, measuring 65 feet overall, with 14-foot 3-inch beam and 8-foot 4-inch draft, she was considerably smaller than the great pre-war mega-yachts. She was a yawl, with auxiliary power from a General Motors diesel engine. Her main saloon was painted white with mahogany trim, and furnished with settees and pilot's berths with navy blue upholstery. There was a mahogany table and polished brass fireplace.

The yacht's original owner was not Rockefeller. She went into the water six days before the 1950 Bermuda race, in which she participated, coming in third. It was soon after that Rockefeller purchased her, and he had her until 1978. Alton Torrey, however, died in 1962.

### Vanda

The power yacht *Vanda*, launched in 1929, was the first of several yachts, including *Hi-Esmaro* and *Corsair IV*, built by Bath Iron Works just before and after the start of the Great Depression. It was the first launching at the yard since 1925, following which the firm went into receivership, and the building

*8.21 The Vanda was the first of a series of yachts launched at Bath Iron Works on the eve of the Great Depression. Courtesy of Deer Isle-Stonington Historical Society*

of luxury yachts was seen as a way of reviving the company. The strategy proved successful, despite the onset of economic hard times. *[See photo 8.21]*

*Vanda* was built not only to start Bath Iron Works on the road to recovery, but also to prove that an American yard could build a luxury yacht every bit as good, if not more so, than those which U S. millionaires routinely purchased abroad. *Vanda's* future owner, Mr. Ernest B. Dane of Brookline, Massachusetts, and Seal Harbor on Mount Desert Island, was convinced, and so the work began. The new boat measured 240-feet 2-inches in overall length, with a 36-foot 4-inch beam, and 14-1/2 foot draft. Gross tonnage was 1,620. She was unusual in having a straight stem, as on a naval or merchant ship, rather than the clipper bow common on private yachts. For power, she had two 3,000 horsepower Cooper Bessemer diesels, with twin screws, that could top a speed of 16 knots. At her regular cruising speed of 12 knots, she had a range of 7,500 miles.

No expense was spared in finishing the boat. Her dining saloon, which measured 45 by 27 feet, was paneled in black walnut. Her smoking room, 23 by 16 feet, was done in fumed oak. Mr. Dane's personal stateroom was 23 by 15 feet.

Like so many of the other private yachts, *Vanda* served in World War II as USS *San Bernardino* (p. 59). Converted for naval use in Thomas Shipyard in New London, she served as a patrol gunboat, and as a weather station in the Pacific. She survived the war, was decommissioned in 1946, and sent to the Maritime Commission for disposal. Her ultimate fate is unknown.

Though *Vanda's* captain was not from Deer Isle, her Chief Mate, Elmer Dow (father of "Mike"), was. Other islanders in her crew were George Barbour, George Lane Beck, Pearl Eaton, Gilbert and Herbert Marshall, Kenneth Pickering, Bradley and Clarence Sawyer and Ralph Thompson. Of these, Clarence Sawyer also saw service on *Viking*, and George Lane Beck would later be in the crew of *Elpetal* (Chapter 9). Others probably saw service on other yachts as well. In the 1938 hurricane, her crewmen had to lie prone on deck, hanging on to whatever they could, to avoid being blown overboard.

Elmer Dow was one of six sons whose father, Dudley Dow, was himself a mariner. Married twice, Dudley died around 1907. Three years later, the *1910 Register* shows four of his sons, including Elmer, still unmarried, and living in the house with Dudley's widow (who died in 1937 at age 90). This was on a piece of land from the farm of Dudley's great-great-grandfather Nathan, who came to Deer Isle

*8.22 Joseph Pulitzer's yacht Discoverer. Courtesy of Deer Isle-Stonington Historical Society*

in 1797. Near the end of the present Dow Road, the area was once referred to as "Dow Town," owing to the number of Nathan's descendants still living there.

Not only was Elmer's father a mariner, so were three of his brothers; one (Winfield) is listed in the *1910 Register* as yachting, another (Charles) as fisherman, and a third as a steamer captain living in Panama. This was George C. Dow, who in 1914 piloted the first merchant vessel ever to pass through the Panama Canal (its captain was also from Deer Isle). A year later, George was in command of a large government tug operating in the Canal Zone, and then a lighter carrying what at that time was the world's largest crane. A fourth brother (Clarence) is listed in 1910 as a boat builder in Bristol, Rhode Island (in the Herreshoff yard?). Prior to this he, too, had gone to sea, as a member of the crew on the yacht *Sapphire* (photo 4.11), and on the *Constitution*, a yacht trying out in 1901 for another defense of the America's Cup. On this, he was joined by his brother Winfield. The fifth brother (Theodore) is listed as a farmer.

About Elmer himself we have little information, save that by 1910 he was already known as a yacht captain. Clearly, he was well seasoned in yachting by the time he signed on as mate on the *Vanda*. After leaving his ancestral home, he took up residence in a house on the outskirts of Deer Isle village, now (2014) the home of The Turtle Gallery.

## Joseph Pulitzer II and the Yacht *Discoverer*

Despite the popularity of big power yachts among those of wealth and power, not all such people abandoned sail altogether. As we have seen, George Baker had his *Ventura*, in addition to the more grandiose *Viking*. Another was Joseph Pulitzer II, heir to his father's publishing empire. Each summer was spent by the Pulitzer family in Bar Harbor in their castle-like "cottage," Chatwold. Offshore, the senior Pulitzer's 268-foot steam yacht *Liberty* was kept moored, as its owner was never happier than when at sea. His son, then, also developed a liking for yachting, and at the age of 18 was given his own sailboat. In it, he could sail from New York to Bar Harbor. After his father's death in 1913, Pulitzer took over the Bar Harbor property, but the *Liberty* was sold. Instead, Pulitzer, who really loved sailing, did his yachting in a 70-foot yawl, which he hung onto even when he felt the financial pinch of the depression. *[See photo 8.22]*

Though far less ostentatious than the big power yachts of the day, Pulitzer's yacht *Discoverer* still required a professional crew, even if relatively small. Her Captain, William Conary, was from the village of Sunshine in the town of Deer Isle. The relationship between him and the boat's owner is worth looking at, as it is another example of the kind of relationship that existed between Willie Greene and the owner of the yacht *Akela*.

William Irving Conary, familiarly known as "Willie I," was born in 1873 to Captain William Wallace Conary and his first wife, Frances (Westcott). One of eleven children born to this couple (William W. fathered one more by his second wife, Daisy), Willie I grew up in Deer Isle's "golden age" of seafaring. His father, a master mariner, followed the sea for many years before coming ashore to run a general store and post office in Sunshine at Conary's Landing. Even then, he was active in the fishing industry.

In the *1910 Register*, four of Willie's brothers have yachting listed as their occupation, and another is listed as a fisherman. Willie himself was also listed as a fisherman, although he had earlier been involved in yachting, and would be again. In 1899, he and his brother Alva both served in the all-Deer Isle crew of the America's Cup defender *Columbia*. *[See photo 8.23]*

Willie I's later career in yachting was as captain of Pulitzer's yacht *Discoverer*. Besides his love of sailing, Pulitzer, who was 12 years younger than his captain, was quite sociable and liked to host dinner parties. Many such parties were at his Bar Harbor mansion, but he also hosted them aboard his boat. One such event was noted in the local Deer Isle paper (January 2, 1932):

Likes Our Fish Chowder.

Deer Isle yacht stewards as well as captains are occasionally getting appreciative words from those to whom they cater. Last summer Explorer R.E. Byrd was a guest on the yacht *Discoverer*, Capt. Wm. I. Conary, on which Alva Conary was Steward. Recently the steward received a letter from the Admiral in which he said: "I want you to know how very greatly I have enjoyed your dinners, especially your fish chowder. It is wonderful and those of us on the expedition would like to have you go south with us."

Willie's brother Alva was older by eight years and, though serving in a lesser capacity, a master mariner in his own right. After 40 years of yachting, poor health eventually forced him ashore where he helped his father in the lobster business, the general store and post office.

The relationship between Captain Willie and Joseph Pulitzer went beyond the formal one between master and owner. They genuinely enjoyed one another's company. On numerous occasions, the yacht was anchored off Sunshine, and the two men would visit ashore, sitting and "shooting the breeze" on Willie's porch. One incident recalled by Marshall Rice Jr., Willie's nephew, is of a time when Pulitzer walked up to the house, where

*8.23 Willie I. Conary, captain of the yacht Discoverer. Courtesy of Deer Isle-Stonington Historical Society*

Willie had several fish hung out on clothes lines to dry. Pulitzer asked: "Willie, what's that god awful smell?" To which Willie replied: "It's dried fish, awfully good," whereupon he peeled the skin off one and proceeded to chew on it. "Ya oughta try one, you'll like it!" Pulitzer was dubious, but after some hesitation, he tried some. When he went back to the yacht, he was seen carrying three dried fish with him, smell and all.

Later on, during the same summer, Willie I gathered several men and boys in the Sunshine community for "haying time." The fields had been cut and the hay winnowed and dried. Willie had already taken a day in July and "hooked up" a mess of scallops so his wife Lizilla (Stevens) could cook up a scallop chowder—scallops, chunked and sliced potatoes, milk, cream, and seasoning—along with hot buttered biscuits.

The men had gathered around the table and Joe Pulitzer was there among them when the chowder was served. Willie asked one of the men what he thought of having a scallop chowder in haying time-scallops were only supposed to be caught during the winter months, so what Will had done was somewhat illegal. The old man cleared his throat and finally said, "Well, Will, it does well enough."

The meal was chowder and biscuits alone. Joe Pulitzer ate only one bowl and sat there quietly while others had seconds and thirds. Finally Lizilla called from the kitchen: "I hope everyone is ready for dessert!" She saw Pulitzer signal her and she asked him, "Is everything all right, Joe?" "Oh yes, mam, but dessert now?" was the reply. "Yes, why?" she asked. "Well, mam, we've only had the first course."

Apparently, Joe was used to having a three- or four-course meal. So he decided to have a couple more bowls of chowder and then apple pie with home-cranked vanilla ice cream for dessert before walking back down the path to the shore. There he climbed into his dinghy and rowed out to his yacht. Later in the evening he rowed back ashore and walked up through the woods to Will and Lizilla's house for another meal and more dessert, this time blueberry pie and ice cream.

Willie I and Lizilla had three sons and two daughters. Their third son they named Joseph Pulitzer Conary, in honor of their friend. As for *Discoverer*, by 1941 she had a new captain. As reported in an October issue of the *Deer Isle Messenger*:

> Capt. Maynard Conary has brought the yacht *Discoverer* to the Stonington-Deer Isle Yacht Basin to be hauled up for the winter.

Maynard was the son of Herbert, an older brother of Willie I, who also went yachting.

The *Discoverer* may seem like an anachronism in the age of really big power yachts. In fact, she was a harbinger of things to come. As a consequence of the depression, World War II and changed tax policies, the era of the big yachts was doomed. After the war, as we will see in the next chapter, private yachts were far more like *Discoverer*, Rockefeller's *Nirvana* or George Baker's *Ventura*, than like *Viking*, *Hi-Esmaro* or *Corsair*.

# Chapter 9: The Post War Period and the End of Yachting

*World War II scattered the great yachts far and wide.... Crews for luxury yachts could no longer be found, and even if they were available, wages for a large crew would break all but a few of the world's multi- millionaires. As an example of how times changed, the roster of the New York Yacht Club included only five power yachts over 100 feet by 1968....*

Bill Robinson, *Legendary Yachts*, p. 175.

The outbreak of World War II pretty much brought to a halt the era of the "mega-yachts." Most of those still in operation were acquired by the Navy, and many—like *Hi-Esmaro* and *Noparo* (ex *Viking*)—were lost in the conflict. Those that came through the war unscathed—like *Corsair IV* and *Camargo*—went into commercial service. One exception to this was the yacht *Elpetal*, of which more below. On Deer Isle, it became rare in the 1940s to see notices of men going yachting. After the war, some men went back to it, but far fewer than before. Moreover, the yachts then in service tended to be far smaller than the "floating palaces" of the 1930s.

## *Elpetal*

One notable exception was the yacht *Elpetal*. She was built in 1930 as the steel-hulled *Reveler* at Friedrick Krupp Germania Werke in Kiel, Germany, for the chairman of the Packard Car Company. With a displacement of 1,434 tons, she was 226 feet in length, had a beam of 34 feet, and a 12-foot 8-inch draft. Propelled by two 2,200 horsepower Krupp diesels with twin screws, she made a speed of 15.5 knots.

A year after she was built, *Reveler* was sold to Charles McCann of the Woolworth five and ten cent store chain and renamed *Chalena* (for Charles and Helena McCann). In 1939, she changed hands again, being sold to Leon Mandel and renamed *Carola* for his wife. This ownership lasted until the vessel was acquired by the Navy in 1942. This saw her conversion into a patrol gunboat at Gibbs Engine Company in Jacksonville, Florida. With this went another name change, to USS *Beaumont* (PG-60). The Navy decommissioned the ship early in 1946, and a year later she was transferred to the War Shipping Administration for disposal. Then, in 1949, she was sold to Norman B. Woolworth's Elpetal Corporation; the name comes from Norman's three best friends: El for Eliot Fox, his neighbor and stock broker; pe for Peter Walton, an artist and art teacher from Middlebury, Vermont; and tal for Talbot Malcolm, his attorney. Renamed for the corporation, and overhauled at Bath Iron Works, she replaced Woolworth's earlier *Noparo*, lost in the late war. His ownership lasted until 1957, and several Deer Isle men were in her crew. Her next owner was a Greek shipping business man, until 1983, when she was purchased by an Australian

*9.1 Elpetal, about to pass under the Deer Isle-Sedgwick Bridge. Courtesy of Deer Isle-Stonington Historical Society*

impresario, film and music producer. He renamed her *Jezebel*. In 1993 she went to yet another owner, J. Paul Getty Jr., who changed her name yet again, to *Talitha G*. He had her overhauled at Plymouth, England, where two new 1,400 horsepower Caterpillar diesels replaced the original engines. With the end of the 20th century, she was still sailing as a private yacht. *[See photo 9.1]*

As already noted, a number of Deer Isle men served on *Elpetal* in the 1950s. First Mate was Arthur Cabot ("Dud") Haskell Jr., Second Mate was Ernest Smith (once mate on *Viking*), Robert Thompson was radio officer (as he had been earlier on *Viking)*, and Frank Allen was Second Engineer (again, as earlier on *Viking*).

Seamen were Emery Gray, Myron Hardy, Wayne Ciomei, and Percival ("Bud") Knowlton; Launchmen were Charles Stanley, Fulton Gross and George Lemoine. George Lane Beck, Linwood Gross, Charles Poitras and Herbert ("Buster") Aldrich were Oilers. In the Steward's department (briefly) was Bernard Spofford.

Arthur Cabot ("Dud") Haskell Jr. was the oldest child of Arthur Cabot and Beatrice (Pickering) Haskell. Both were descendants of mariners, so Dud was following a traditional calling. Dud's father was a son of Judson T. Haskell, whose father was George Dudley Haskell, who we met in the last chapter. Always a mariner, "Cap'n Jud" generally sailed as a yacht captain. He and his first wife, Rose Weed, named Arthur Cabot after the owner of one of the yachts he skippered. Arthur Cabot Sr. was a marine engineer.

Born at home in 1920, Dud boasted that the fee charged by the physician who presided at his birth worked out to exactly one dollar per pound of his birth weight. He graduated in 1938 from Deer Isle's McKinley High School, where he was a proud member of the band (he played trombone). Soon after graduation he began his career as a mariner, as a crew member on *Camargo*. In 1940, he went to work for Merchant and Miners Co. climbing the hawse pipes on several ships. With the entry of the United States in World War II he went to the United States Maritime Officers Training School in New London, where a four-month course qualified him for third officer. As third mate, he shipped aboard the *Alcoa Polaris*, a military cargo ship. This took him through the Panama Canal, around the world and back to the U.S. The ship was then converted to a troop transport, on which he served as Second Mate. On her, he saw action in the islands of the western Pacific. *[See photo 9.2]*

Dud's yachting career took off in the postwar period, and in 1945, he earned his unlimited master's license. In the 1950s, he was captain of yachts cruising the Atlantic and Caribbean. This included, in 1955, the *Souris II*, reputed to be the largest yacht ever brought into the United States from abroad (Emery Gray of Stonington was mate). While serving on *Elpetal*, returning to the states from Europe, he suffered an acute attack of appendicitis, requiring emergency surgery. The appendectomy was performed on board by an intern, assisted by the mate and the owner's wife.

In the 1960s, Dud left yachting and returned to

# The Post War Period

*9.2 Captain Arthur Cabot Haskell Jr. For a picture of his house, see photo 2-13 on page 25. Courtesy of Eric Ziner*

merchant vessels, until his retirement in 1980. After retirement, to the home in which he was born, he was active ashore in the Memorial Ambulance Corps. He earned his EMT and served on the board of directors. He mentored several school children, and was a driving force in the restoration of the old Shakespeare school *[see photo 2.14 on page 25]*. On warm sunny days, he would "hold court" on a bench in his barn door *[see photo 2.13 on page 25]*. A story told by Carroll M. Haskell (distantly related) is typical of the man:

> I had junked a VW front-wheel-drive sedan in Philadelphia, and I brought the rear suspension cross-member and rear-axle assembly up to Deer Isle in the 1966 Ford Fairlane wagon. I made a new boat trailer using that rear suspension and some oak boards that Joe Judkins had sawn out for me with his sawing machine. It was an ugly trailer, but it worked well enough, and I have used it for many things.
>
> The Galley used to be a grocery store in Deer Isle village, and there used to be a cast-iron-framed wooden bench out in front, where Captain Arthur Haskell and others would gather to pass the time of day, gossiping and telling stories. I drove into the village to mail some letters, and Captain Arthur, known as "Dud," hollered at me, "Hey, Cabbage! You ain't a native no more!"

I asked, "Why's that, Arthur?"

"Well, you've been away; ya hafta be back here fifty years to be a native agin!" ignoring that he had been away at sea almost all his adult years.

Several days later, I hauled a load of brush down to the Deer Isle recycling center (read "dump"), and Dud was down there fibbing with Frankie Davis, the attendant at that time. Arthur saw me, and as I was getting ready to leave, he shouted, "Cabbage, did ya make that thing?" (indicating my crude-but-it-works trailer).

"Why, yes, Arthur, I did."

"Well, then! You're a native!" he replied, with emphasis on the last three words. Undeterred, I went back for another load.

Captain Dud is eighty-eight years old, and his health and stamina have deteriorated. But he doesn't give up. He still opens the cow-barn door to hold court, but not every nice day!

Captain Arthur Cabot Haskell Jr. died in 2010.

## Other Yachts of the Postwar Era

In the postwar era, *Elpetal* and *Souris II* were anachronisms. Most yachts were very much smaller, more like Rockefeller's *Nirvana*, generally less than one hundred feet in length. Commensurate with their smaller size, they carried much smaller crews.

Typical of the era was the yacht *Antonia*, owned by Herbert Bryant. She was a houseboat, built by New York Ship and Light on the Hudson River. Eighty-two feet in length, she had a dining room forward of the pilot house, aft of which was a lounge and, on the quarterdeck, some wicker chairs and a table, shaded by the boat deck above. The captain's bunk was in the pilot house, on the starboard side. On the port side, outside, was a ladder giving access to the boat deck and flying bridge. *[See photo 9.3]*

*9.3 The yacht Antonia, the first on which Carroll Haskell served, was typical of the smaller yachts of the post-World War II era. Courtesy of Carroll M. Haskell*

Below the main deck forward, just aft of a chain locker and below the dining room was the galley. Four bunks for the crew were aft of the galley, with a tiny washbasin and cramped toilet. Behind them was the engine room, originally equipped with Krupp diesels but later replaced by two General Motors 6-71s. There were two tiny staterooms behind this, each with its own tiny bathroom. Astern was the master stateroom with its own bathroom. In the very stern was a lazarette, used for storage and housing the steering mechanism.

The only Deer Islander in the crew was Carroll M. ("Cabbage") Haskell, born in Stonington and a 1945 graduate of its high school. After some years of clamming, fishing and working on the granite quarry, he was aboard from 1953 to 1954. The captain was from Great Bruin, a small out-port on Newfoundland, totally obliterated by a tsunami in the early 20th century. The auxiliary helmsman was from Norway, as was one sailor. Another was a Swede. Haskell was hired, as the captain knew Maurice Eaton (a veteran of *Camargo*) who later was captain of a lobster carrier on which Haskell had been cook. In 1954, Bryant sold *Antonia* and bought a new boat, assumed to have been owned at one time by the actor Errol Flynn. This was the *Tonga*, a 60-foot gaff-rigged ketch with an auxiliary gasoline engine. She made one trip to Havana, Cuba, before being sold. *[See photo 9.4]* After this came the *Margo*, a 60-foot houseboat built by John Trumpy and Sons of Annapolis, Maryland. All three yachts were berthed on the Potomac and cruised from there to Florida in and out of the inland waterway. On Haskell's first trip south on *Antonia* they stopped off in Morehead City, North Carolina, for a break and to take on fuel. By chance, Alton Torrey and Mike Dow aboard *Nirvana* (Chapter 8) were also there. Before their arrival, Torrey and Dow had rescued a downed pilot off the coast. A helicopter that had been searching for him rendezvoused with the yacht, sent an airman down with a winch, and lifted the wounded man up into the "chopper." *[See photo 9.5]*

By 1955, Haskell had had enough of Bryant's yachts and obtained a waiter's job on the yacht *Addonoway*, berthed at City Island, New York. Owned by Donnelly Outdoor Advertising, she was almost a twin to the *Antonia*, being a product of the same builder. She cruised Long Island Sound and on to Cape Cod and Nantucket. By this time, Haskell was about ready to quit yachting altogether. But then, he got a call from the captain he had

# The Post War Period

*9.4 The yacht Tonga, Carroll Haskell's second yacht. Courtesy of Carroll M. Haskell*

*9.5 Carroll Haskell sailing south from Morehead City, North Carolina, aboard Tonga. Courtesy of Carroll M. Haskell*

sailed with on the three Bryant yachts, inviting him to join the crew of a brand new boat, the *Electron*. This was built in Nevins' yard on City Island for the Radio Corporation of America (RCA), and was equipped with state-of-the-art electronics, even including a large, ornate stereo console in the aft saloon. On this, General Sarnoff (chairman of the RCA board of directors) liked to play classical music at full volume. On the ship's shakedown cruise, "Cabbage" and the captain were joined by Haskell's cousin Captain Walter ("Dan") Billings, the chef and another deckhand. Captain Dan departed soon after, at which time a professional waiter from Scotland came on board. Before long, the waiter departed, as his anti-Semitism was not compatible with Sarnoff's Judaism. At that point, Haskell was offered the job, and for this was given special training by an English butler, known solely as "Marston" at RCA's headquarters at Rockefeller Center. *[See photo 9.6]*

Haskell stuck it out on the *Electron* for exactly a year, traveling between New York, Nantucket, the

*9.6 Carroll Haskell as General Sarnoff's personal waiter aboard Electron. Courtesy of Carroll M. Haskell*

Bahamas and Cuba, catering to the whims and eccentricities of various RCA executives, their families and guests. There was also the tedium of waiting around at various marinas for passengers to show up for cruises. By then, he had really had enough. Leaving the ship in Florida, he traveled to Philadelphia, married, and began a career with the telephone company. After service in the engineering department, he retired in 1991, at the age of 65.

## George Lane Beck and *Alva*

As Carroll Haskell was new to yachting in the post-World War II period, George Lane Beck was by then a veteran. He first served on the *Vanda*, followed by *Hi-Esmaro* and then *Elpetal*. His last yacht was the *Alva*, launched in 1949. She was in marked contrast to those earlier yachts: built by John Trumpy and Sons, she was 60 feet overall, with a beam of just over 16 feet, and drew an inch over 4 feet. With a wooden hull, she had a top speed of 15.75 knots, with a crew of two and accommodations for a party of four. Her owner was Edward E. Dickinson Jr. of Essex, Connecticut. He was the third generation of the family that was the world's largest supplier of witch hazel. The firm was begun by his grandfather, the Reverend Thomas Newton Dickinson, who had made a fortune selling uniforms to the Union forces in the Civil War. Thomas' son Edward reorganized the firm in 1875 as E.E. Dickinson Co. and expanded its operations. In 1929 his son took over, passing it on to his son after World War II. The *Alva* was the fifth yacht designed by Sparkman and Stephens for the second Edward Dickinson.

George Lane Beck was named for his great uncle, a highly respected sea captain. One of eight children, the captain went to sea at age 16 with his father, on a schooner packet running between Deer Isle and Rockland. He went on to serve as mate under Captain Judson Torrey on a three-master, becoming its captain at the age of 21. He sailed until retiring at age 35, at which point he became collector of customs, and went into the hardware business with M.D. Joyce (purchased in 1932 by Arthur Barter). He also served as an undertaker until his death, another example of the occupational versatility of Deer Isle mariners. The building that housed the

*9.7 George Lane Beck. Courtesy of Deer Isle-Stonington Historical Society*

undertaking business, called "The Casket House," was behind the hardware store in Deer Isle village. It was subsequently moved to Mountainville, near the Sunshine causeway, where it became the summer home of Arthur Barter's family. More recently it was moved again to become Nervous Nellie's Jams and Jellies.

Captain Beck's brother, Fred, ran a grocery and meat business in Deer Isle that was begun by his father. A third brother Charles, known as "Cuff", assisted in the store. Cuff, who was something of a prankster, lived in Sunset, and usually traveled home by a shortcut through the woods. One winter night, he donned his big bear skin coat and set out for home. Part way through the ink black woods he heard someone approaching from the opposite direction. He waited until a figure loomed up in front of him, whereupon he rose up with a throaty growl and wrapped his bear skin clad arms around Merle Greene, hugging him tightly. It is said that Merle's feet only touched the ground twice from the time Cuff grabbed him until he reached Deer

# The Post War Period

Isle village. This was the same Merle Greene we encountered in previous chapters.

The store was later taken over by Fred's son Harry, who previously had gone yachting. It was Harry who named his son after his (Harry's) uncle. The younger George Lane, after his employment on *Hi-Esmaro*, married, and went into the armed forces in World War II. After the end of that conflict, he took over the operation of the family's meat and grocery business for a short period, before selling it to Randall Haskell and returning to yachting. After *Elpetal*, his career ended on the *Alva*. In 1969, at the age of 50, he died. *[See photo 9.7]*

## Yachting's Aftermath

In the years following World War II, substantial changes came to Deer Isle. To a large extent, these were unintended consequences of the previous emphasis on yachting, now in decline. So long as islanders went to sea in family-owned and -operated vessels, as they did for many years, they maintained a great deal of self-sufficiency. But as more and more men went yachting, they became ever more dependent on wages. Another contributor was the change in commercial shipping, as corporations became the major owners of cargo vessels. In a wage economy, it became easier for islanders to pay for food, goods and services, instead of providing for themselves. They could pay others to do the things, like producing food that they had previously done for themselves.

Just as islanders became more caught up in a cash economy, there came the loss of significant income as yachting declined. Some islanders found continued employment in commercial shipping. Many of these were seasoned sailors, who had been on ships, commercial or otherwise, before the war. Many, like Weston Small and Kenneth Greenlaw, rose to high positions in their profession. But many islanders, especially younger ones, turned to fishing in local waters. Instead of sailing all over the world, as their ancestors had, they stayed home, and became more insular.

This new insularity on the part of islanders is ironic, given the connection to the mainland brought about by the opening of the Deer Isle-Sedgwick Bridge in 1939. The conventional wisdom would see this event as opening up the outside world to the islanders. After all, they could now come and go to and from the island at any time of day or night, any day of the week. No longer were they at the mercy of ferry or steamboat schedules, which did not run at all hours, nor events such as storms or winter ice that shut down service altogether. Without question, this was an enormous improvement, but it did not "open up the world" to islanders. The outside world had already been opened up, for over 150 years. *[See photo 9.8]*

If the bridge did not open up the outside world to islanders, it did open up the island to people from places like Boston, New York and Philadelphia. To be sure, people from the large eastern cities began to come here as steamboats made the island accessible after the Civil War. This led to the development of enclaves of "summer people," most notably at Eggemoggin and the Dunham's Point area. For the most part, though, these outsiders knew their place and did not seriously interfere with island life. And just as the local people were a source of fascination for the summer folks, so were the activities of the latter a source of amusement for the locals.

After World War II, slowly at first but more rapidly after the mid-1950s, more and more outsiders came to Deer Isle. Unlike the established summer people, they did not always understand island ways, and brought in ideas not always welcomed by the locals. Previously, islanders had the ability to choose which ideas and things from the outside world they wished to bring into their own lives, and those they wished to reject. Now, more and more, outside ideas and goods were thrust upon them.

Because the wages from yachting were drying up, the money that outsiders brought in to the local economy was welcome. Moreover, farming, which had still been important through the war, underwent a decline in the years following. By the 1950s, it was no longer a significant element in the economy. As a consequence, people no longer needed all the acres of the old family farms. This did provide another source of cash, however, as there were lots of people from away eager to own a piece of the island. So, many of the old family

*9.8 The Deer Isle-Sedgwick Bridge, soon after its construction, looking towards the mainland. Courtesy of Deer Isle-Stonington Historical Society*

holdings were subdivided and sold off. Thus, for example, the old farm at North Deer Isle established by Peter Hardy and home to five generations of his descendants was sold off to outsiders. Today, none of his descendants live there.

One other consequence of the bridge may be mentioned here. As people began to come and go from the island freely, it became easier for them to buy the things they wanted in places like Bangor and Ellsworth. As more and more people did so, it drained local businesses. Deer Isle village, once a vibrant commercial center, is now a virtual ghost town in winter. Stonington, too, lost its variety of furniture, clothing and other stores. Most businesses there now cater to tourists and other island visitors.

No longer does the island provide for almost all the community's needs and services. *[See photos 9.9 and 9.10]*

What happened, then, with the demise of yachting was the end of the old maritime/farming economy. In its place today is one based on lobstering and catering to tourists and other vacationers. Although islanders were never totally self-sufficient, they are certainly less so today than they were only sixty or seventy years ago. Whether all this is a good thing or not depends on one's perspective, but it certainly is different. One thing that has survived, however, is a stubborn streak of independence, which sometimes leads to clashes with more recent immigrants to the island.

# The Post War Period

*9.9, 9.10 Deer Isle Village, as it used to be, and is now. Main Street in winter, shortly before the bridge was built. Businesses on the left side included a fish market, Haskell and Pickering's Garage, Ned Haskell's barber shop and variety store (with seasonal dentist upstairs), Norman Powers' news stand, a restaurant, the newspaper office and gift shop, with the Lynnmore Hotel (by then serving as a storehouse for Barter Lumber Co.) at the end of the street. Coming up the right hand side of the street is the post office, the White Front Sweet Shop (with the telephone office upstairs), Malcolm Carman's cobbler shop; Beck's Market, M.D. Joyce Hardware, and Walker Pickering's IGA store (meats and groceries). Courtesy of Deer Isle-Stonington Historical Society Below: the same view in April 2014. Note the lack of cars compared to the earlier photo. Photo by William A. Haviland.*

# Appendix I

## S. Appel & Co., by Clayton H. Gross (Reprinted from Gross, 1982)

One of the illusions owning a yacht gave its owner may have been one of power. Each individual yachtsman was in a sense a "commodore" and he vied with his rivals in the way he outfitted his crew in quasi naval uniforms.

To obtain the uniforms and crew he often would turn to a most unusual firm, S. Appel & Co., which specialized in haberdashery, military, naval and yachting uniforms. It was not only an outfitting firm but an informal employment agency as well.

Yachting jobs were usually "fully found," that is board and all necessary uniforms were part of the employment package. Appel's got the edge on their competitors by offering not only to supply the uniform but also a reliable person to fill it. Therefore when a young man from Deer Isle went to New York to seek his fortune in yachting, he reported as soon as possible to S. Appel & Co. at 16-18 Fulton St. On the main floor of their three-story establishment, there was a large smoking room next to Ben Appel's office. He had a preferred list of captains, deck officers, engineers, cooks, stewards and sailors, most of whom came from Deer Isle. In the spring when yachts were being placed in commission the room would be thronged with men waiting for jobs. Calls were constantly coming in and almost everyone ended up getting a job. In return for the favor of filling the job, both the employer and employee agreed to fill their clothing needs for the season from S. Appel & Co. Appel's supplied uniforms and jobs for Deer Isle seamen from 1887 until the eve of World War II. During the war they supplied navy and maritime commission uniforms to those going off to war. Unfortunately Appel's is no longer with us as it was absorbed recently by another firm. The writer has been told that its name recently disappeared from the yellow pages. Ben Appel visited Deer Isle twice; once as the guest of Capt. Edwin Haskell; and again as the guest of Capt. Willie Greene.

# Appendix II

## From William to Edwin and Kenneth: A Greenlaw Genealogy

(italics mark the male line of descent to George Edward and his sons)

### The First Generation

*William* and Jane Greenlaw, born in Scotland, emigrated with their sons to Warren, Maine, in 1753. Moved to Deer Isle in 1761, where William died ca. 1783.

Children of *William* and Jane (all born in Scotland):

1. James, b. ca. 1732.

2. William, b. ca. 1734.

3. *Jonathan*, b. ca. 1736.

4. Ebenezer, b. ca. 1738.

5. Charles, b. ca. 1740.

6. Alexander, b. ca. 1742.

### The Second Generation

*Jonathan* Greenlaw, b. ca. 1736, married Elizabeth Lamb in 1759 in Portland. Moved from Deer Isle to Castine after 1779, then to St. Andrews, New Brunswick, in 1783, where he died in 1818.

Children of *Jonathan* and Elizabeth:

1. *William*, b. 1761.

2. Ebenezer, b. ca. 1763.

3. Moses, b. ca. 1767.

4. John, b. ca. 1769.

5. Richard G., b. 1772, d. 1841.

6. Sarah.

7. Jonathan, b. 1777.

8. Elizabeth.

9. Jean.

10. Rebecca, b. ca. 1780.

11. Joanna

All were born on Deer Isle, excepting Joanna, who was probably born in Castine.

### The Third Generation

*William* Greenlaw, b. 1761 on Deer Isle, d. 1832 on Deer Isle. A farmer, he married Rebecca Babbidge in 1780 in Castine. In 1783, he went to St. Andrews, New Brunswick, with other loyalists, returned to Deer Isle in 1784. His brother Richard returned ca. 1790, and three of his sons established farms near *William's* in the Greenlaw District.

Children of *William* and Rebecca:

1. William, b. 1781, d. 1804, lost at sea on a whaling voyage.

2. Capt. John Babbidge, b. 1783, Deer Isle, d. 1870, Deer Isle.

3. James, b. 1785, d. 1833, drowned at Norfolk, Virginia.

4. Margaret, b. 1788, d. after 1880 in Surry.

5. Capt. Jonathan Babbidge, b. 1790.

6. Ebenezer, b. 1792, d. 1826.

7. Capt. *Richard*, b. 1795 in Deer Isle, d. 1860 in Deer Isle.

8. Thomas, b. 1797, d. 1817, drowned.

9. Capt. Walter, b. 1800, d. 1852 of yellow fever in Jacksonville, Florida.

10. Levi, b. 1802, d. 1888.

11. William, b. 1806, inherited his father's farm, d. 1875.

### The Fourth Generation

Capt. *Richard* Greenlaw, b. 1795, Deer Isle, d. 1860, Deer Isle. Married first Sarah Gold Robbins in 1817, she d. 1847; married second Mehitable Jordan in 1849.

Appendix II

Children of *Richard* and Sarah:

1. William, b. 1818.

2. Thomas R., b. 1820, d. 1889.

3. Prescott, b. 1821.

4. Jonathon Solomon, b. 1825 in Deer Isle, d. 1864, lost at sea.

5. Susan, b. 1827, d. July 1909.

6. Hannah Antinette, b. 1833.

7. Capt. *Nelson R.*, b. 1836 in Deer Isle, d. 1880.

8. Mary Elizabeth, b. 1840.

There were no children with Mehitable.

**The Fifth Generation**

Capt. *Nelson* Greenlaw, b. 1836, Deer Isle; married Elizabeth Pressey in Deer Isle in 1856; d. Deer Isle 1880.

Children of *Nelson* and Elizabeth:

1. Carrie Eva, b. 1857.

2. Capt. Frederick Richard, b. 1859.

3. Mehitable, b. 1861.

4. Capt. *George Edward*, b 1862, d. 1916.

5. Harry, b. 1865, d. 1887.

6. Capt. Alfred, b. 1869.

**The Sixth Generation**

Capt. *George Edward* Greenlaw, b. 1862, Deer Isle, married first in 1884 Zara F. Thompson of Biddeford, who died in 1897. He married second in Boston Caroline Elizabeth Monnier from Switzerland; d. in 1916 at Deer Isle.

Children of *George Edward* and Zara:

1. Harold Redman, b. 1893; raised by his aunt Carrie Greenlaw Gray.

Children of *George Edward* and Caroline Elizabeth:

1. Capt. *Edwin Berger*, b. 1899, Deer Isle, d. 1991, Deer Isle.

2. Lillian Marion, b. 1905, Deer Isle, d. 2000, Deer Isle.

3. Capt. *Kenneth Nelson*, b. 1906, Deer Isle, d. 1988 in California.

**The Seventh Generation**

Capt. *Edwin Berger*, b. 1889, Deer Isle, married Ada Jacobsen, 1927, d. 1991, Deer Isle.

Children of *Edwin Berger* and Ada:

1. Sonya, b. 1930, Brooklyn, New York, d. 1997, Luverne, Alabama.

Capt. *Kenneth Nelson*, b. 1906, Deer Isle, married in 1929 Lyndell L. Stinson in Deer Isle, d. 1988 in California.

Children of Kenneth Nelson and Lyndell:

1. Barbara Lillian, b. 1930, Stonington.

2. Col. Kenneth Nelson Jr., b. 1931, Stonington.

3. Roger Lee, b. 1936, New London, Connecticut.

# Bibliography

**Aldrich, James M.**

1985. *Centennial: A History of Island Newspapers.* Stonington, ME.: Penobscot Bay Press.

1991. *Fair Winds and Stormy Seas: 50 Years of Maine Maritime Academy.* Stonington, ME.: Penobscot Books.

**Anonymous**

1938. Hurricane and Flood. *The Connecticut Circle Magazine*: 1-4.

1973. Steam Yacht Caused Stir in Rockland. Rockland, ME.: *Courier Gazette, Coastal Courier Edition*, Aug. 19: 25.

1954. The Isthmian Steamship Company. Brochure.

n.d. Liberty Ships and Victory Ships, America's Lifeline in War. *National Park Service, U.S. Department of the Interior, Teaching with Historic Lesson Plans.* Website.

n.d. Liberty Ships and Victory Ships, Setting the Stage. *National Park Service, U.S. Department of the Interior, Teaching with Historic Lesson Plans.* Website.

**Bray, Maynard and Carlton Pinheiro**

1989 Herreshoff of Bristol: A Photographic History of America's Greatest Yacht and Boat Builders. Brooklin, ME.: Wooden Boat Publishing.

**Britton, Barbara L.**

2011. Yachting with Three Greenlaws from Sunset. *Island Ad-Vantages*, July 21: 5; July 28: 5; August 4: 5.

**Burg, Amos**

1934. Color Glimpses of the Changing South Seas. *National Geographic* LXV (3): I-VIII.

**Buxton, Henry**

1937. Capt. William S. Greene Famous Yacht Skipper. *Bangor Daily News*, June 30.

**Chatto and Turner**

*1910 Register of the Towns of Sedgwick, Brooklin, Deer Isle, Stonington and Isle au Haut.* Brooklin, ME.: Friend Memorial Library.

**Dietz, Lew**

1956. The Skipper Goes Ashore. *Down East*, 11 (8): 32-35.

**Eaton, Cyrus**

1851. *Annals of the Town of Warren.* Hallowell, ME.: Masters Smith and Co.

**Eskew, Garnett Laidlaw**

1958. *Cradle of Ships.* New York: G. P. Putnam's Sons.

**Fleischmann, Julius**

1935. *Footsteps in the Sea.* New York: G. P. Putnam's.

**Fox, William**

*1986. Always Good Ships: A History of Newport News Shipbuilding and Drydock Company.* Virginia Beach, VA.: The Donning Company.

**Gabrielson, Mark J.**

2013. *Deer Isle's Undefeated America's Cup Crews.* Charleston, SC: History Press.

**Gallet, Edna and Helen MacKay**

2011. Essie Beck, A Life Dominated by the Sea. In: *Island Heritage: Reminiscences on Island Life,* Caroline Spear, Ed. Stonington, ME.: Penobscot Books, pp. 1-7.

# Bibliography

**Greenlaw, Capt. Edwin Berger**

n.d. *Memories and Nostalgia*. Unpublished manuscript on file with Barbara L. Britton.

**Gross, Clayton H.**

1967. Treasure Island? *Island Ad-Vantages*, April 2: 5.

1979. Islanders had Luck Riding Out '38 Hurricane. *Island Ad-Vantages*, Sept. 28: 5.

1982. Yachting and Capt. Willie Greene. *Island Ad-Vantages*, Aug. 26: 5.

1983. Yachting. *Island Ad-Vantages*, June 16: 4.

**Gross, Gilbert**

1932. *My Trip Around the World on the Camargo*. Diary in possession of Tinker Crouch, Stonington.

**Gross, Nancy**

2014. The Birds are Coming Back Rather Slowly. *Island Ad-Vantages*, April 17: 4.

**Haskell, Carroll M.**

2011. *Growing Up on an Island off the Coast of Maine*. Solon, ME.: Polar Bear and Co.

**Haviland, William A.**

2009. The Early Coming (and Going) of the Greenlaws. *Island Ad-Vantages*, June 11: 5.

2010. A remembrance of Monty Haskell: Crew Member of the America's Cup Defender *Columbia*. *Island Ad-Vantages*, April 22: 5 and 29: 4.

2011. Charles H. Scott of the all Deer Isle America's Cup Crews. *Island Ad-Vantages*, Jan. 13: 4.

----. Captain A. L. Haskell and the Yacht *Tarantula*. *Island Ad-Vantages*, Aug. 18: 4.

2012. Reflections on Deer Isle in the Yachting Era. *Island Ad-Vantages*, July 19: 5.

----. Greenlaw Houses in the Greenlaw District. Manuscript on file, Deer Isle-Stonington Historical Society.

2013. *A History of the Hardy Farm at North Deer Isle*. Manuscript on file, Deer Isle-Stonington Historical Society.

**Herreshoff, Rebecca C.**

1982. *Navette*. Herreshoff Museum Chronicle, No. 7.

**Hickman, Kennedy**

n.d. World War II: The Liberty Ship Program. *About.com Military History*. Website.

**Hosmer, George L.**

1886. *An Historical Sketch of the Town of Deer Isle, with Notices of its Settlers and Early Inhabitants*. Boston: Press of Stanley and Usher.

**Hunter, Joyce**

2011. Captain George Washington Torrey, Jr. A Seafaring Man from a Seafaring Family. In: *Island Heritage: Reminiscences on Island Life*, Caroline Spear, Ed. Stonington, ME.: Penobscot Books, pp. 133-138.

**Jaffe, Walter W.**

2004. *The Liberty Ships from A to Z*. Palo Alto, CA.: Glencannon Press.

**Kearney, Peg**

2009. *Land, Loyalty and Self-Interest: One Family's Journey from Neutrality to Exile*. Master's Thesis, University of Maine, Orono.

**Lewis, Skip**

2003. The History of the Isthmian Steamship Company. *Isthmian Lines.com*. Website.

**Lloyd's Register of American Yachts**

1911, 1912, 1924, 1964, 1967. New York: Lloyd's Registry of Shipping.

**MacKay, Gordon**

1952 On the Side. *Island Ad-Vantages*, Oct. 9: 1.

**Manning's Yacht Register**

1883, 1901, 1903 and 1907. New York: Manning's Yacht Agency.

**Manry, Robert**

1965. *Tinkerbelle*. New York: Harper and Rowe.

**Obituary**

2010. Arthur Cabot "Dud" Haskell, Jr. *Island Ad-Vantages*, Compass section, March 11: 4.

**Phillips, Richard and Stephen Talty**

2010 *A Captain's Duty*. New York: Hyperion Books

**Rice, Marshall Jr. and William A. Haviland**

2011. Deer Isle in the Yachting Era: William Irving Conary. *Island Ad-Vantages*, July 7: 4.

**Robinson, Bill**

1978. *Legendary Yachts*. New York: David McKay Co, Inc.

**Rodengen, Jeffrey L.**

1994. *The Legend of Electric Boat*. Fort Lauderdale, FL.: Write Stuff Syndicate.

**Rowe, W. H.**

1948. *The Maritime History of Maine*. New York: W. W. Norton.

**Sables, Robert P.**

2005. "Overdue Atlantic": USS Cythera (PY 26). *NavSource Naval History*. Website.

**Scott, Capt. Walter**

1960. Letter. *Island Ad-Vantages* 25: 2

n.d. Letter of the Week. *Island Ad-Vantages*, date unknown, collection of William A. Haviland.

**Shanabrook, Paul E.**

1979. *The Boston*. Boston: The Boston Yacht Club.

**United States Census**

1850. Hancock County. Collections of the Deer Isle-Stonington Historical Society.

1860, 1870, 1880. Deer Isle and Isle au Haut, Maine. Collections of the Deer Isle-Stonington Historical Society.

**Wasson, George S.**

1949. *Sailing Days on the Penobscot*. New York: W. W. Norton.

**Whipple, A. B. C.**

1980. *The Racing Yachts*. Alexandria, VA.: Time-Life Books.

**Wisner, Bill**

1975. The Golden Age of Yachts. *Motor Boating and Sailing*, December: 23-29, 66-69.

*Photo by Jeremiah Savage*

# About the Authors

**William A. Haviland** is Professor Emeritus of Anthropology at the University of Vermont. Although schooled in Philadelphia, his summers were always spent with his family on Deer Isle. Their neighbors there were all islanders, many of them close friends. They included three members of the all Deer Isle crews that defended the America's Cup, as well as others who went yachting, including the captain of the yacht *Hi-Esmaro*. Having grown up in the midst of these mariner-farmers, Haviland has long been fascinated with the unique culture that developed on the island around these pursuits.

After coming of age, Haviland continued living summers on Deer Isle, and any other time he could get there. He and his wife now live there full time, and he has served on the Deer Isle Conservation Commission, on the board, and as President of Island Heritage Trust. Currently, he is on the boards of the Deer Isle-Stonington Historical Society and the Abbe Museum in Bar Harbor.

**Barbara L. (Greenlaw) Britton** enjoyed a professional career in healthcare as Vice-president, Facilities, Support Services and Construction at Mercer Medical Center, a 365-bed hospital in Trenton, New Jersey. Born on Deer Isle, Barbara lived the first years of her life with her parents, brother and extended family in her grandmother Greenlaw's house on Sunset Road; the family's move to New London, Connecticut, followed in December 1935. Her father served as crew member and then deck officer aboard the yacht *Cythera*, from 1927 to 1942. During his career, yachting dominated the cycle of family life and connections to the island remained strong. Close friends and family members in New London were islanders who shared news from "down home," and the weekly island newspaper kept the family in touch with larger community issues.

*The Mainstay*, a gift from her aunt Lillian Greenlaw when she died in 2000, brought Barbara and her husband back to Sunset as summer residents. Barbara serves as a dedicated volunteer at the Deer Isle-Stonington Historical Society, is treasurer of the Greenlaw Family Association and editor of the Greenlaw Newsletter, and actively pursues research germane to Island history.

# Other titles available from Penobscot Books

If you've enjoyed reading this book, check out these other island-themed books from Penobscot Books. Visit *penbaypress.me* for full descriptions of these and other books we offer.

*Island Naturalist* — 2015 Maine Literary Awards Winner
by Kathie Fiveash $27.95

*An Island Sense of Home: Stories from Isle au Haut*
by Harold S. van Doren $37.95

*I Loved This Work....I have been delightfully busy*
by John T. Crowell with accompanying DVD $49.95

*Island Heritage: Reminiscences on Island Life*
by Joyce Hunter, Linda Nelson, Caroline Rittenhouse and Jessica Brophy $23.95

*Centennial: A Century of Island Newspapers*
by James M. Aldrich $24.95

*Island Chronicles*
by Clayton Gross $9.95

*Stonington Past & Present*
by the Stonington Centennial Committee $16.95

**Order online at *penbaypress.me* or call 207-374-2341.**

**Penobscot Books**
A division of Penobscot Bay Press
P.O. Box 36, 69 Main St.
Stonington ME 04681
*books@pbp.me* • *penobscotbaypress.com*
207-367-2200